AGE OF APOCALYPSE

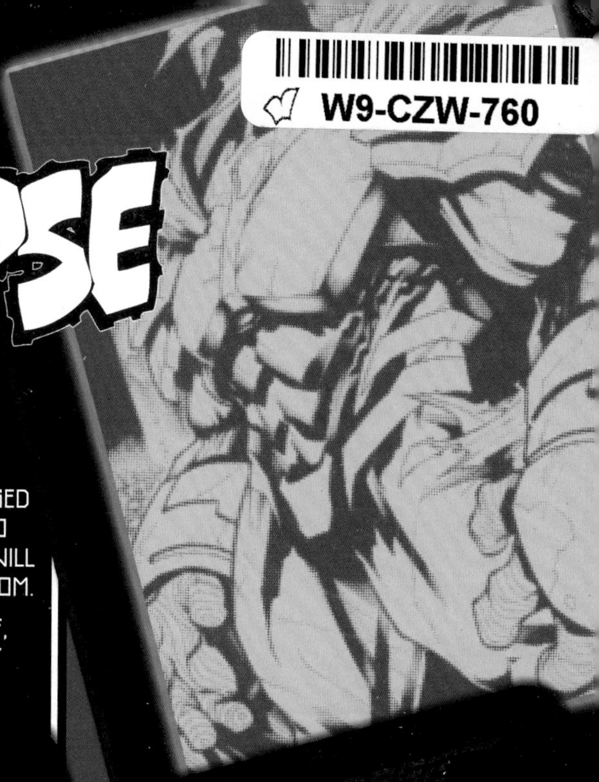

THE MULTIVERSE WAS DESTROYED

NOW, ALL THAT REMAINS...
IS BATTLEWORLD!

A MASSIVE, PATCHWORK PLANET COMPOSED OF FRAGMENTS FROM WORLDS THAT NO LONGER EXIST, MAINTAINED BY THE IRON WILL OF ITS GOD AND MASTER, VICTOR VON DOOM.

EACH REGION IS A DOMAIN UNTO ITSELF, BUT NONE IS RULED MORE RUTHLESSLY THAN THE REALM OF
EN SABAH NUR, APOCALYPSE.

FABIAN NICIEZA WRITER
GERARDO SANDOVAL (#1-3) & IBAN COELLO (#4-5) ARTISTS
DAVID CURIEL COLORIST

VC'S CLAYTON COWLES LETTERER
GERARDO SANDOVAL & DAVID CURIEL COVER ART
XANDER JAROWEY & CHRISTINA HARRINGTON
ASSISTANT EDITORS
KATIE KUBERT
EDITOR

JENNIFER GRÜNWALD
COLLECTION EDITOR
SARAH BRUNSTAD
ASSISTANT EDITOR
ALEX STARBUCK
ASSOCIATE MANAGING EDITOR
MARK D. BEAZLEY
EDITOR, SPECIAL PROJECTS
JEFF YOUNGQUIST
SENIOR EDITOR, SPECIAL PROJECTS
DAVID GABRIEL
SVP PRINT, SALES & MARKETING
JAY BOWEN
BOOK DESIGNER

AXEL ALONSO
EDITOR IN CHIEF
JOE QUESADA
CHIEF CREATIVE OFFICER
DAN BUCKLEY
PUBLISHER
ALAN FINE
EXECUTIVE PRODUCER

GE OF APOCALYPSE: WARZONES! Contains material originally published in magazine form as AGE OF APOCALYPSE 1-5. First printing 2015. ISBN# 978-0-7851-9862-8. Published by MARVEL WORLDWIDE, INC., a subsidiary of MARVEL NTERTAINMENT, LLC. OFFICE OF PUBLICATION: 135 West 50th Street, New York, NY 10020. **Printed in anada.** ALAN FINE, President, Marvel Entertainment; DAN BUCKLEY, President, TV, Publishing and Brand Management; OE QUESADA, Chief Creative Officer; TOM BREVOORT, SVP of Publishing; DAVID BOGART, SVP of Operations & rocurement, Publishing; C.B. CEBULSKI, VP of International Development & Brand Management; DAVID GABRIEL, SVP rint, Sales & Marketing; JIM O'KEEFE, VP of Operations & Logistics; DAN CARR, Executive Director of Publishing echnology; SUSAN CRESPI, Editorial Operations Manager; ALEX MORALES, Publishing Operations Manager; STAN LEE, hairman Emeritus. For information regarding advertising in Marvel Comics or on Marvel.com, please contact Jonathan heingold, VP of Custom Solutions & Ad Sales, at jrheingold@marvel.com. For Marvel subscription inquiries, please call 00-217-9158. **Manufactured between 9/11/2015 and 10/19/2015 by SOLISCO PRINTERS, SCOTT, QC, CANADA.**

0 9 8 7 6 5 4 3 2 1

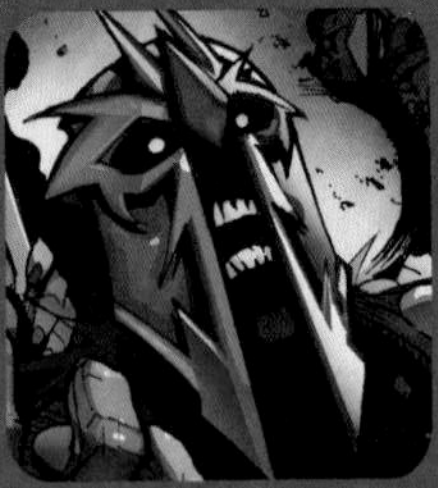

MAGNETO
MAX EISENHARDT
A.K.A. ERIK LEHNSHERR

CAPACITIES: Generates and controls magnetic fields.
PROFILE: Leader of the X-MEN, named after his deceased friend (see XAVIER, CHARLES). Magneto has recruited and trained young terrorist rebels who have opposed the rightful rule of Baron Nur.

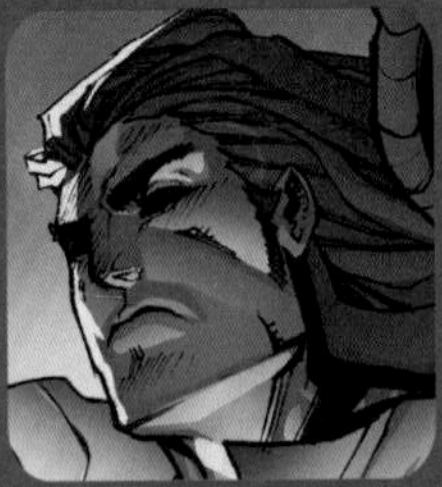

DR. PETER CORBEAU

PROFILE: Human physicist who has earned some favor from Baron Nur due to their mutual affinity for science. Corbeau is the elected leader of the Human Community, but is also suspected of fomenting the underground terrorist group known as The Friends of Humanity.

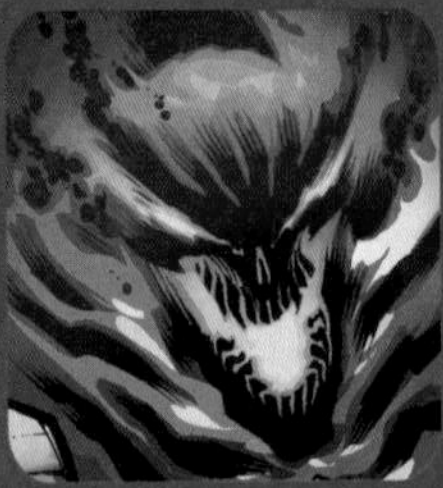

HOLOCAUST
WILLIAM ROLFSON

CAPACITIES: Generates bio-nuclear microwave energy blasts.
PROFILE: The son of Baron Nur and the most powerful of the FOUR HORSEMEN. He is a ruthless killing machine who becomes more powerful with every death he causes.

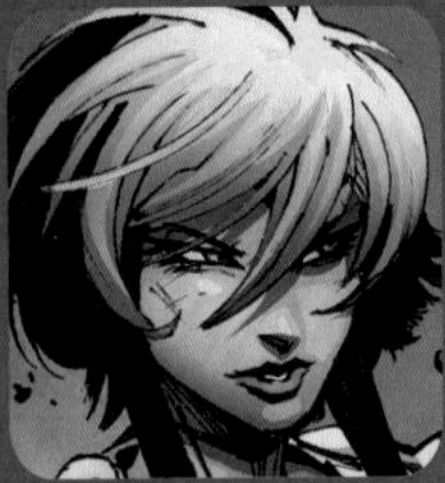

ROGUE

CAPACITIES: Uncontrolled ability to absorb the powers or memories of any living being on contact; flight, enhanced strength.
PROFILE: Long-standing member of the X-Men, Rogue remains deeply embittered over the death of Remy LeBeau, the man she loved. Should the opportunity present itself, she is a prime candidate to turn against Magneto.

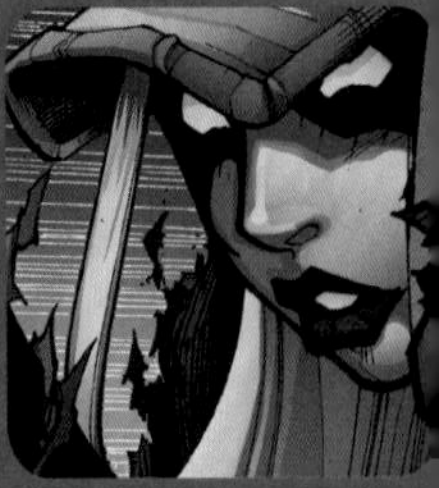

CAROL DANVERS

PROFILE: The Rules Enforcement Officer of the Human Community, Danvers is also suspected of being the leader of the growing underground terrorist group known as The Friends of Humanity.

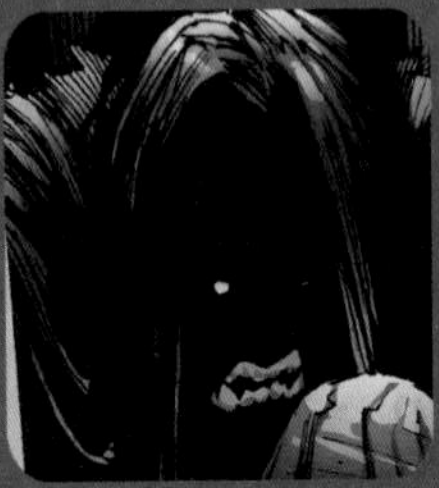

DARK BEAST
HANK McCOY

CAPACITIES: Enhanced strength and agility; chemically self-augmented appearance; alleged great intellect.
PROFILE: The pernicious Mengele Puppet who dances on Lord Essex's strings, McCoy is an expert at biogenetic archiving and Reclamations responsible for cataloging and experimenting on hundreds of thousands of DNA samples.

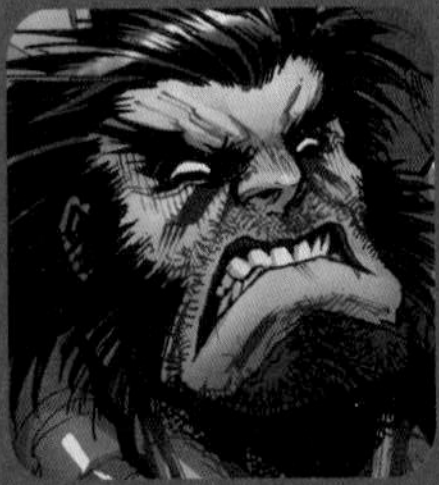

WOLVERINE
JAMES "LOGAN" HOWLETT

CAPACITIES: Enhanced senses, agility, strength and regenerative healing factor; Adamantium skeleton and claws.
PROFILE: Former "recruiter" for the biological experiments of Lord Essex. Years ago, Logan betrayed his master when he fell in love with a young recruit named Jean Grey. He failed her, lost his hand while escaping and joined Magneto's X-Men.

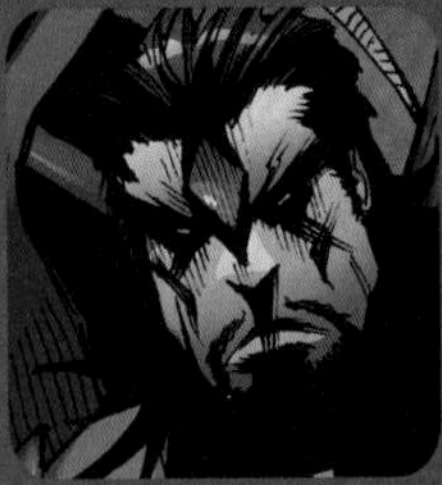

ESSEX
NATHANIEL ESSEX

CAPACITIES: Telepath, telekinetic, shape-shifter, teleporter; scientific genius.
PROFILE: A human who experimented on fellow humans in the 1800s, eventually allying himself with Apocalypse. He became physically transformed and secretly served En Sabah Nur in culling the growing tide of mutants.

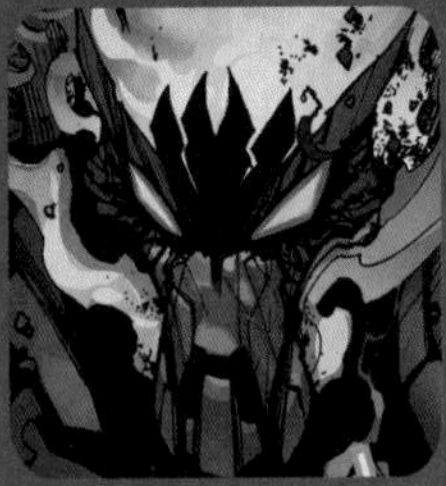

BURNER
REAL NAME UNKNOWN

CAPACITIES: Enhanced agility, strength and speed; able to pyrokinetically charge a target.
PROFILE: An escapee from the bio-labs of Hank McCoy, little is known of the last X-Men recruit. He wears full-body armor, rumored to cover most of his body.

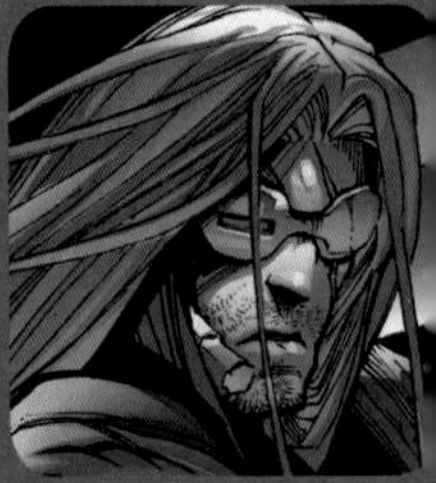

CYCLOPS
SCOTT SUMMERS

CAPACITIES: Generates beams of concussive force from eyes
PROFILE: Favored son of Essex and leader of Apocalypse's Elite Mutant Force. The genetic and moral key to the future. All he has to do is find the door.

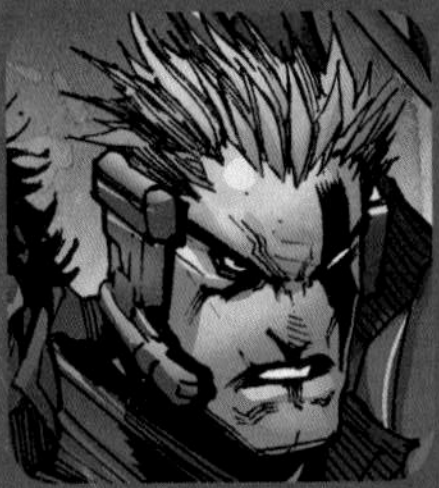

HAVOK
ALEXANDER SUMMERS

CAPACITIES: Transforms cosmic energy into plasma emanation.
PROFILE: Deputy of the EMF, he is bitter and jealous, thinking power is an entitlement. His desperation for validation makes him very dangerous.

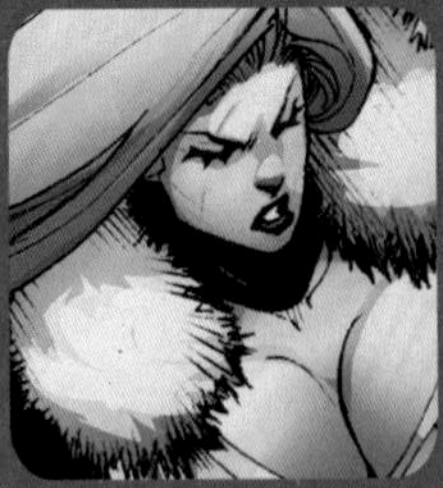

EMMA FROST
FORMERLY MARVEL GIRL

CAPACITIES: Telepath
PROFILE: One of Magneto's original X-Men, Frost has the most powerful mind in the world, but only because contestant #1 was killed twenty years ago and #2 has been de-powered.

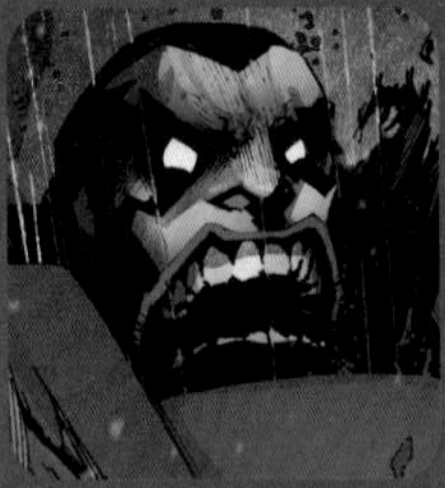

APOCALYPSE
EN SABAH NUR

CAPACITIES: Conscious control of every cell in his body, granting strength, shape-shifting, energy blasts and more.
PROFILE: Baron Nur rules the domain of Apocalypse with an iron fist. Believing only in the survival of the fittest, Nur single-handedly carved out a savage empire where mutants rule over a ghettoized human populace, and all must fight and suffer to prove their worth and earn their place.

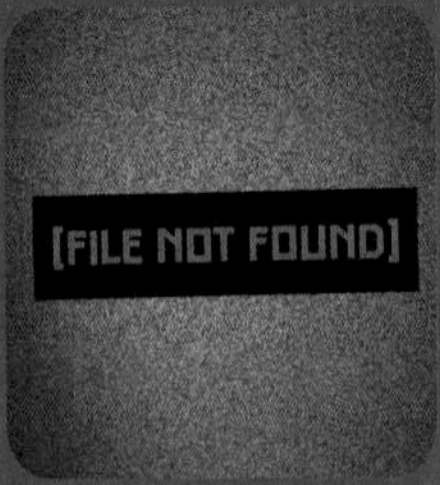
[FILE NOT FOUND]

JEAN GREY

CAPACITIES: Former Omega-level telepath and telekinetic.
PROFILE: Years ago, Lord Essex ordered this girl lobotomized. He so feared her mutant potential that he was willing to incur the wrath of Apocalypse. Jean now works for Angel at his neutral nightclub Heaven,a shadow of her former self.

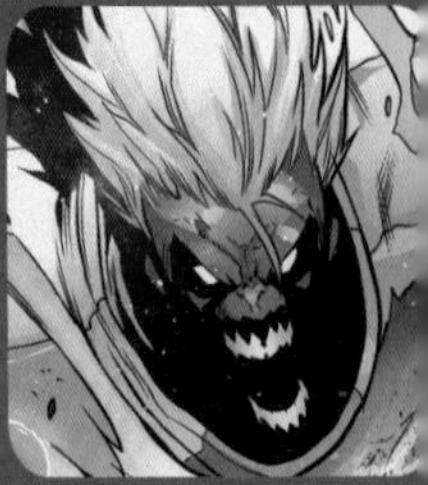

NEMESIS
DR. JAMES BRADLEY

CAPACITIES: Super-scientist, augmented with powers from other mutants.
PROFILE: Believing mutants should use every means at their disposal to evolve, Hank McCoy's assistant James Bradley turned his mutant intellect inward, experimenting on himself and upgrading his body with genetic profiles gleaned from scores of McCoy's mutant specimens.

ONE | STICKS AND STONES...

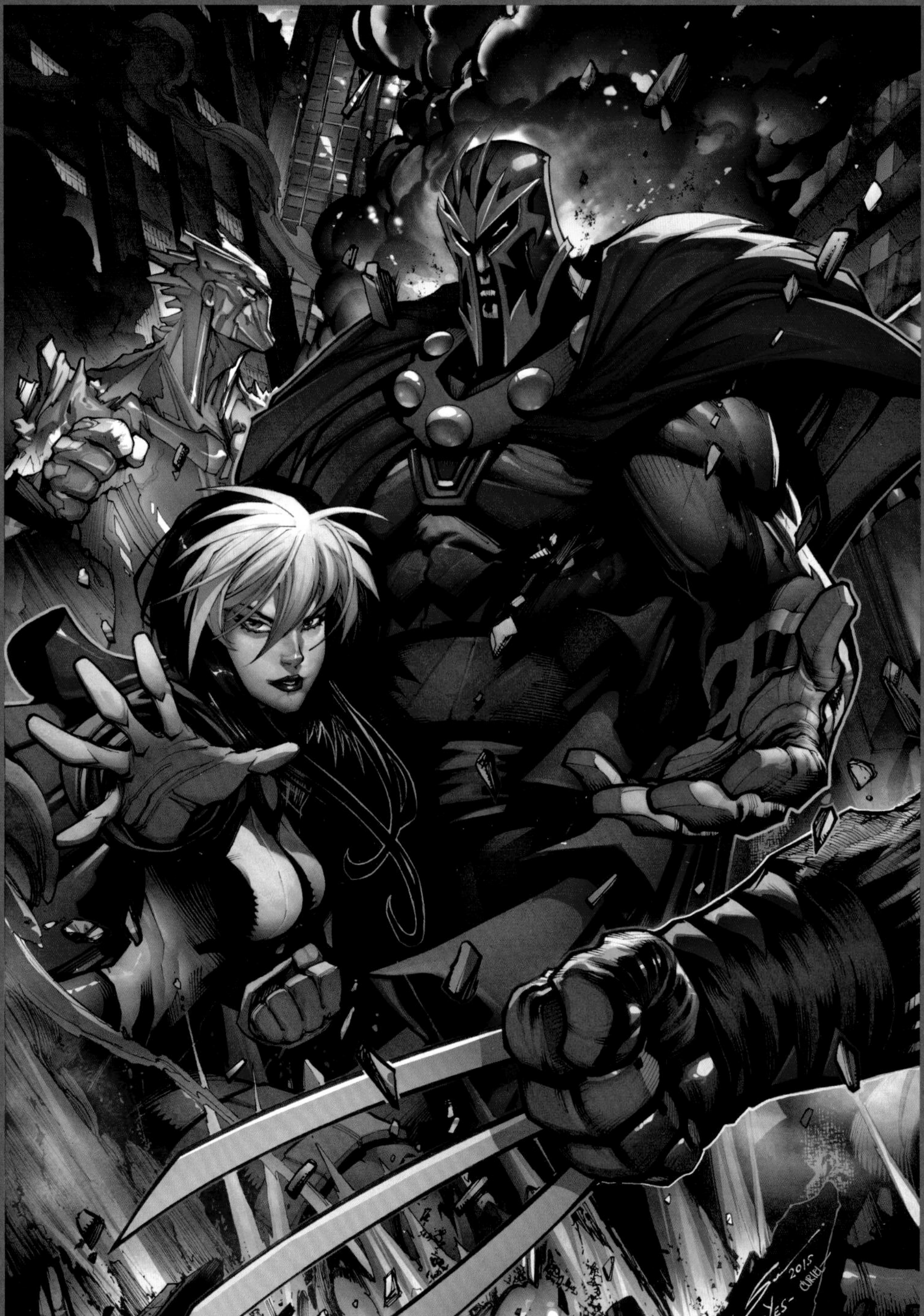

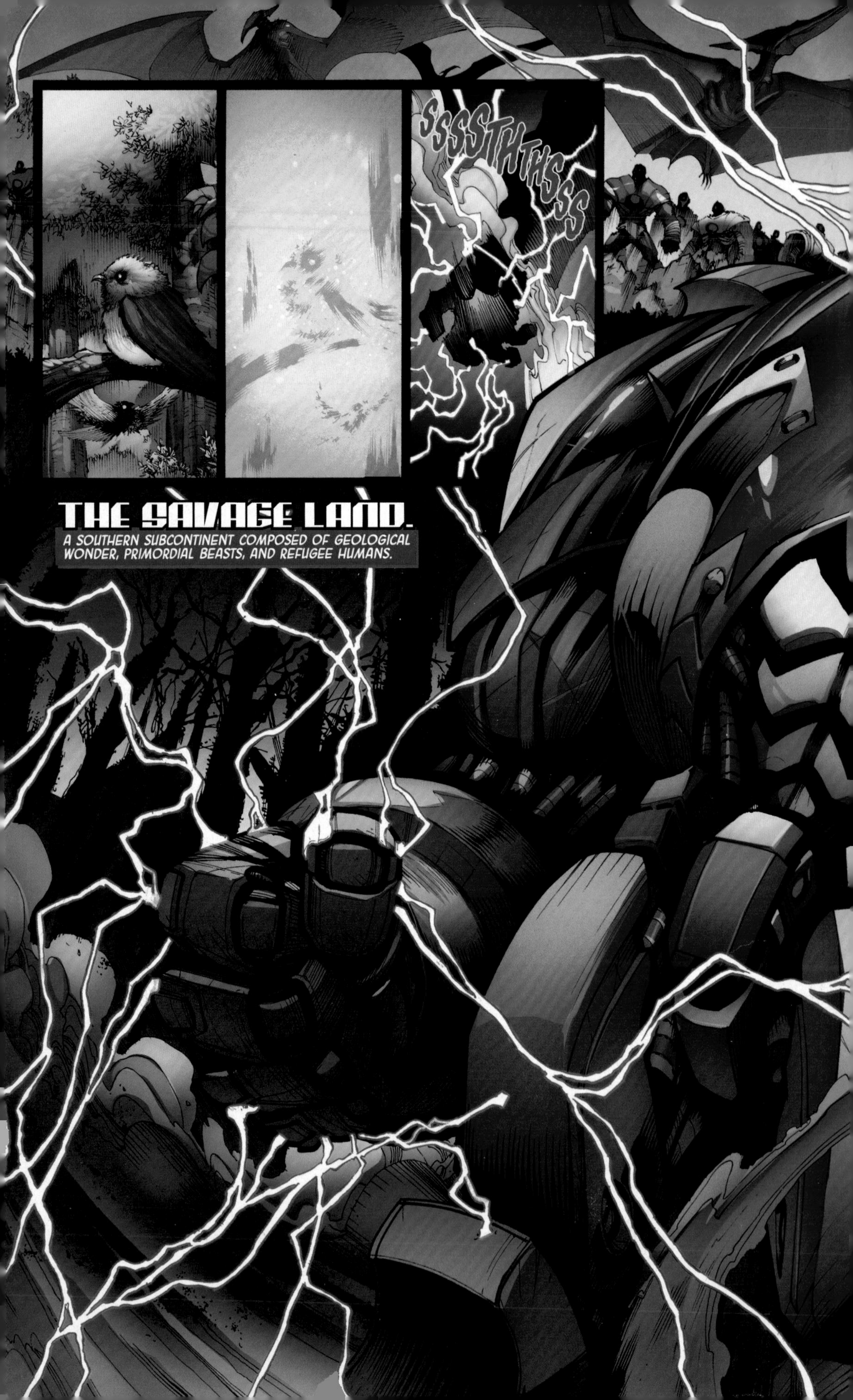
SSSSTHTHSSS
THE SAVAGE LAND.
A SOUTHERN SUBCONTINENT COMPOSED OF GEOLOGICAL WONDER, PRIMORDIAL BEASTS, AND REFUGEE HUMANS.

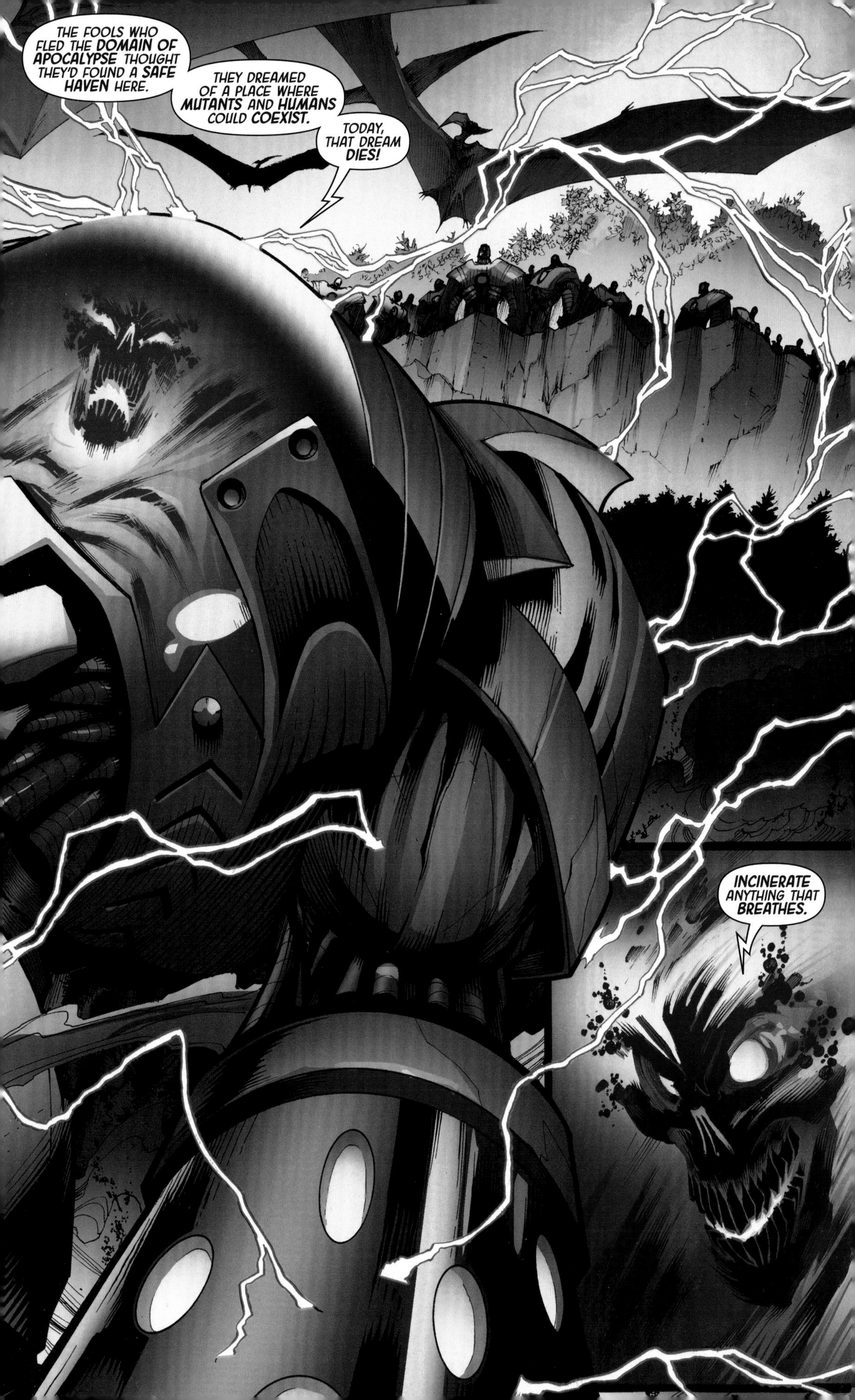
THE FOOLS WHO FLED THE DOMAIN OF APOCALYPSE THOUGHT THEY'D FOUND A SAFE HAVEN HERE.
THEY DREAMED OF A PLACE WHERE MUTANTS AND HUMANS COULD COEXIST.
TODAY, THAT DREAM DIES!
INCINERATE ANYTHING THAT BREATHES.

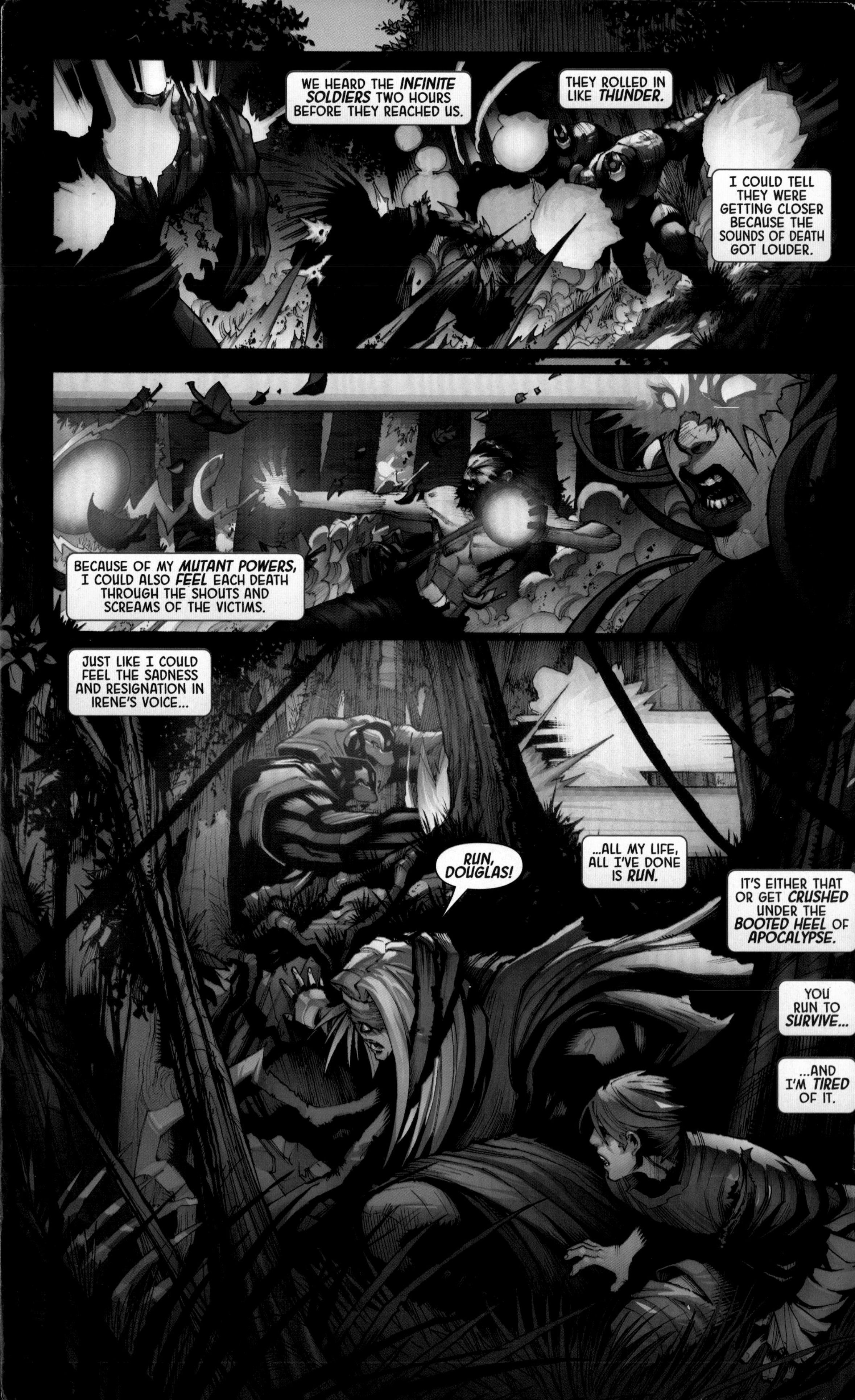
WE HEARD THE INFINITE SOLDIERS TWO HOURS BEFORE THEY REACHED US.
THEY ROLLED IN LIKE THUNDER.
I COULD TELL THEY WERE GETTING CLOSER BECAUSE THE SOUNDS OF DEATH GOT LOUDER.
BECAUSE OF MY MUTANT POWERS, I COULD ALSO FEEL EACH DEATH THROUGH THE SHOUTS AND SCREAMS OF THE VICTIMS.
JUST LIKE I COULD FEEL THE SADNESS AND RESIGNATION IN IRENE'S VOICE...
RUN, DOUGLAS!
...ALL MY LIFE, ALL I'VE DONE IS RUN.
IT'S EITHER THAT OR GET CRUSHED UNDER THE BOOTED HEEL OF APOCALYPSE.
YOU RUN TO SURVIVE...
...AND I'M TIRED OF IT.

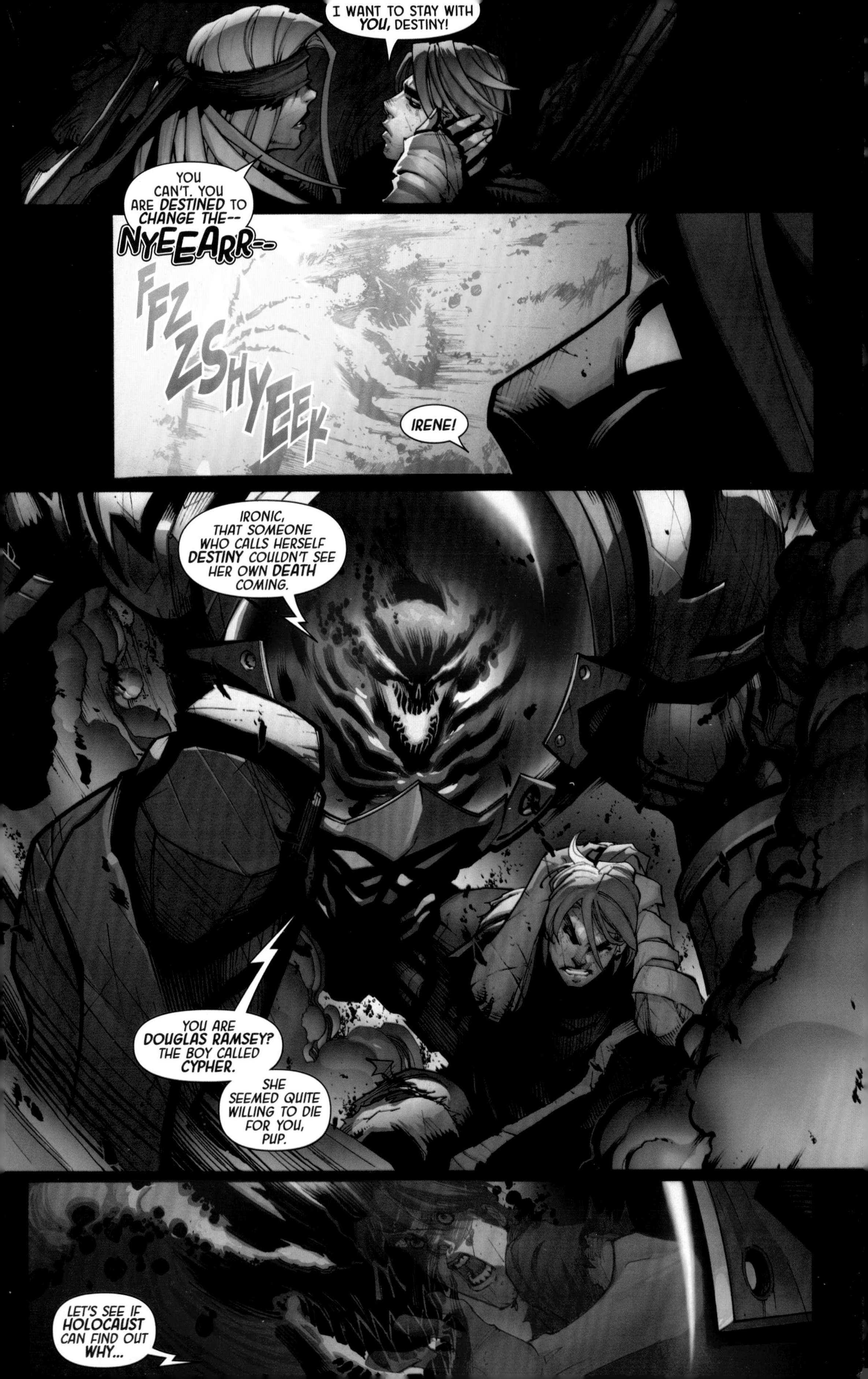

I WANT TO STAY WITH YOU, DESTINY!
YOU CAN'T. YOU ARE DESTINED TO CHANGE THE--
NYEEARR--
FFZ ZSHYEEK
IRENE!
IRONIC, THAT SOMEONE WHO CALLS HERSELF DESTINY COULDN'T SEE HER OWN DEATH COMING.
YOU ARE DOUGLAS RAMSEY? THE BOY CALLED CYPHER.
SHE SEEMED QUITE WILLING TO DIE FOR YOU, PUP.
LET'S SEE IF HOLOCAUST CAN FIND OUT WHY...

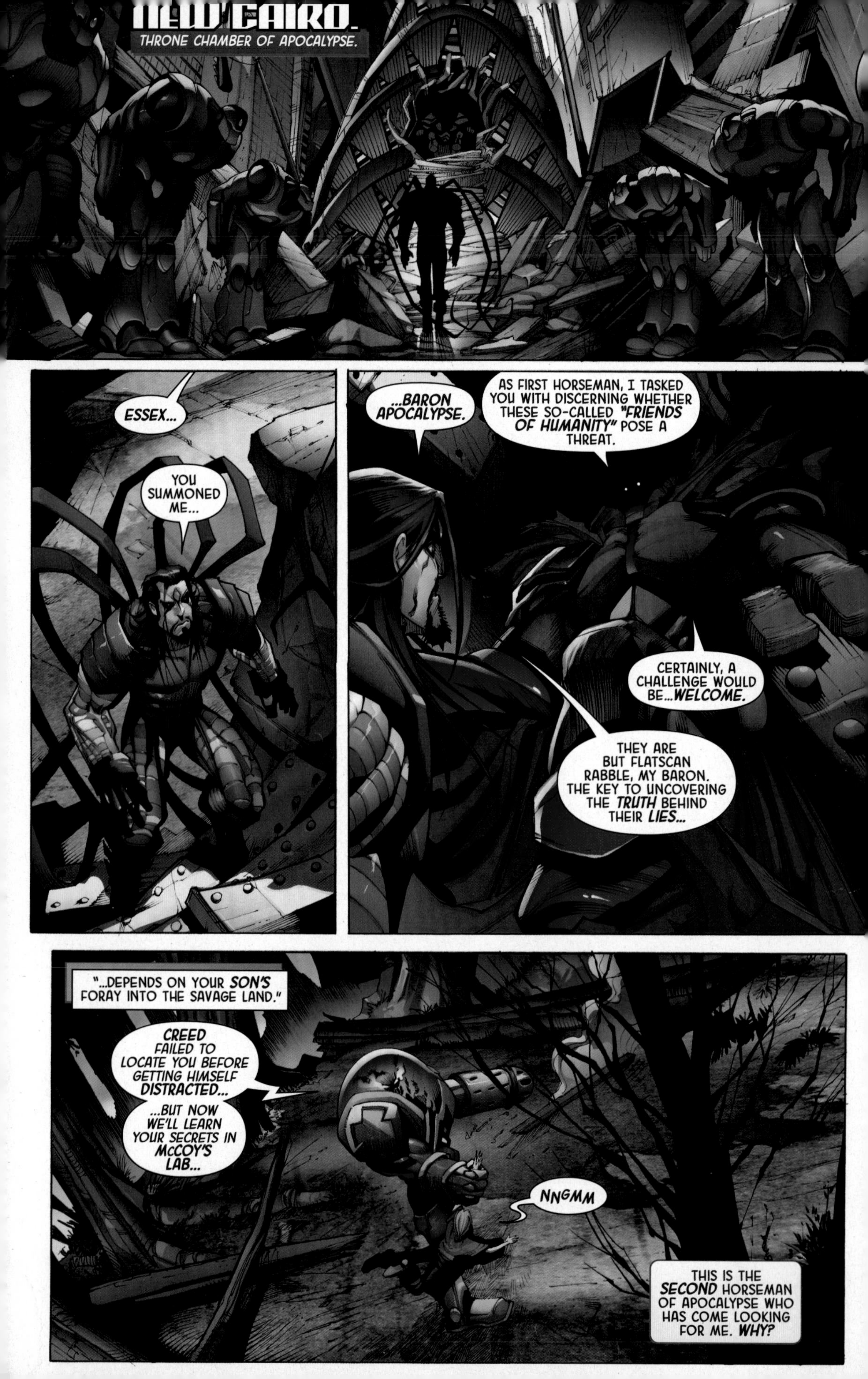
NEW CAIRO.
THRONE CHAMBER OF APOCALYPSE.
ESSEX...
YOU SUMMONED ME...
...BARON APOCALYPSE.
AS FIRST HORSEMAN, I TASKED YOU WITH DISCERNING WHETHER THESE SO-CALLED "FRIENDS OF HUMANITY" POSE A THREAT.
CERTAINLY, A CHALLENGE WOULD BE...WELCOME.
THEY ARE BUT FLATSCAN RABBLE, MY BARON. THE KEY TO UNCOVERING THE TRUTH BEHIND THEIR LIES...
"...DEPENDS ON YOUR SON'S FORAY INTO THE SAVAGE LAND."
CREED FAILED TO LOCATE YOU BEFORE GETTING HIMSELF DISTRACTED...
...BUT NOW WE'LL LEARN YOUR SECRETS IN McCOY'S LAB...
NNGMM
THIS IS THE SECOND HORSEMAN OF APOCALYPSE WHO HAS COME LOOKING FOR ME. WHY?

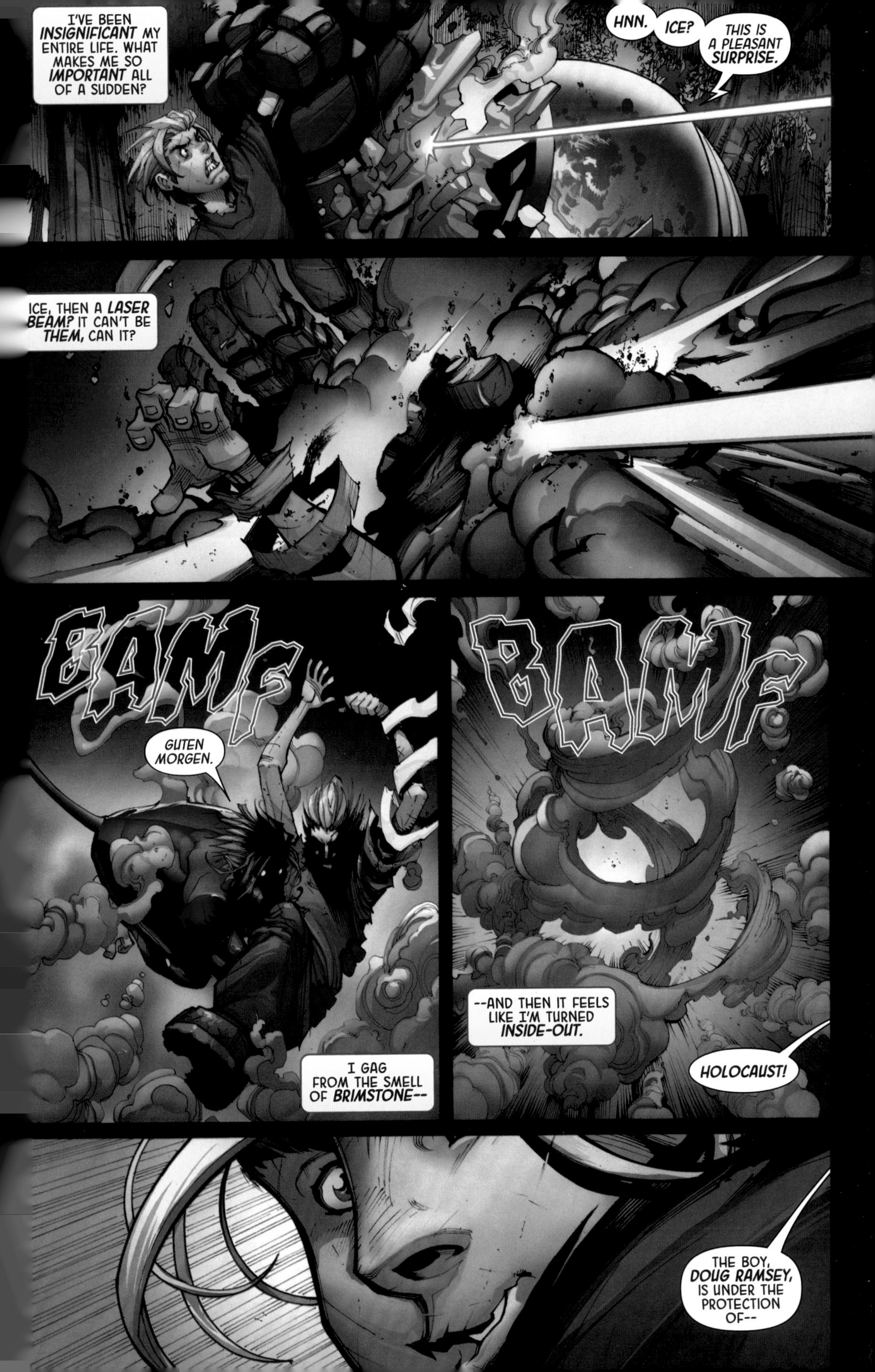
I'VE BEEN INSIGNIFICANT MY ENTIRE LIFE. WHAT MAKES ME SO IMPORTANT ALL OF A SUDDEN?
HNN.
ICE?
THIS IS A PLEASANT SURPRISE.
ICE, THEN A LASER BEAM? IT CAN'T BE THEM, CAN IT?
BAMF
GUTEN MORGEN.
I GAG FROM THE SMELL OF BRIMSTONE--
BAMF
--AND THEN IT FEELS LIKE I'M TURNED INSIDE-OUT.
HOLOCAUST!
THE BOY, DOUG RAMSEY, IS UNDER THE PROTECTION OF--

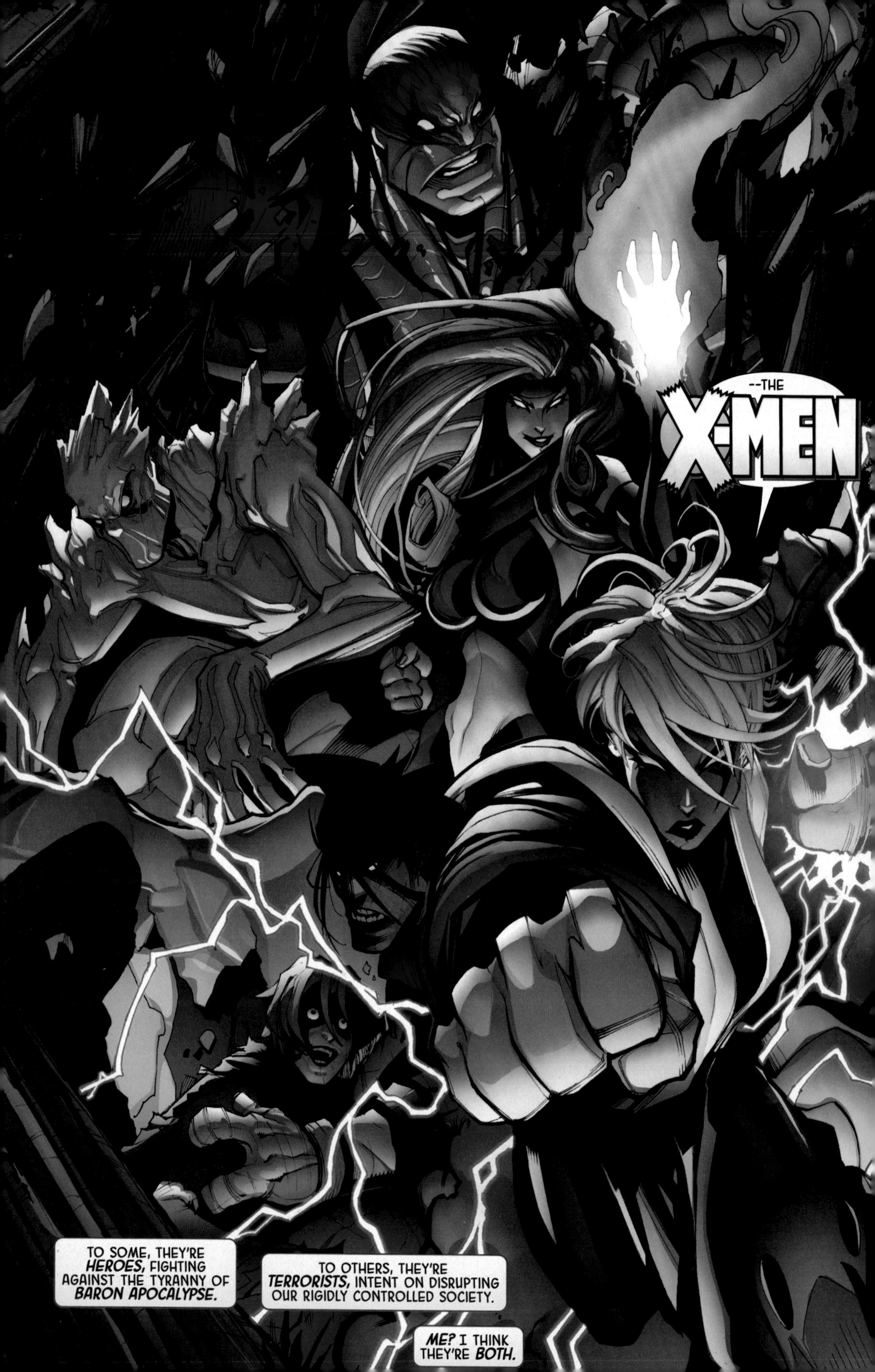
--THE
X-MEN
TO SOME, THEY'RE HEROES, FIGHTING AGAINST THE TYRANNY OF BARON APOCALYPSE.
TO OTHERS, THEY'RE TERRORISTS, INTENT ON DISRUPTING OUR RIGIDLY CONTROLLED SOCIETY.
ME? I THINK THEY'RE BOTH.

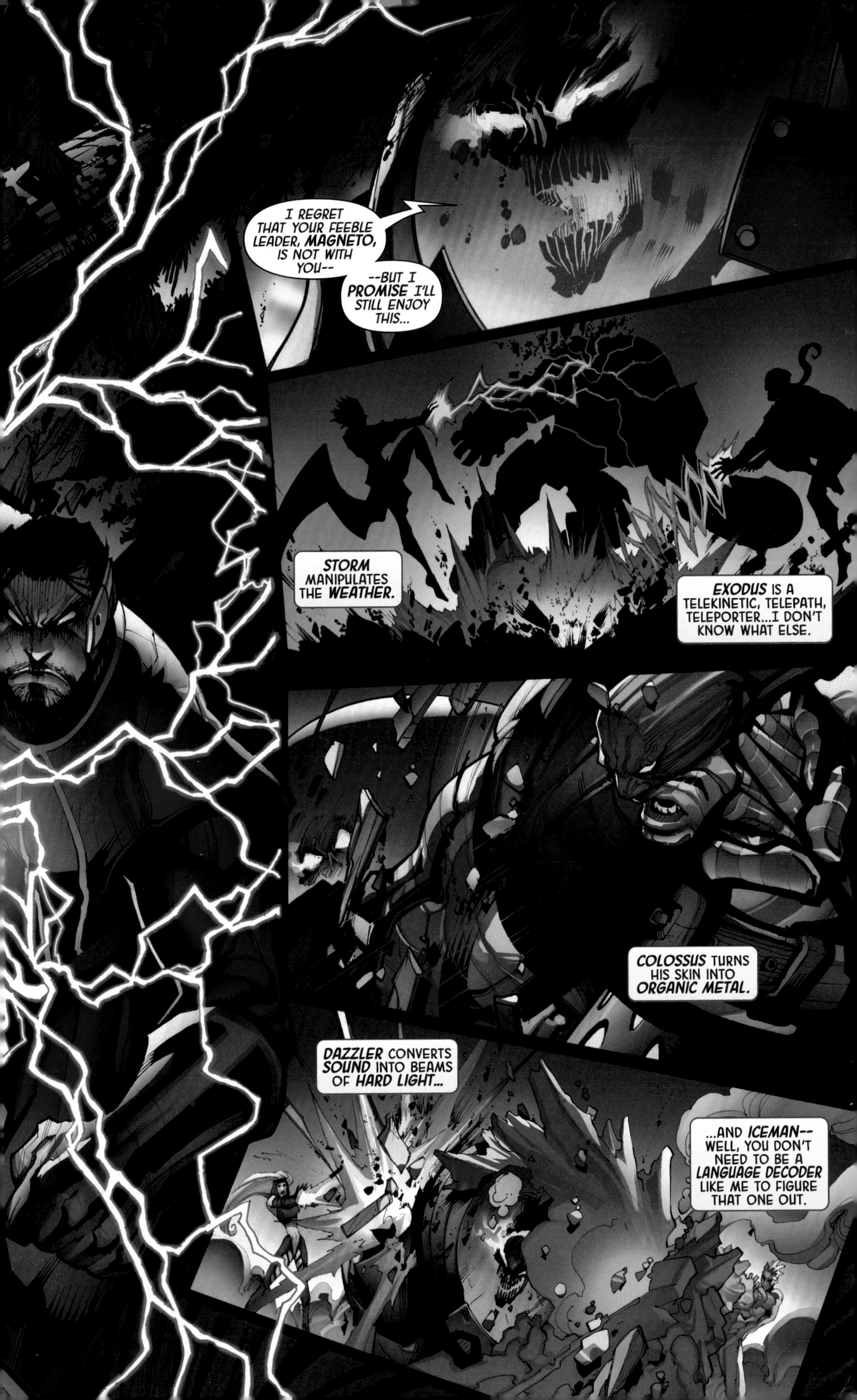
I REGRET THAT YOUR FEEBLE LEADER, MAGNETO, IS NOT WITH YOU--
--BUT I PROMISE I'LL STILL ENJOY THIS...
STORM MANIPULATES THE WEATHER.
EXODUS IS A TELEKINETIC, TELEPATH, TELEPORTER...I DON'T KNOW WHAT ELSE.
COLOSSUS TURNS HIS SKIN INTO ORGANIC METAL.
DAZZLER CONVERTS SOUND INTO BEAMS OF HARD LIGHT...
...AND ICEMAN--WELL, YOU DON'T NEED TO BE A LANGUAGE DECODER LIKE ME TO FIGURE THAT ONE OUT.

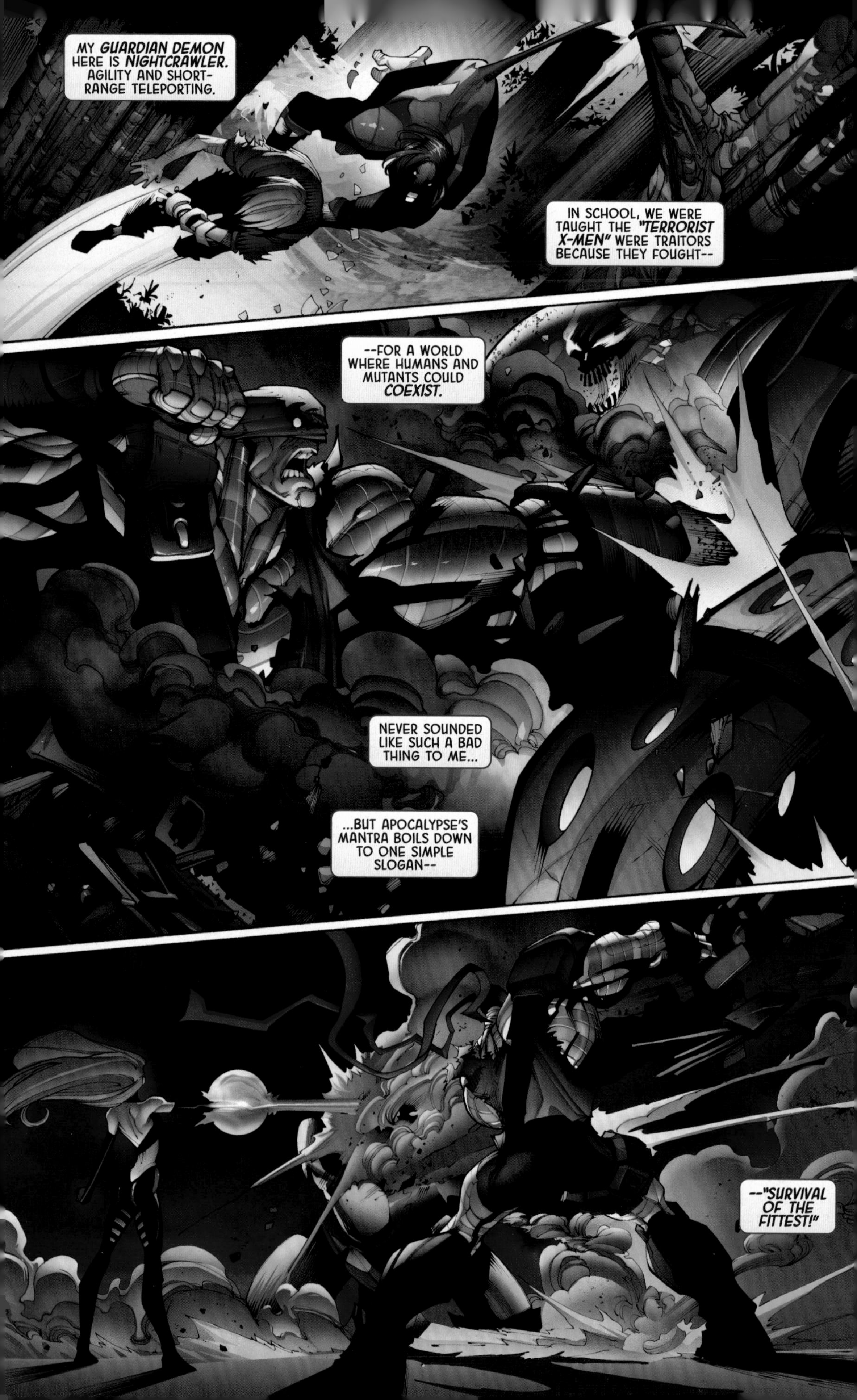
MY GUARDIAN DEMON HERE IS NIGHTCRAWLER. AGILITY AND SHORT-RANGE TELEPORTING.
IN SCHOOL, WE WERE TAUGHT THE "TERRORIST X-MEN" WERE TRAITORS BECAUSE THEY FOUGHT--
--FOR A WORLD WHERE HUMANS AND MUTANTS COULD COEXIST.
NEVER SOUNDED LIKE SUCH A BAD THING TO ME...
...BUT APOCALYPSE'S MANTRA BOILS DOWN TO ONE SIMPLE SLOGAN--
--"SURVIVAL OF THE FITTEST!"

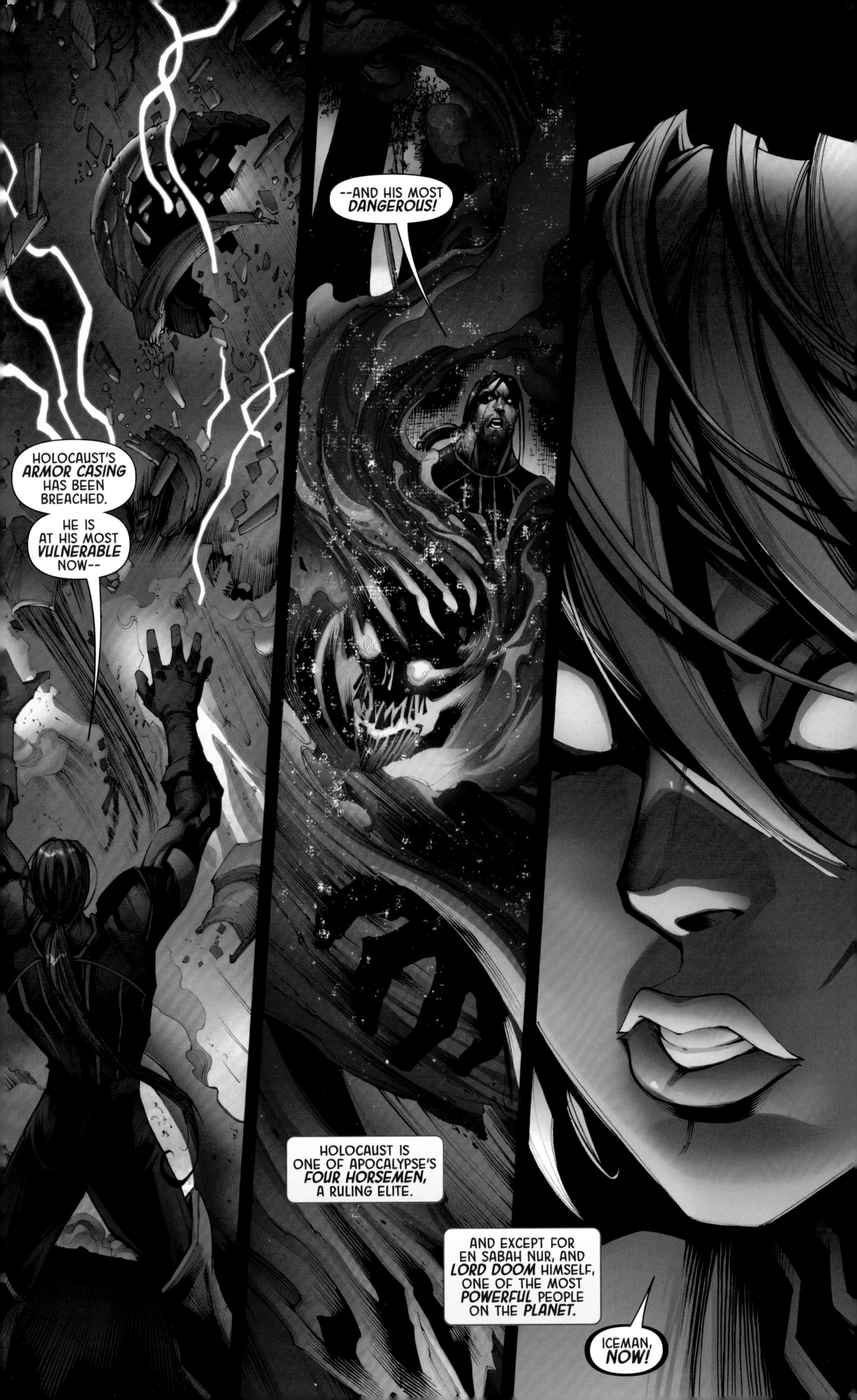

HOLOCAUST'S ARMOR CASING HAS BEEN BREACHED.
HE IS AT HIS MOST VULNERABLE NOW--
--AND HIS MOST DANGEROUS!
HOLOCAUST IS ONE OF APOCALYPSE'S FOUR HORSEMEN, A RULING ELITE.
AND EXCEPT FOR EN SABAH NUR, AND LORD DOOM HIMSELF, ONE OF THE MOST POWERFUL PEOPLE ON THE PLANET.
ICEMAN, NOW!

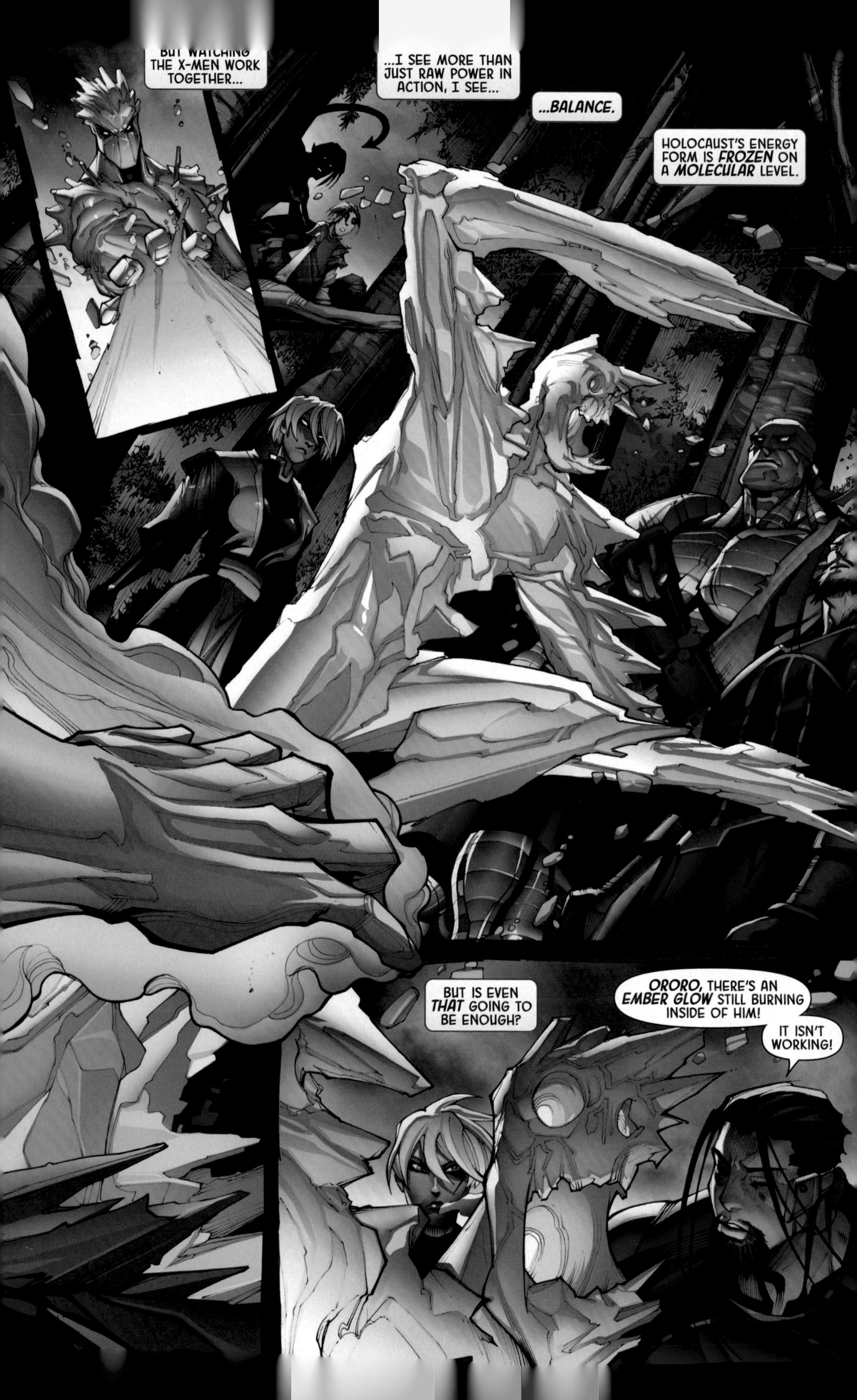

BUT WATCHING THE X-MEN WORK TOGETHER...
...I SEE MORE THAN JUST RAW POWER IN ACTION, I SEE...
...BALANCE.
HOLOCAUST'S ENERGY FORM IS FROZEN ON A MOLECULAR LEVEL.
BUT IS EVEN THAT GOING TO BE ENOUGH?
ORORO, THERE'S AN EMBER GLOW STILL BURNING INSIDE OF HIM!
IT ISN'T WORKING!

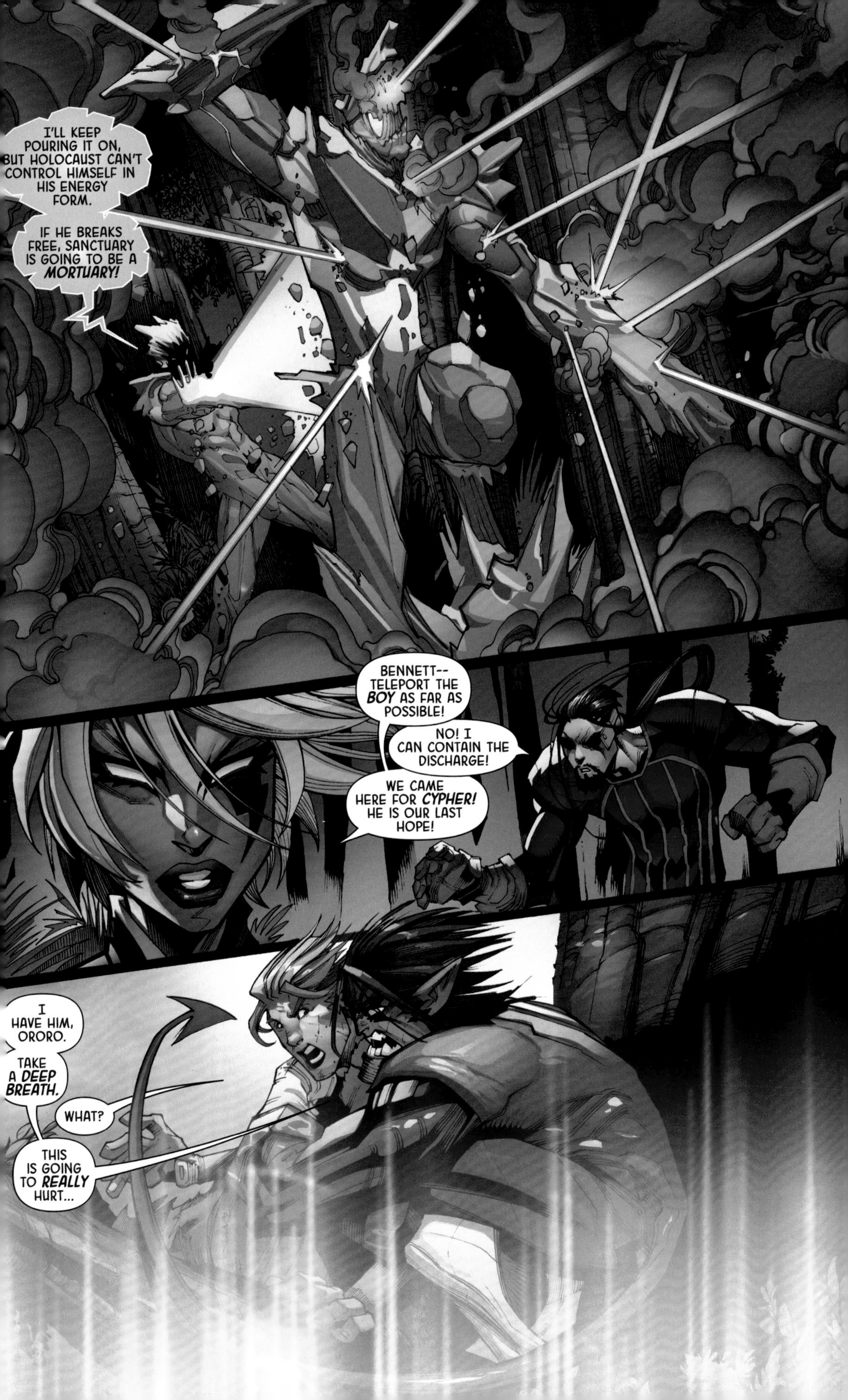

I'LL KEEP POURING IT ON, BUT HOLOCAUST CAN'T CONTROL HIMSELF IN HIS ENERGY FORM.
IF HE BREAKS FREE, SANCTUARY IS GOING TO BE A *MORTUARY!*
BENNETT-- TELEPORT THE *BOY* AS FAR AS POSSIBLE!
NO! I CAN CONTAIN THE DISCHARGE!
WE CAME HERE FOR *CYPHER!* HE IS OUR LAST HOPE!
I HAVE HIM, ORORO.
TAKE A *DEEP BREATH.*
WHAT?
THIS IS GOING TO *REALLY* HURT...

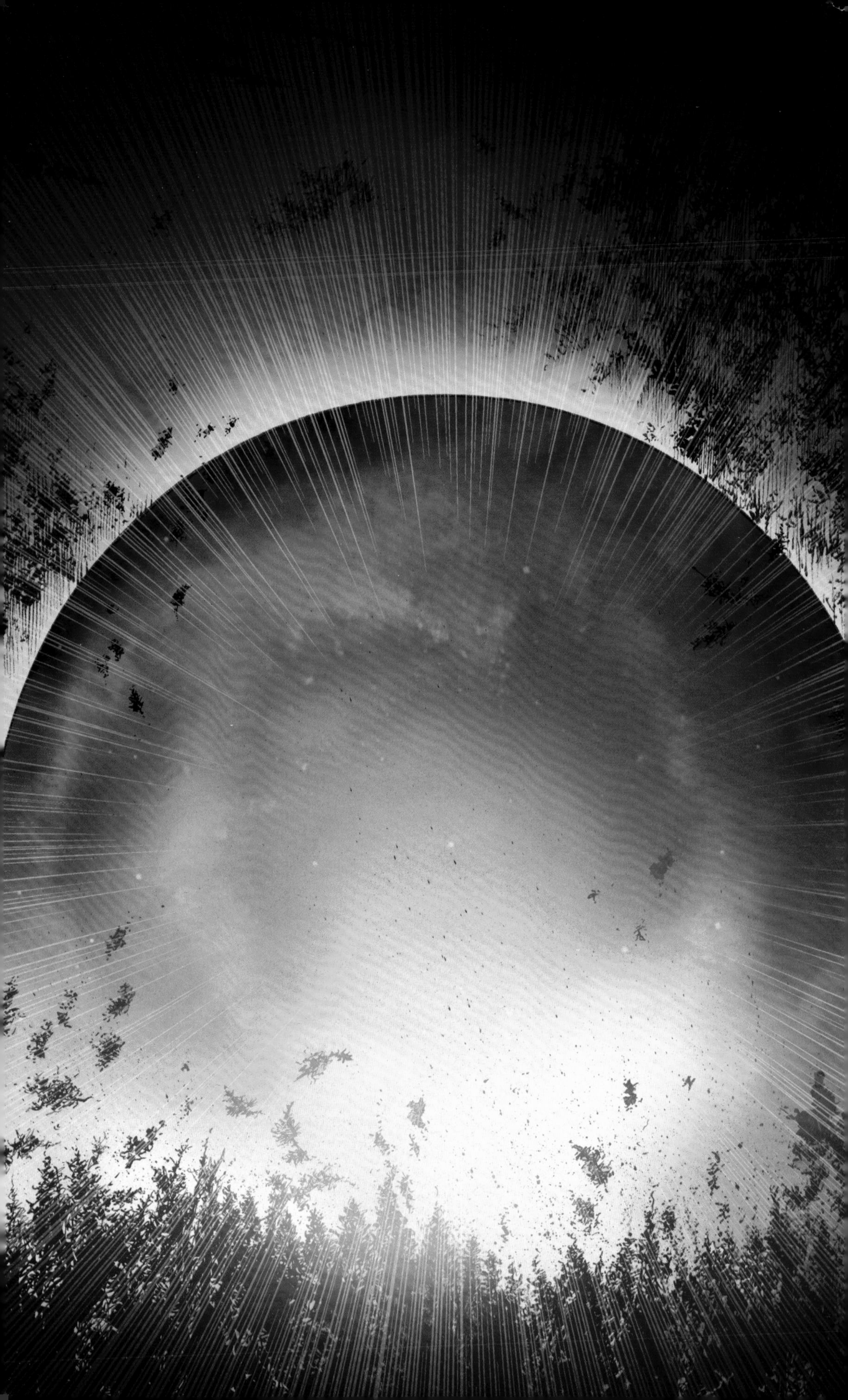

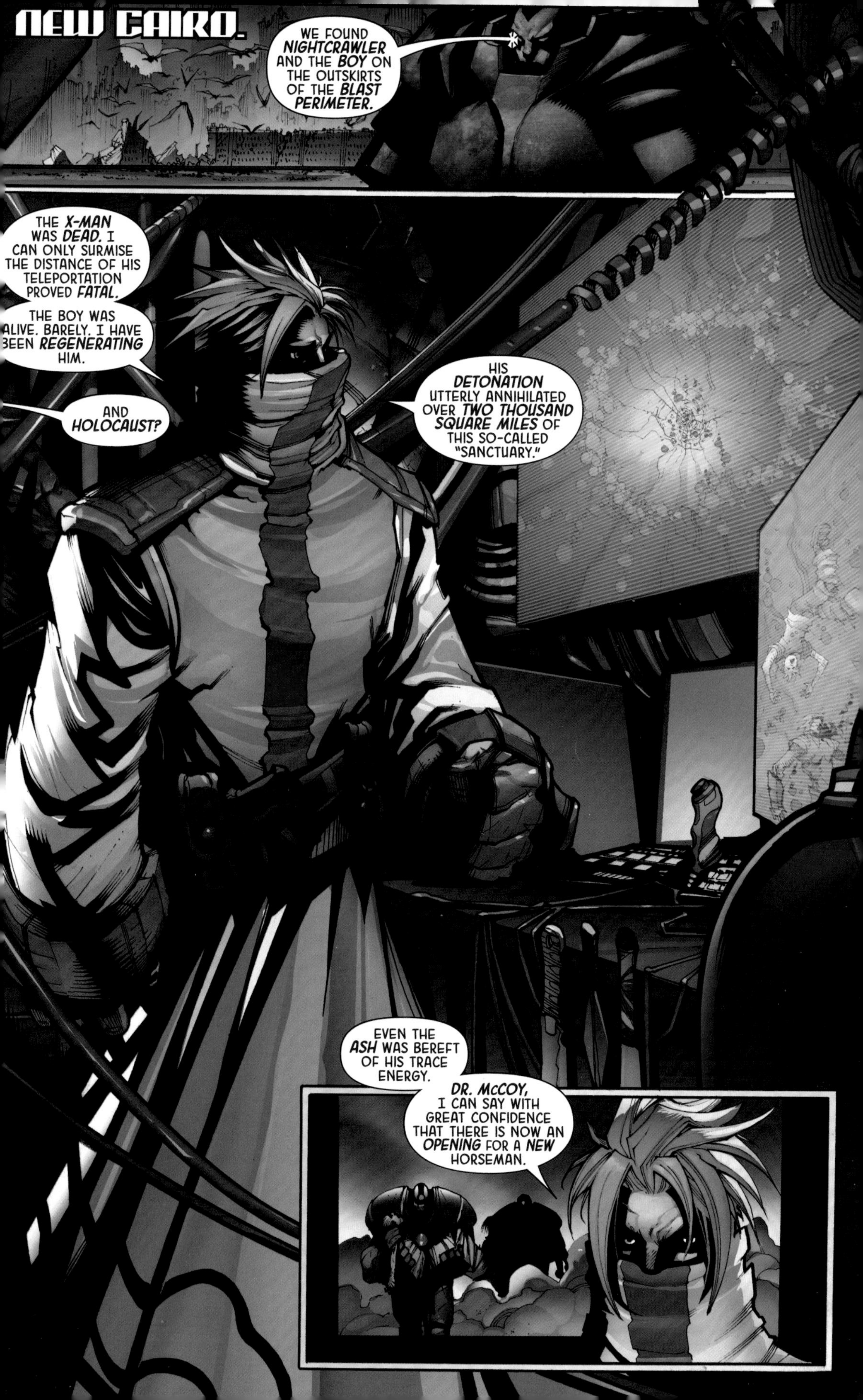
NEW CAIRO.
WE FOUND NIGHTCRAWLER AND THE BOY ON THE OUTSKIRTS OF THE BLAST PERIMETER.
THE X-MAN WAS DEAD. I CAN ONLY SURMISE THE DISTANCE OF HIS TELEPORTATION PROVED FATAL.
THE BOY WAS ALIVE. BARELY. I HAVE BEEN REGENERATING HIM.
AND HOLOCAUST?
HIS DETONATION UTTERLY ANNIHILATED OVER TWO THOUSAND SQUARE MILES OF THIS SO-CALLED "SANCTUARY."
EVEN THE ASH WAS BEREFT OF HIS TRACE ENERGY.
DR. McCOY, I CAN SAY WITH GREAT CONFIDENCE THAT THERE IS NOW AN OPENING FOR A NEW HORSEMAN.

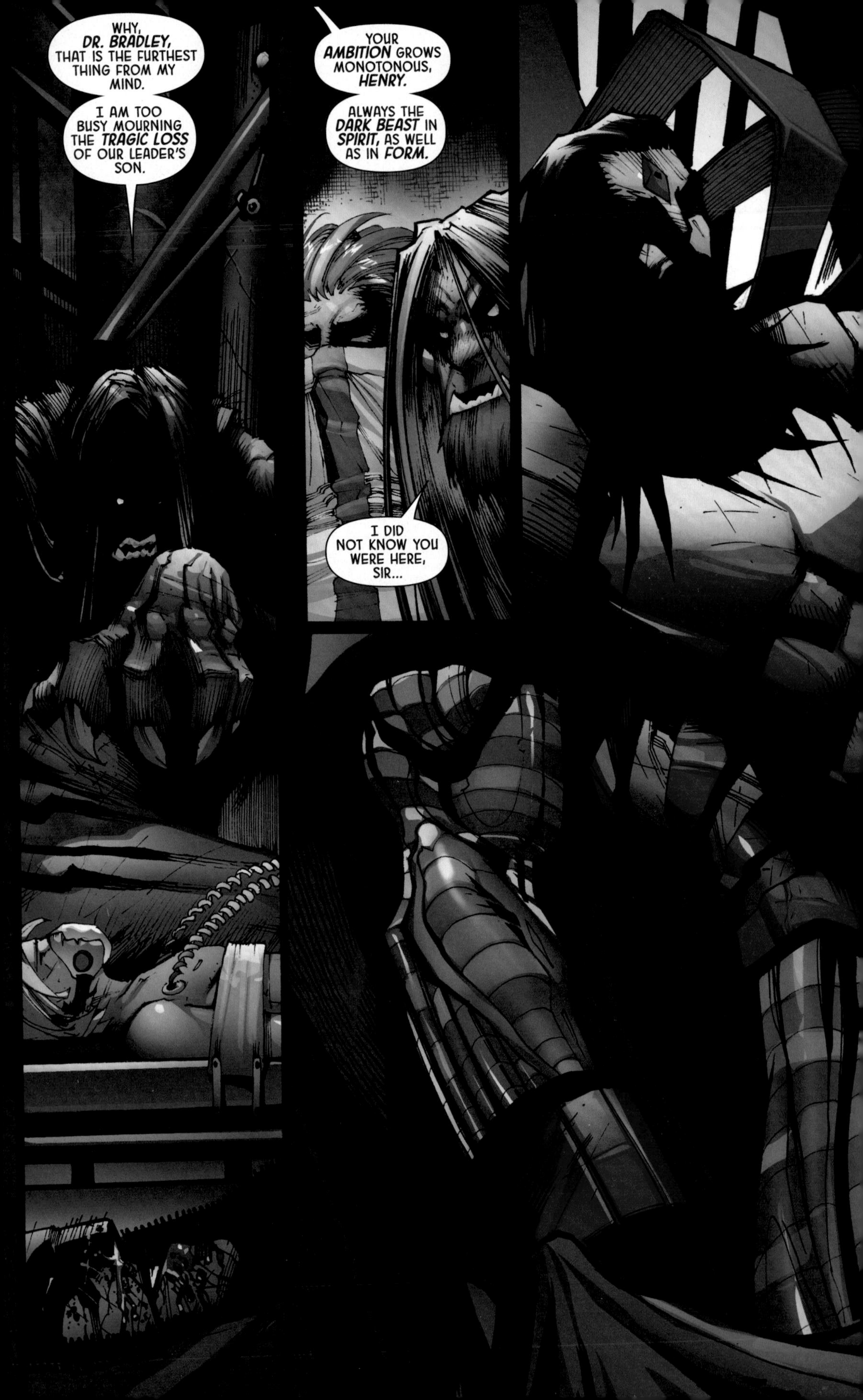
WHY, DR. BRADLEY, THAT IS THE FURTHEST THING FROM MY MIND.
I AM TOO BUSY MOURNING THE TRAGIC LOSS OF OUR LEADER'S SON.
YOUR AMBITION GROWS MONOTONOUS, HENRY.
ALWAYS THE DARK BEAST IN SPIRIT, AS WELL AS IN FORM.
I DID NOT KNOW YOU WERE HERE, SIR...

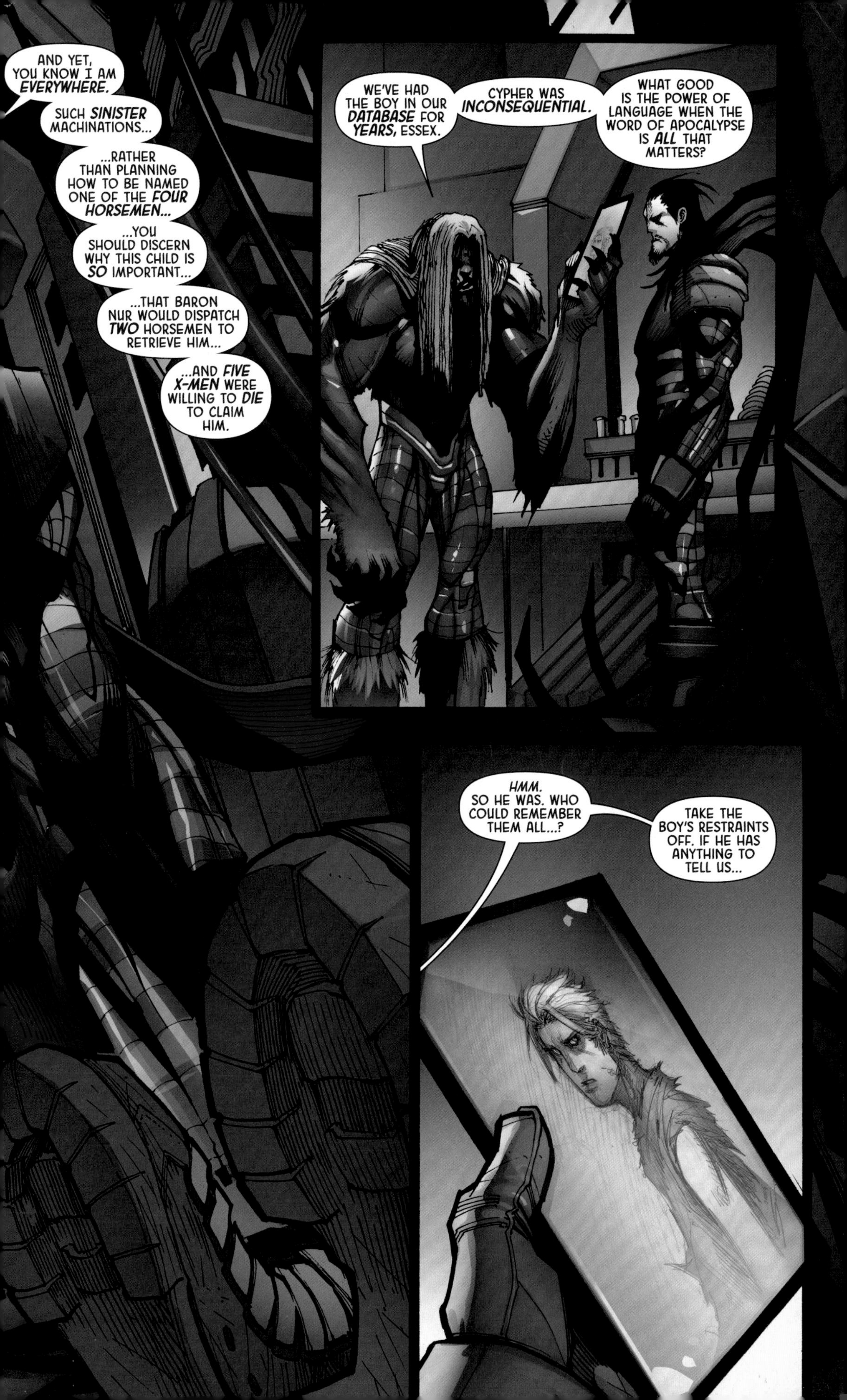
AND YET, YOU KNOW I AM EVERYWHERE.
SUCH SINISTER MACHINATIONS...
...RATHER THAN PLANNING HOW TO BE NAMED ONE OF THE FOUR HORSEMEN...
...YOU SHOULD DISCERN WHY THIS CHILD IS SO IMPORTANT...
...THAT BARON NUR WOULD DISPATCH TWO HORSEMEN TO RETRIEVE HIM...
...AND FIVE X-MEN WERE WILLING TO DIE TO CLAIM HIM.
WE'VE HAD THE BOY IN OUR DATABASE FOR YEARS, ESSEX.
CYPHER WAS INCONSEQUENTIAL.
WHAT GOOD IS THE POWER OF LANGUAGE WHEN THE WORD OF APOCALYPSE IS ALL THAT MATTERS?
HMM. SO HE WAS. WHO COULD REMEMBER THEM ALL...?
TAKE THE BOY'S RESTRAINTS OFF. IF HE HAS ANYTHING TO TELL US...

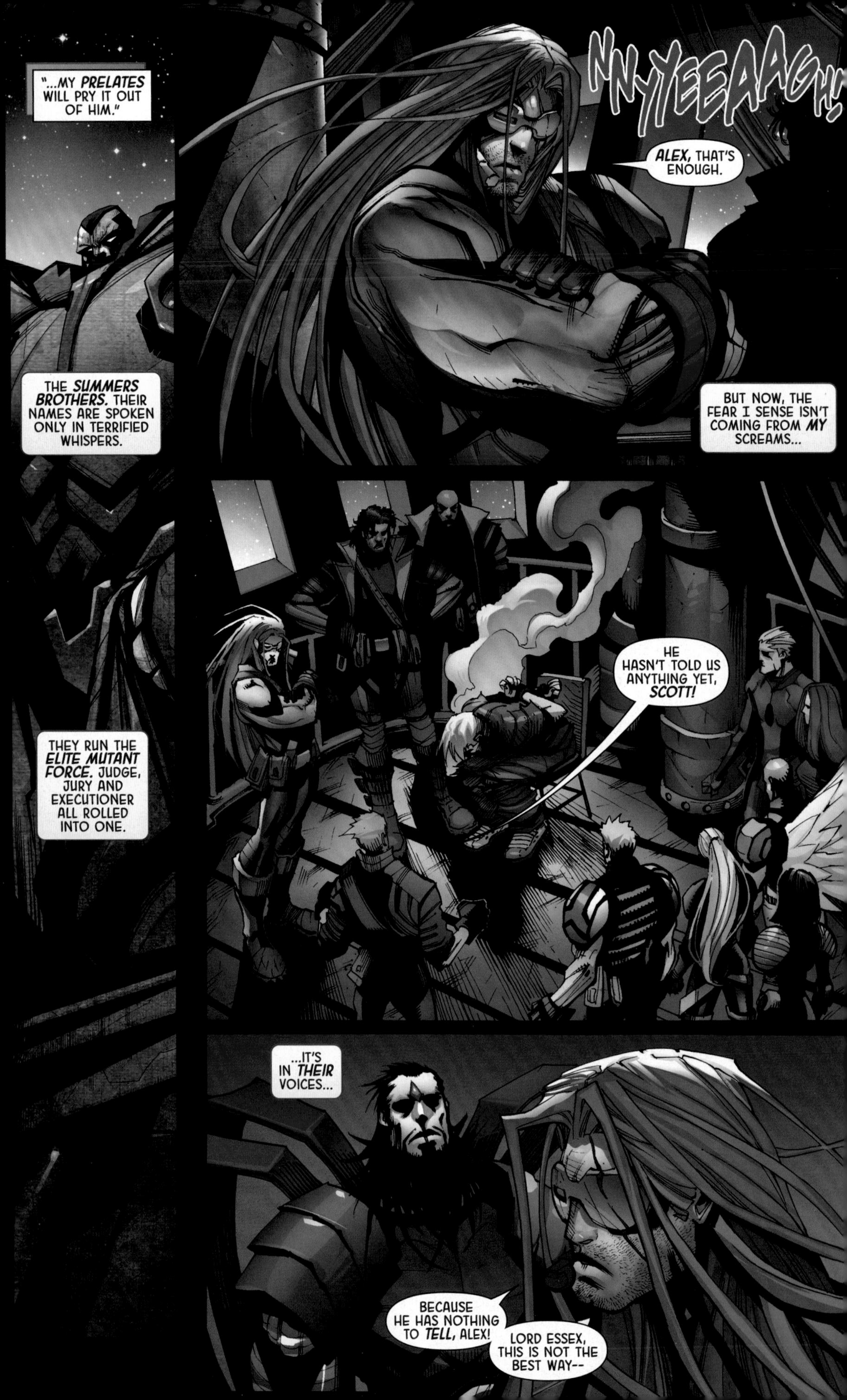

"...MY PRELATES WILL PRY IT OUT OF HIM."
NNYYEEAAAGH!
ALEX, THAT'S ENOUGH.
THE SUMMERS BROTHERS. THEIR NAMES ARE SPOKEN ONLY IN TERRIFIED WHISPERS.
BUT NOW, THE FEAR I SENSE ISN'T COMING FROM MY SCREAMS...
HE HASN'T TOLD US ANYTHING YET, SCOTT!
THEY RUN THE ELITE MUTANT FORCE. JUDGE, JURY AND EXECUTIONER ALL ROLLED INTO ONE.
...IT'S IN THEIR VOICES...
BECAUSE HE HAS NOTHING TO TELL, ALEX!
LORD ESSEX, THIS IS NOT THE BEST WAY--

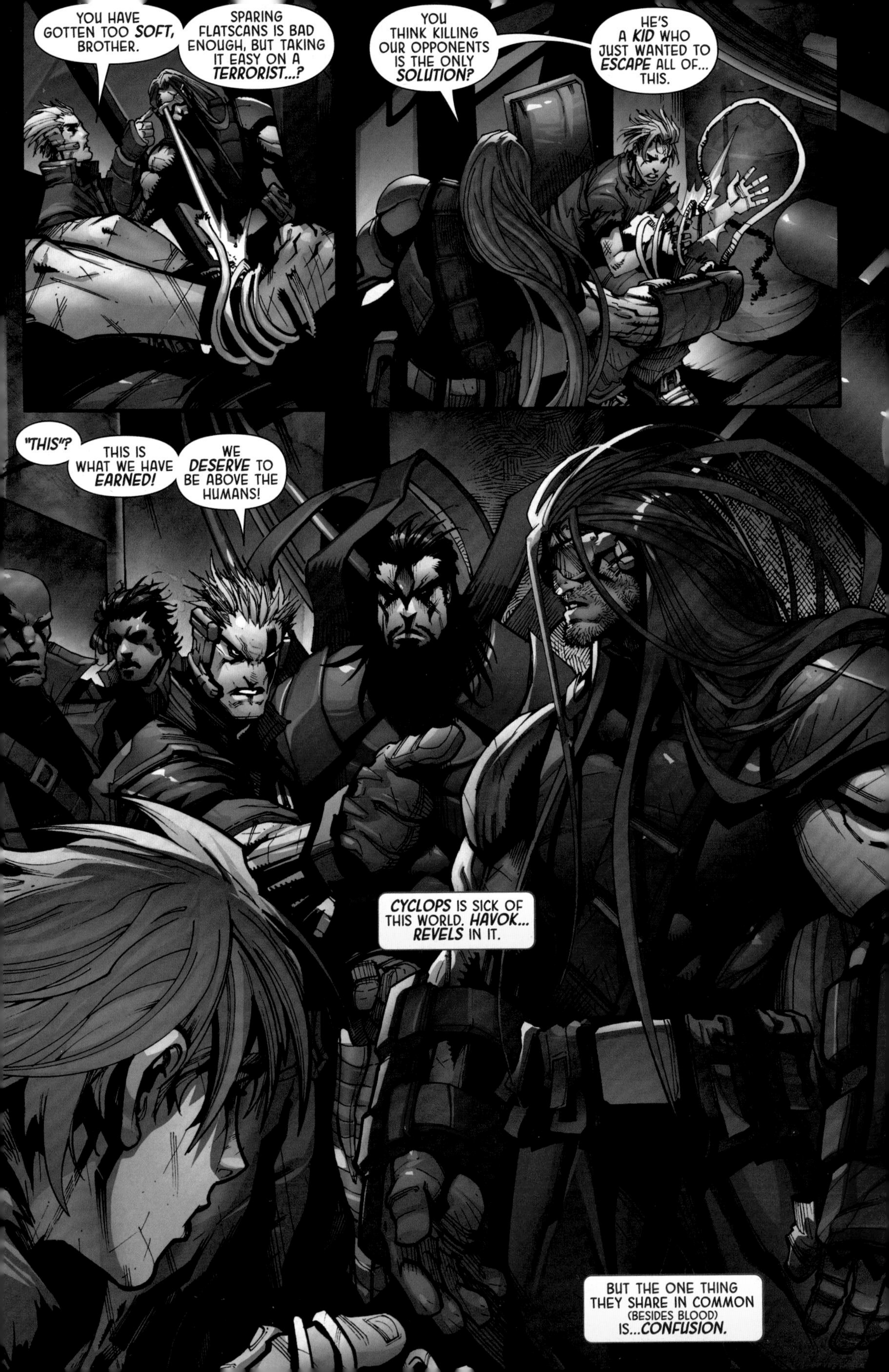

YOU HAVE GOTTEN TOO SOFT, BROTHER.
SPARING FLATSCANS IS BAD ENOUGH, BUT TAKING IT EASY ON A TERRORIST...?
YOU THINK KILLING OUR OPPONENTS IS THE ONLY SOLUTION?
HE'S A KID WHO JUST WANTED TO ESCAPE ALL OF... THIS.
"THIS"?
THIS IS WHAT WE HAVE EARNED!
WE DESERVE TO BE ABOVE THE HUMANS!
CYCLOPS IS SICK OF THIS WORLD. HAVOK... REVELS IN IT.
BUT THE ONE THING THEY SHARE IN COMMON (BESIDES BLOOD) IS...CONFUSION.

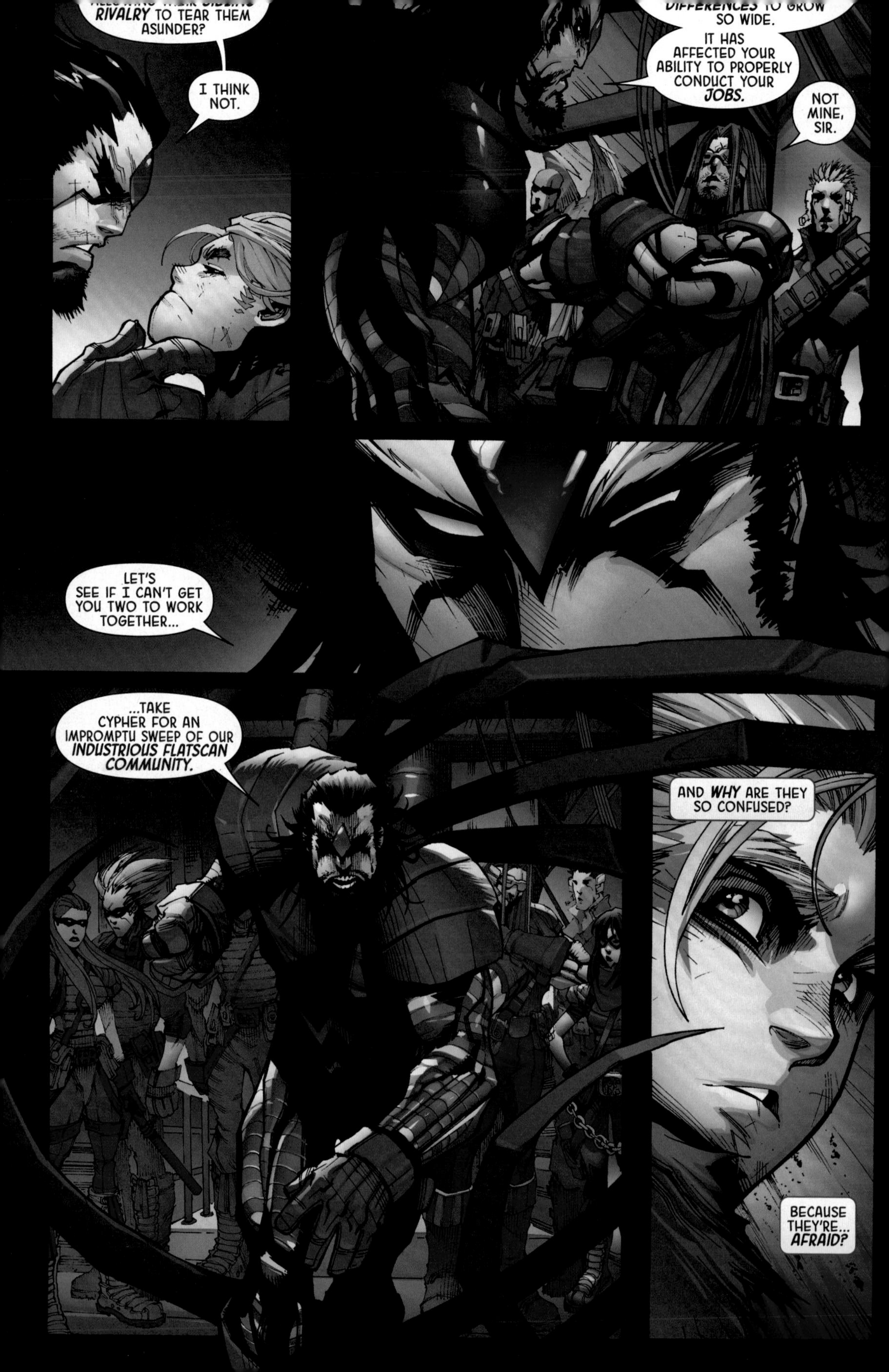
RIVALRY TO TEAR THEM ASUNDER?
I THINK NOT.
DIFFERENCES TO GROW SO WIDE.
IT HAS AFFECTED YOUR ABILITY TO PROPERLY CONDUCT YOUR JOBS.
NOT MINE, SIR.
LET'S SEE IF I CAN'T GET YOU TWO TO WORK TOGETHER...
...TAKE CYPHER FOR AN IMPROMPTU SWEEP OF OUR INDUSTRIOUS FLATSCAN COMMUNITY.
AND WHY ARE THEY SO CONFUSED?
BECAUSE THEY'RE... AFRAID?

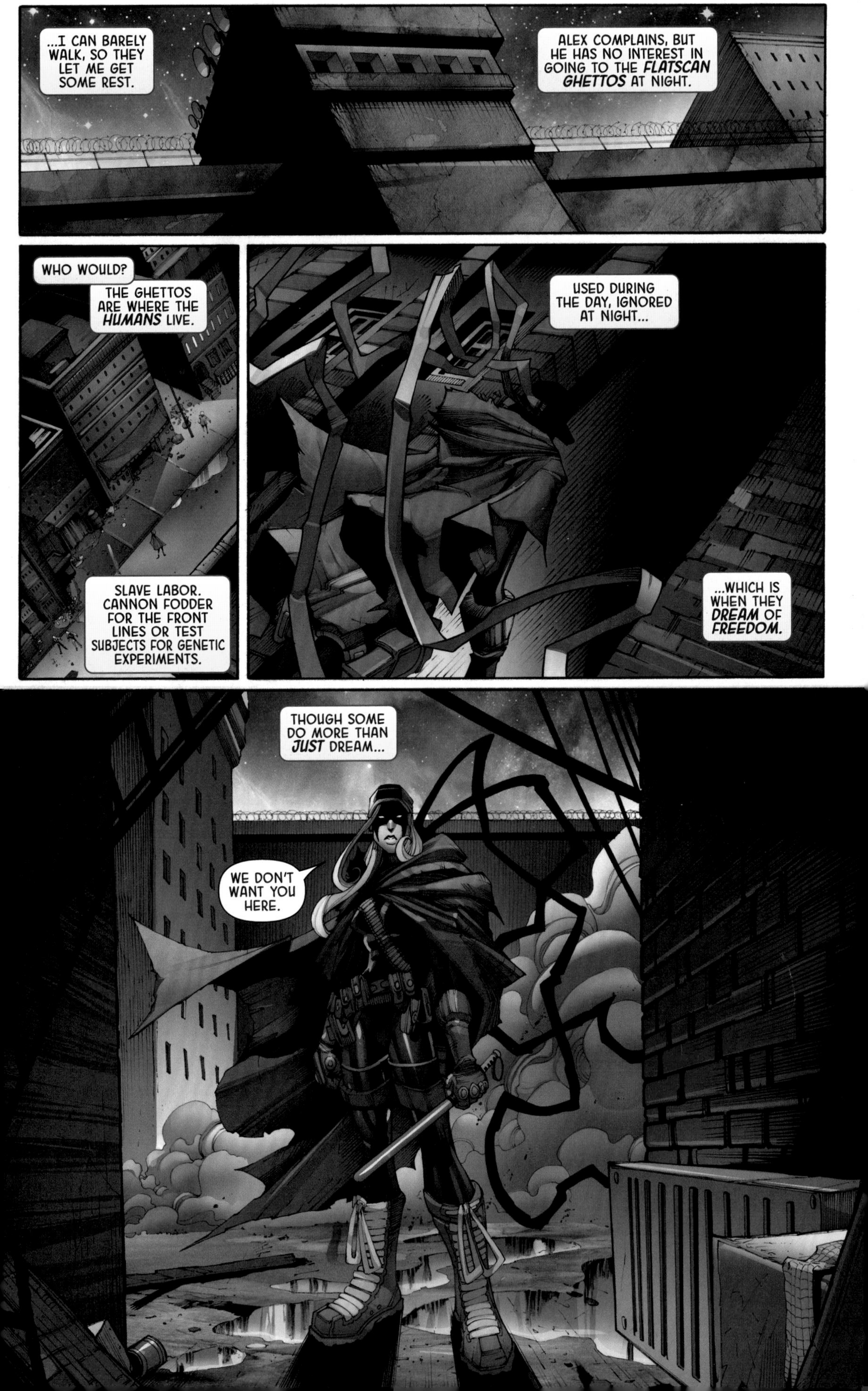

...I CAN BARELY WALK, SO THEY LET ME GET SOME REST.
ALEX COMPLAINS, BUT HE HAS NO INTEREST IN GOING TO THE FLATSCAN GHETTOS AT NIGHT.
WHO WOULD?
THE GHETTOS ARE WHERE THE HUMANS LIVE.
SLAVE LABOR. CANNON FODDER FOR THE FRONT LINES OR TEST SUBJECTS FOR GENETIC EXPERIMENTS.
USED DURING THE DAY, IGNORED AT NIGHT...
...WHICH IS WHEN THEY DREAM OF FREEDOM.
THOUGH SOME DO MORE THAN JUST DREAM...
WE DON'T WANT YOU HERE.

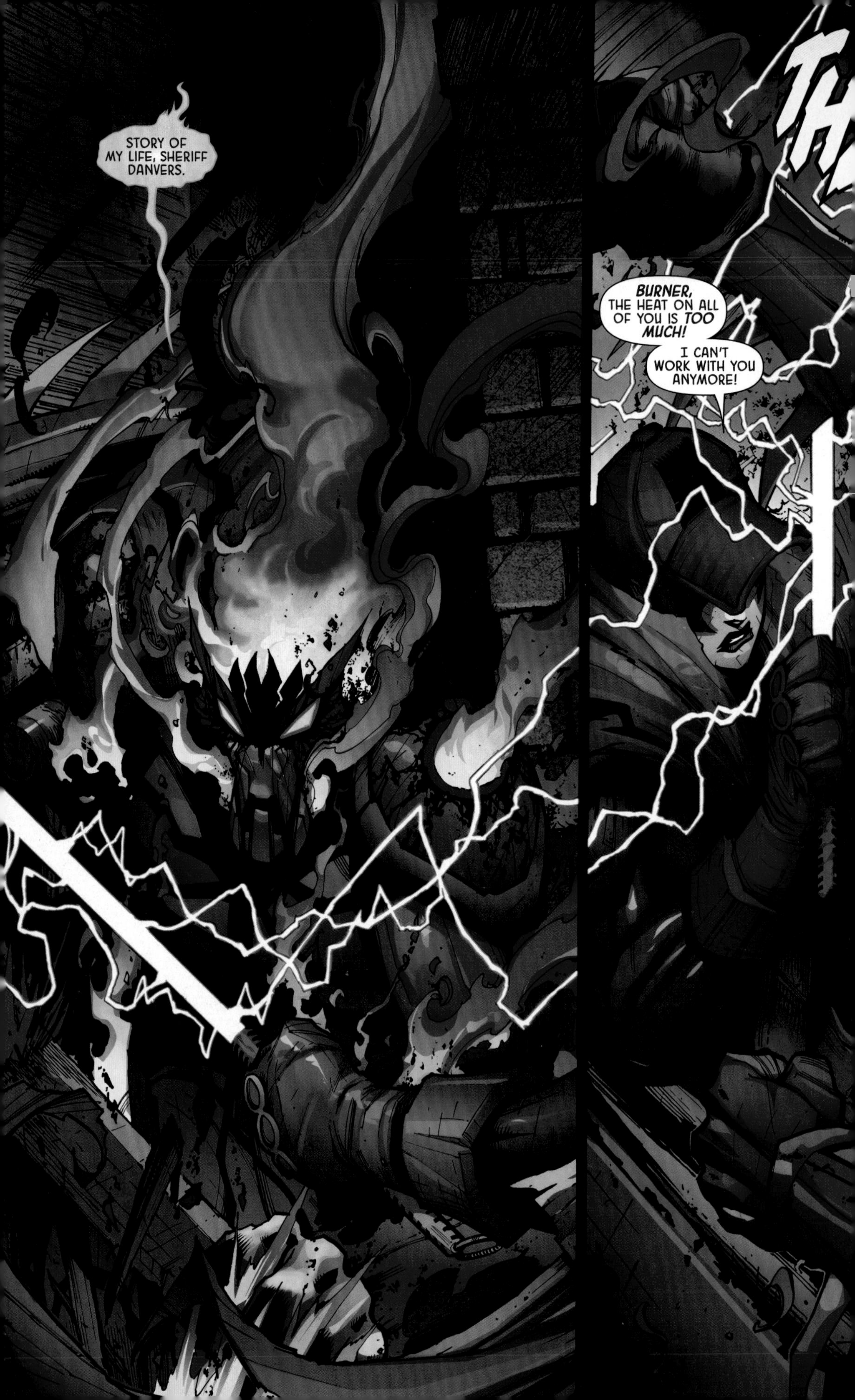
STORY OF MY LIFE, SHERIFF DANVERS.
BURNER, THE HEAT ON ALL OF YOU IS TOO MUCH!
I CAN'T WORK WITH YOU ANYMORE!

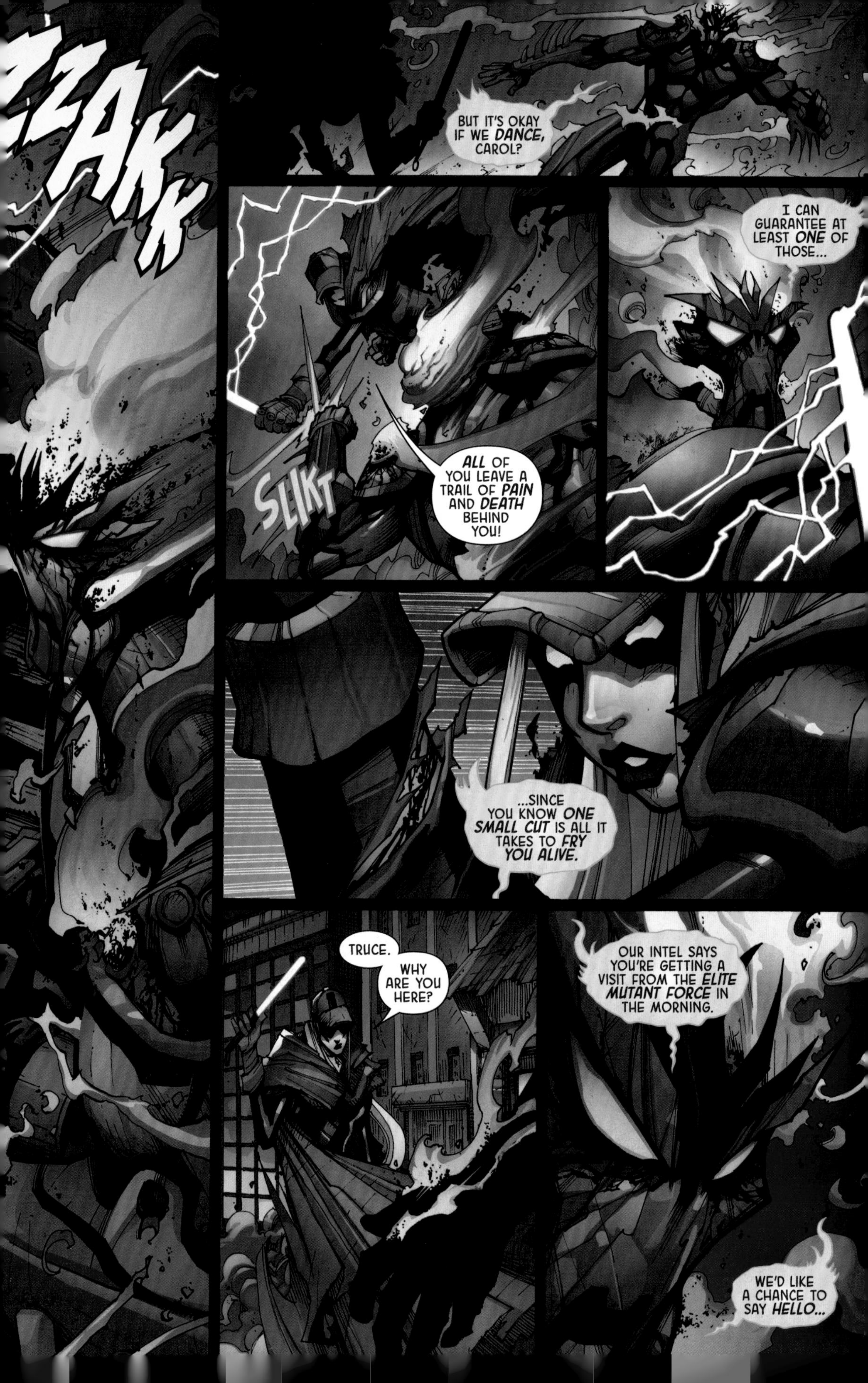

ZZAKK
BUT IT'S OKAY IF WE DANCE, CAROL?
SLIKT
ALL OF YOU LEAVE A TRAIL OF PAIN AND DEATH BEHIND YOU!
I CAN GUARANTEE AT LEAST ONE OF THOSE...
...SINCE YOU KNOW ONE SMALL CUT IS ALL IT TAKES TO FRY YOU ALIVE.
TRUCE.
WHY ARE YOU HERE?
OUR INTEL SAYS YOU'RE GETTING A VISIT FROM THE ELITE MUTANT FORCE IN THE MORNING.
WE'D LIKE A CHANCE TO SAY HELLO...

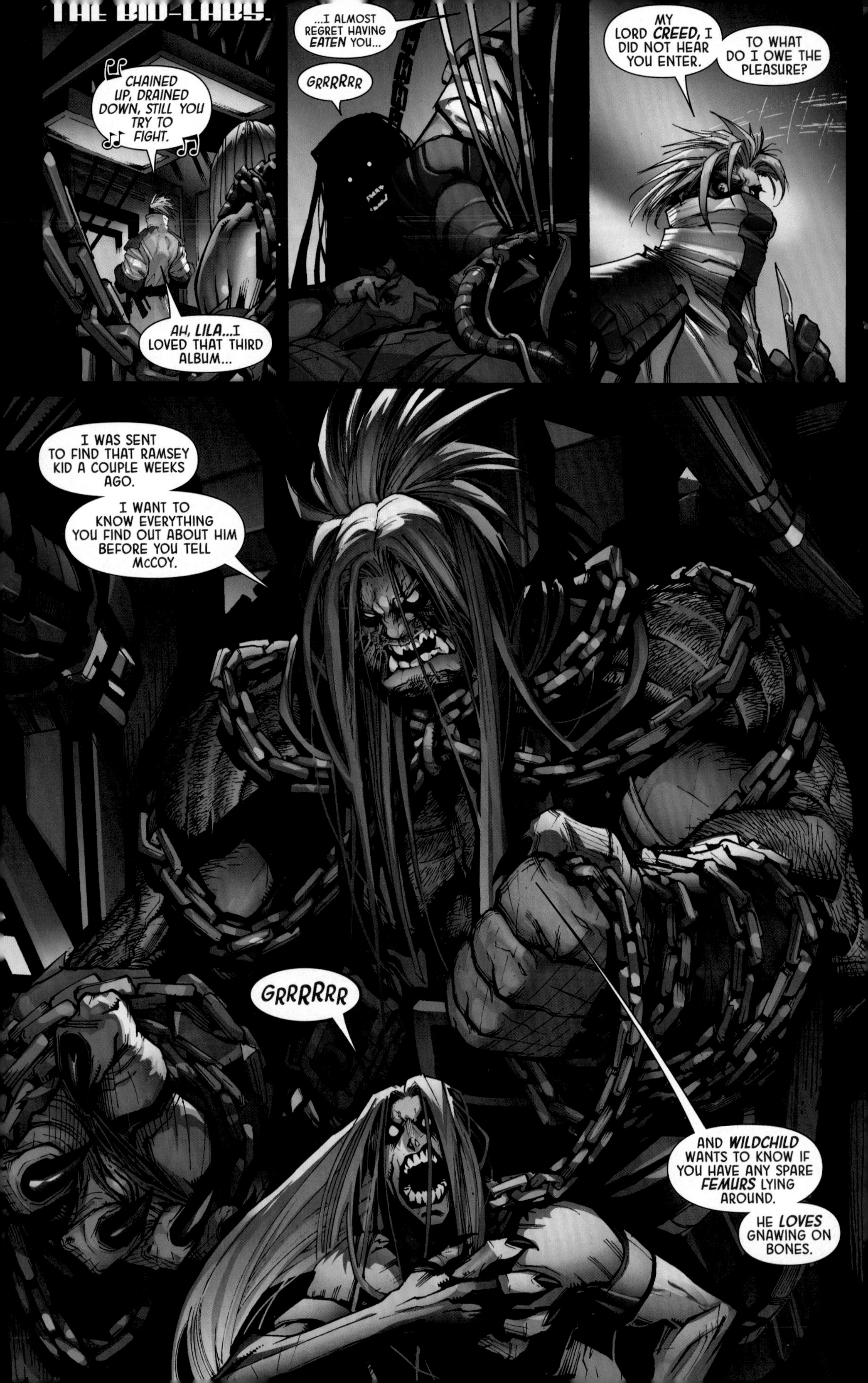
THE BIO-LABS.
CHAINED UP, DRAINED DOWN, STILL YOU TRY TO FIGHT.
AH, LILA...I LOVED THAT THIRD ALBUM...
...I ALMOST REGRET HAVING EATEN YOU...
GRRRRRR
MY LORD CREED, I DID NOT HEAR YOU ENTER.
TO WHAT DO I OWE THE PLEASURE?
I WAS SENT TO FIND THAT RAMSEY KID A COUPLE WEEKS AGO.
I WANT TO KNOW EVERYTHING YOU FIND OUT ABOUT HIM BEFORE YOU TELL McCOY.
GRRRRRR
AND WILDCHILD WANTS TO KNOW IF YOU HAVE ANY SPARE FEMURS LYING AROUND.
HE LOVES GNAWING ON BONES.

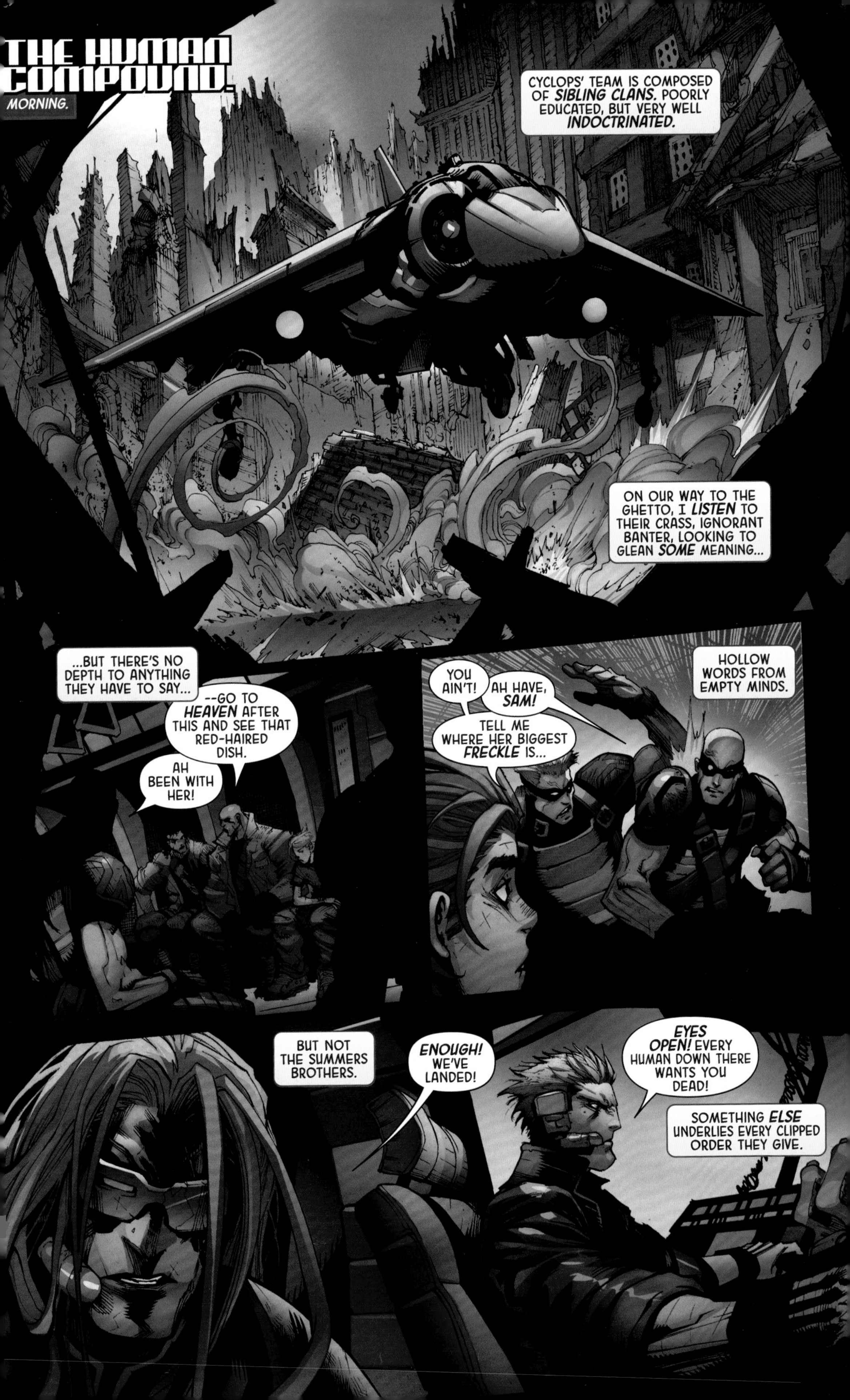
THE HUMAN COMPOUND.
MORNING.
CYCLOPS' TEAM IS COMPOSED OF SIBLING CLANS. POORLY EDUCATED, BUT VERY WELL INDOCTRINATED.
ON OUR WAY TO THE GHETTO, I LISTEN TO THEIR CRASS, IGNORANT BANTER, LOOKING TO GLEAN SOME MEANING...
...BUT THERE'S NO DEPTH TO ANYTHING THEY HAVE TO SAY...
--GO TO HEAVEN AFTER THIS AND SEE THAT RED-HAIRED DISH.
AH BEEN WITH HER!
YOU AIN'T!
AH HAVE, SAM!
TELL ME WHERE HER BIGGEST FRECKLE IS...
HOLLOW WORDS FROM EMPTY MINDS.
BUT NOT THE SUMMERS BROTHERS.
ENOUGH! WE'VE LANDED!
EYES OPEN! EVERY HUMAN DOWN THERE WANTS YOU DEAD!
SOMETHING ELSE UNDERLIES EVERY CLIPPED ORDER THEY GIVE.

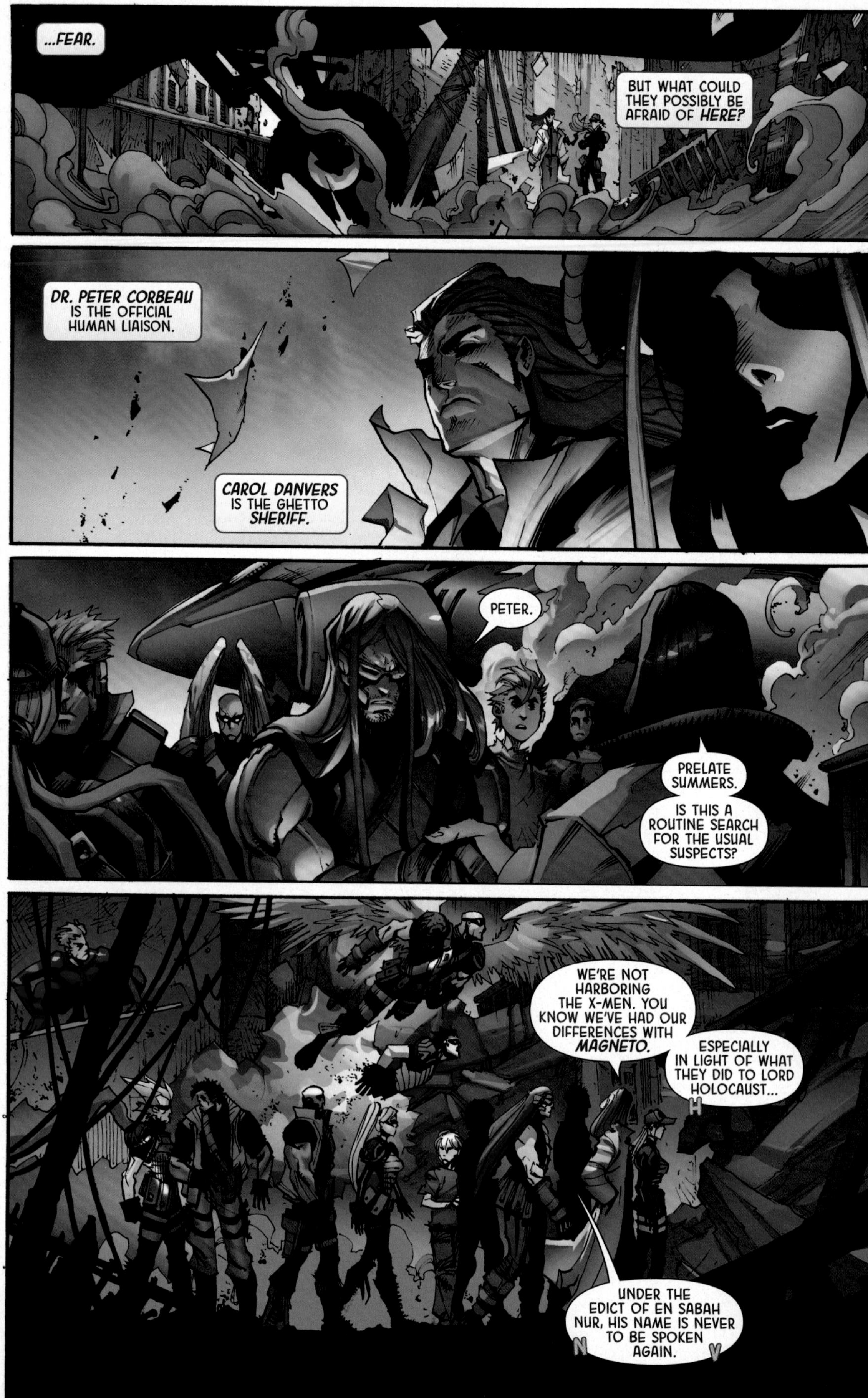
...FEAR.
BUT WHAT COULD THEY POSSIBLY BE AFRAID OF HERE?
DR. PETER CORBEAU IS THE OFFICIAL HUMAN LIAISON.
CAROL DANVERS IS THE GHETTO SHERIFF.
PETER.
PRELATE SUMMERS.
IS THIS A ROUTINE SEARCH FOR THE USUAL SUSPECTS?
WE'RE NOT HARBORING THE X-MEN. YOU KNOW WE'VE HAD OUR DIFFERENCES WITH MAGNETO.
ESPECIALLY IN LIGHT OF WHAT THEY DID TO LORD HOLOCAUST...
UNDER THE EDICT OF EN SABAH NUR, HIS NAME IS NEVER TO BE SPOKEN AGAIN.

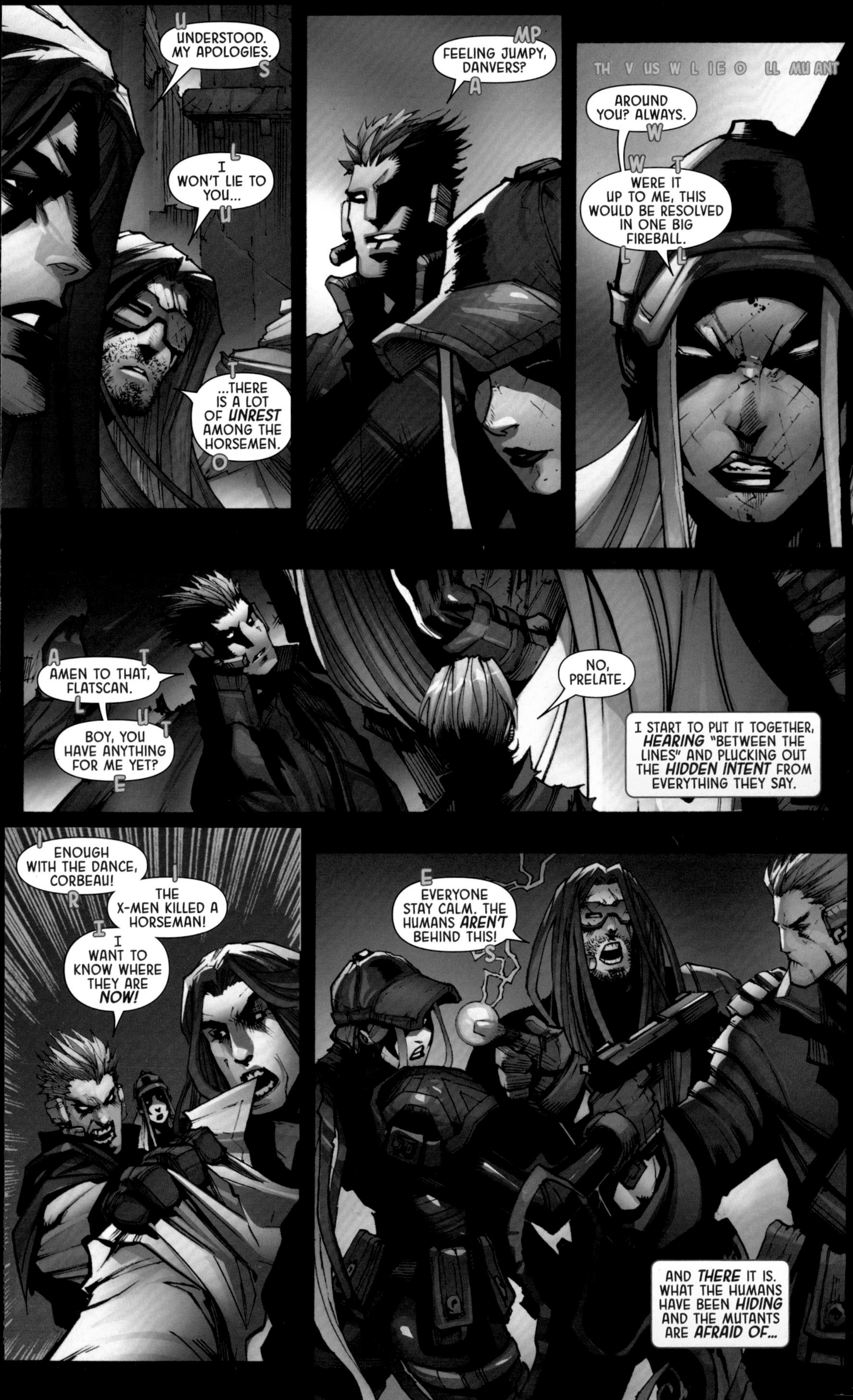
UNDERSTOOD. MY APOLOGIES.
I WON'T LIE TO YOU...
...THERE IS A LOT OF *UNREST* AMONG THE HORSEMEN.
FEELING JUMPY, DANVERS?
AROUND YOU? ALWAYS.
WERE IT UP TO ME, THIS WOULD BE RESOLVED IN ONE BIG FIREBALL.
AMEN TO THAT, FLATSCAN.
BOY, YOU HAVE ANYTHING FOR ME YET?
NO, PRELATE.
I START TO PUT IT TOGETHER, *HEARING* "BETWEEN THE LINES" AND PLUCKING OUT THE *HIDDEN INTENT* FROM EVERYTHING THEY SAY.
ENOUGH WITH THE DANCE, CORBEAU!
THE X-MEN KILLED A HORSEMAN!
I WANT TO KNOW WHERE THEY ARE *NOW!*
EVERYONE STAY CALM. THE HUMANS *AREN'T* BEHIND THIS!
AND *THERE* IT IS. WHAT THE HUMANS HAVE BEEN *HIDING* AND THE MUTANTS ARE *AFRAID OF...*

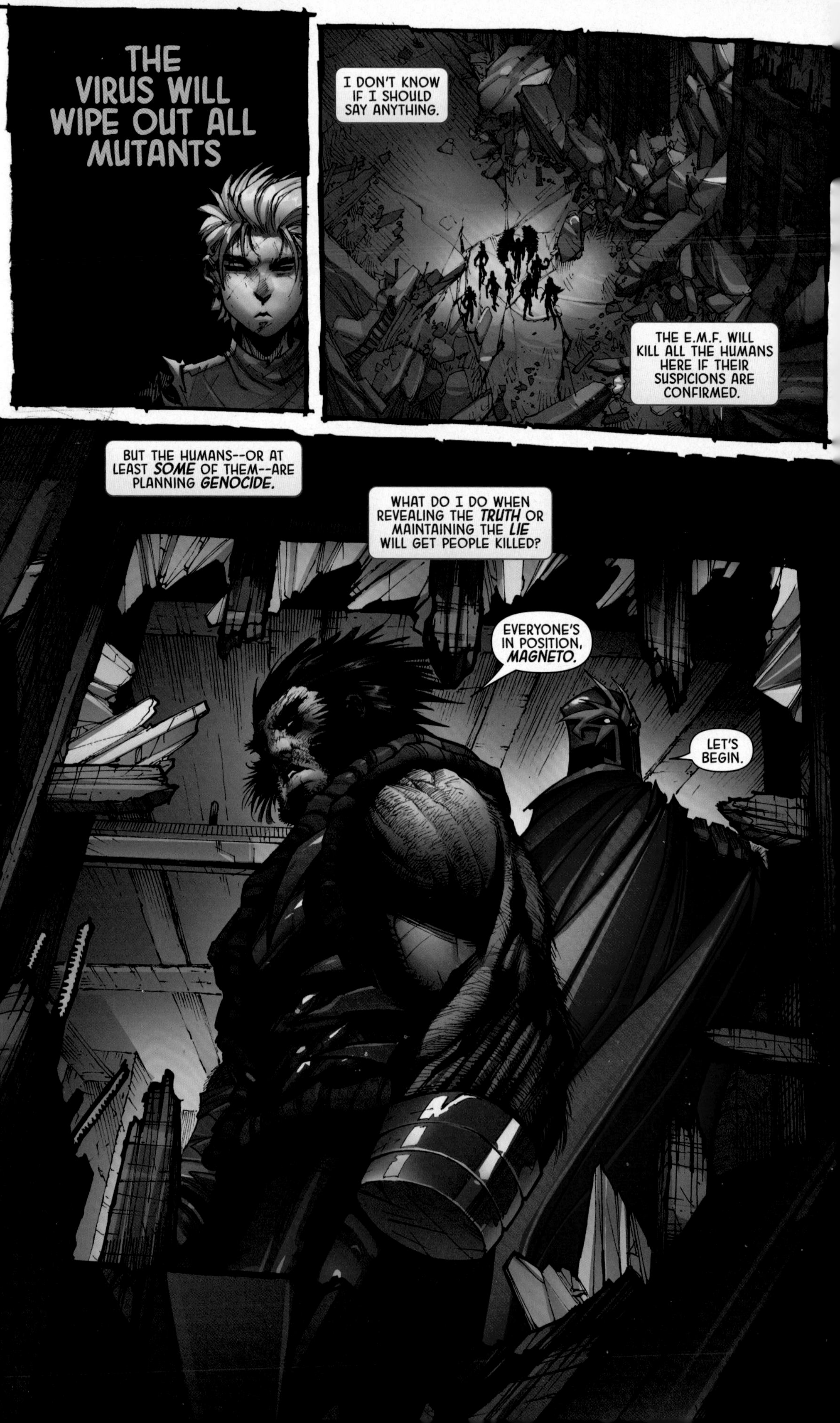
THE VIRUS WILL WIPE OUT ALL MUTANTS
I DON'T KNOW IF I SHOULD SAY ANYTHING.
THE E.M.F. WILL KILL ALL THE HUMANS HERE IF THEIR SUSPICIONS ARE CONFIRMED.
BUT THE HUMANS--OR AT LEAST SOME OF THEM--ARE PLANNING GENOCIDE.
WHAT DO I DO WHEN REVEALING THE TRUTH OR MAINTAINING THE LIE WILL GET PEOPLE KILLED?
EVERYONE'S IN POSITION, MAGNETO.
LET'S BEGIN.

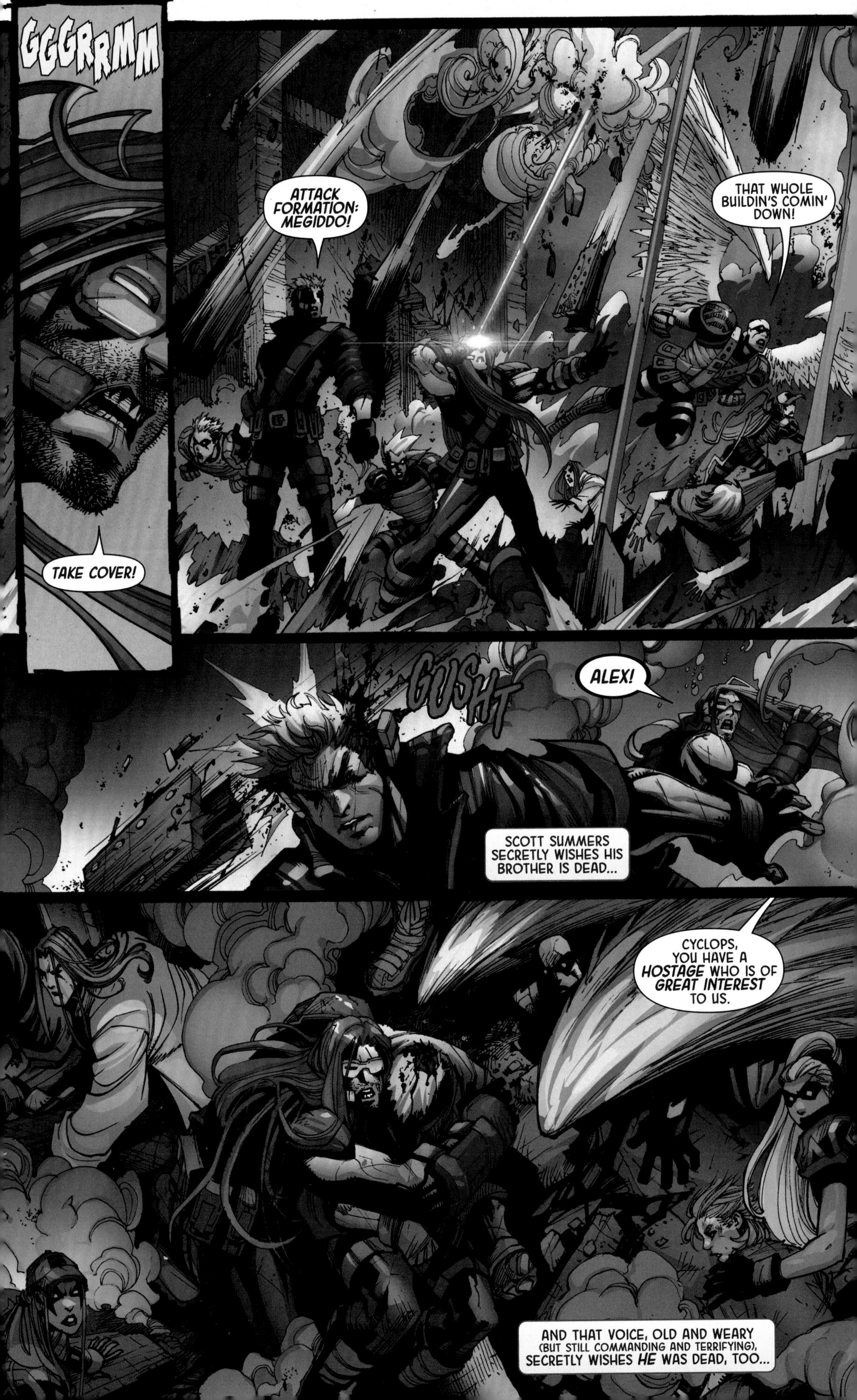
GGGRRMM
TAKE COVER!
ATTACK FORMATION: MEGIDDO!
THAT WHOLE BUILDIN'S COMIN' DOWN!
GUSHT
ALEX!
SCOTT SUMMERS SECRETLY WISHES HIS BROTHER IS DEAD...
CYCLOPS, YOU HAVE A HOSTAGE WHO IS OF GREAT INTEREST TO US.
AND THAT VOICE, OLD AND WEARY (BUT STILL COMMANDING AND TERRIFYING), SECRETLY WISHES HE WAS DEAD, TOO...

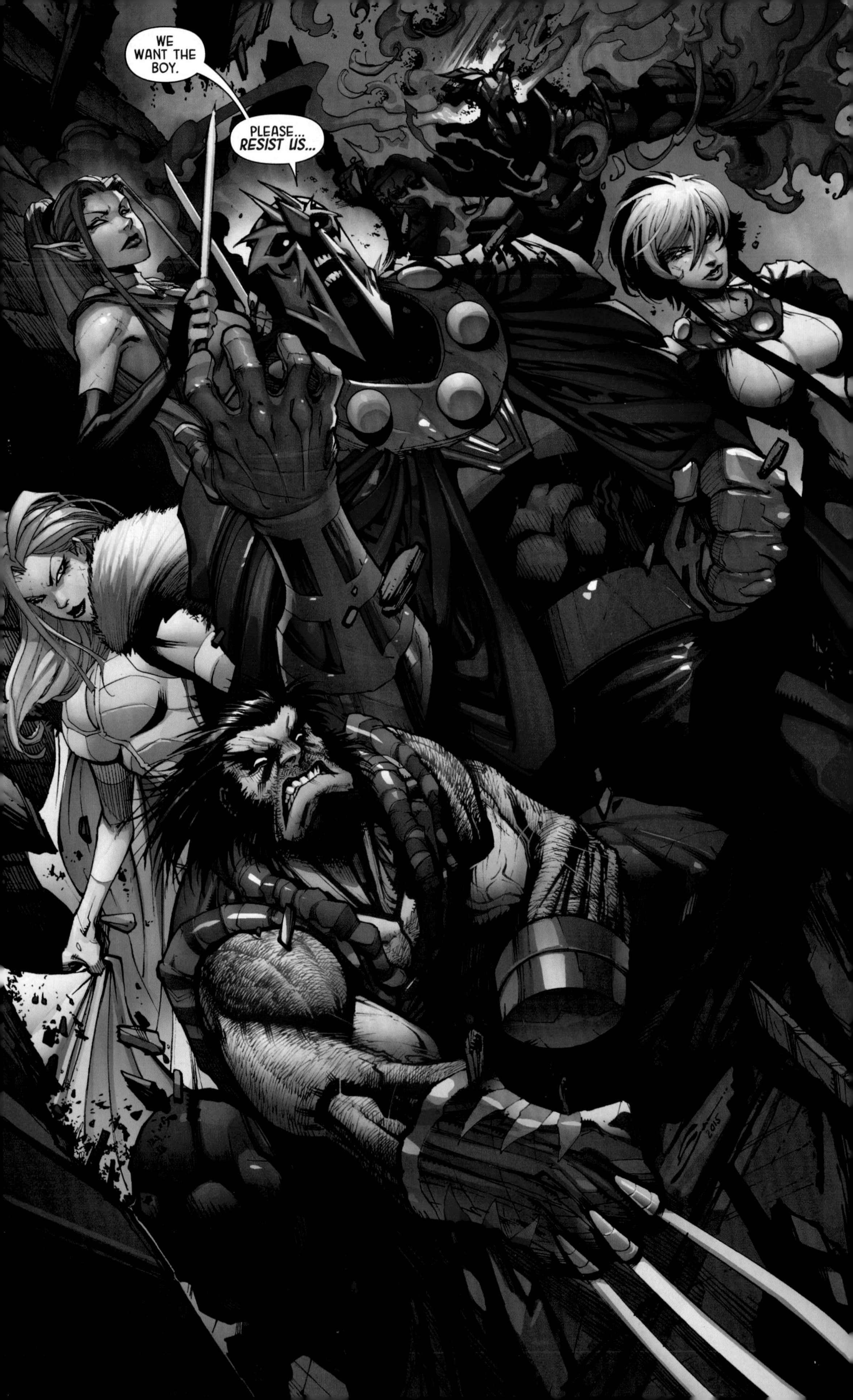
WE WANT THE BOY.
PLEASE... RESIST US...

FORGE

TWO | MUTUALLY ASSURED DESTRUCTION

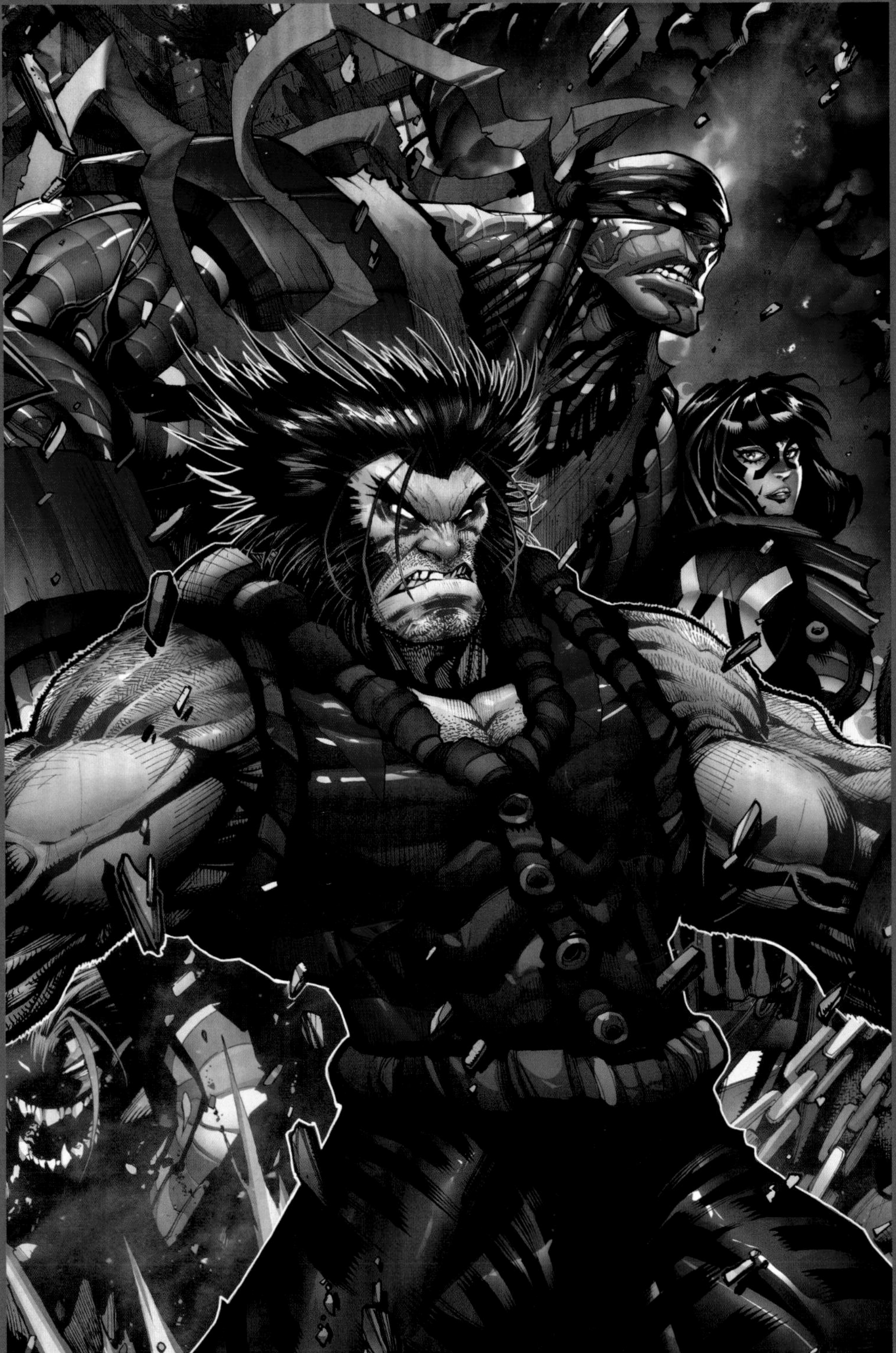

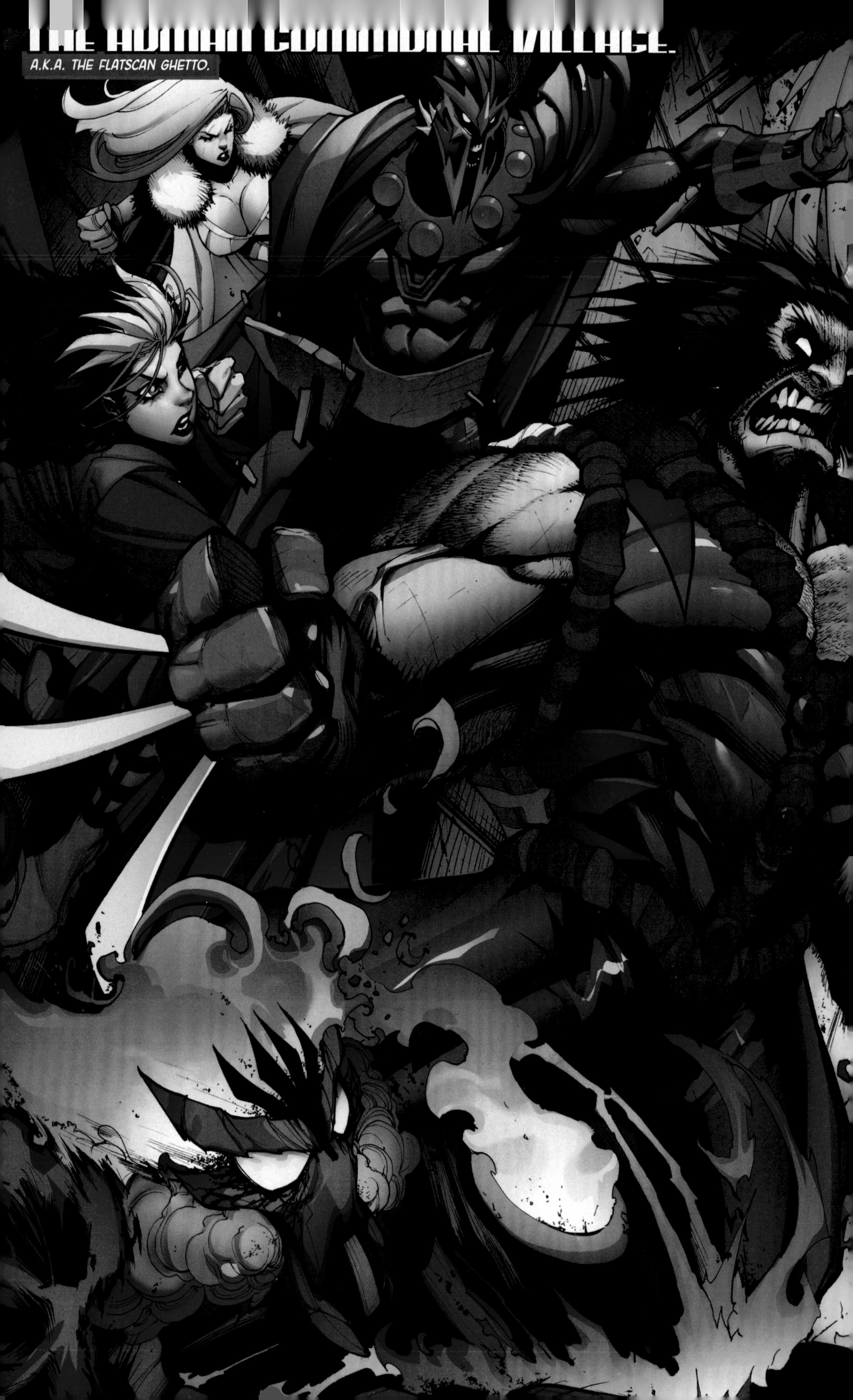
THE HUMAN COMMUNAL VILLAGE.
A.K.A. THE FLATSCAN GHETTO.

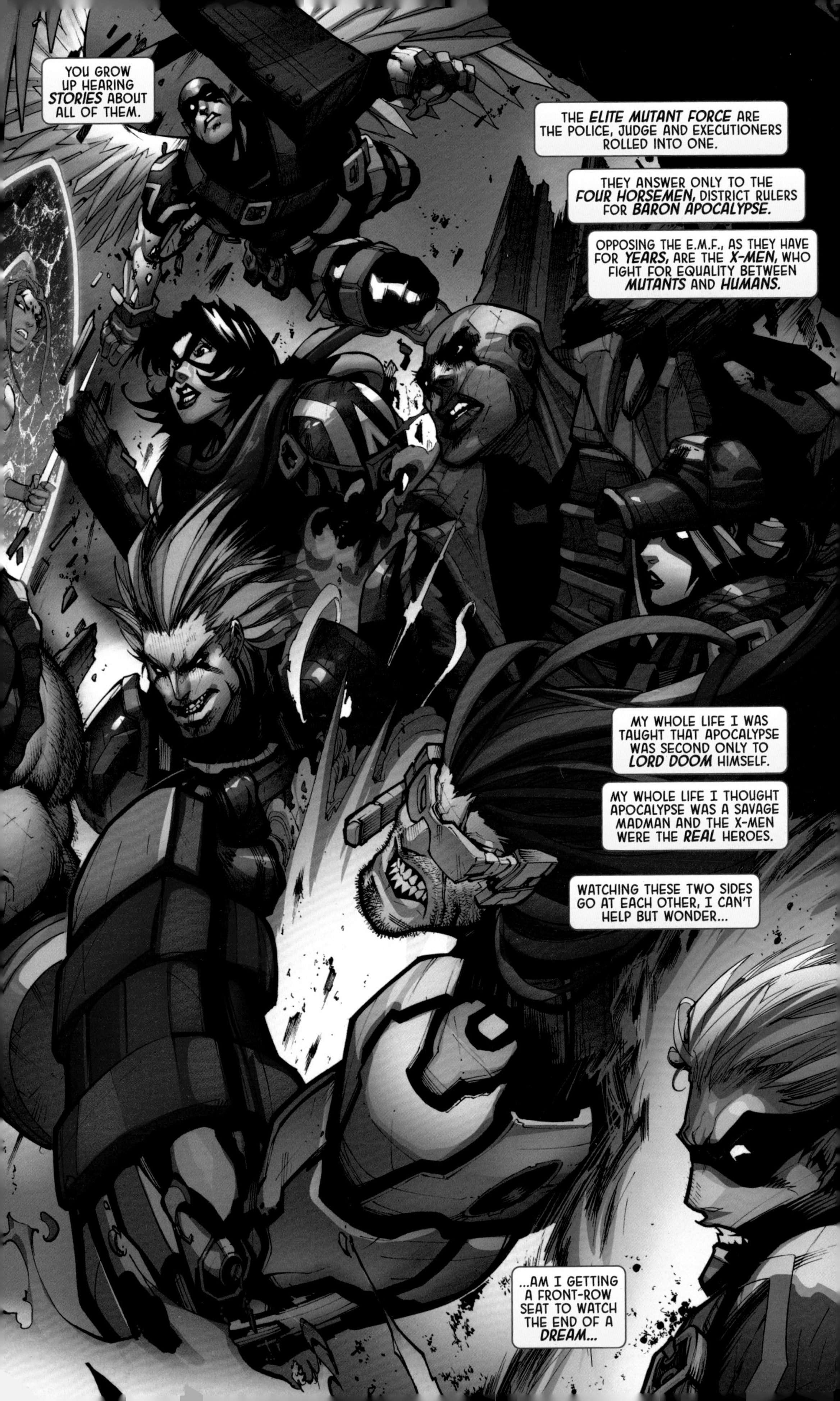
YOU GROW UP HEARING STORIES ABOUT ALL OF THEM.
THE ELITE MUTANT FORCE ARE THE POLICE, JUDGE AND EXECUTIONERS ROLLED INTO ONE.
THEY ANSWER ONLY TO THE FOUR HORSEMEN, DISTRICT RULERS FOR BARON APOCALYPSE.
OPPOSING THE E.M.F., AS THEY HAVE FOR YEARS, ARE THE X-MEN, WHO FIGHT FOR EQUALITY BETWEEN MUTANTS AND HUMANS.
MY WHOLE LIFE I WAS TAUGHT THAT APOCALYPSE WAS SECOND ONLY TO LORD DOOM HIMSELF.
MY WHOLE LIFE I THOUGHT APOCALYPSE WAS A SAVAGE MADMAN AND THE X-MEN WERE THE REAL HEROES.
WATCHING THESE TWO SIDES GO AT EACH OTHER, I CAN'T HELP BUT WONDER...
...AM I GETTING A FRONT-ROW SEAT TO WATCH THE END OF A DREAM...

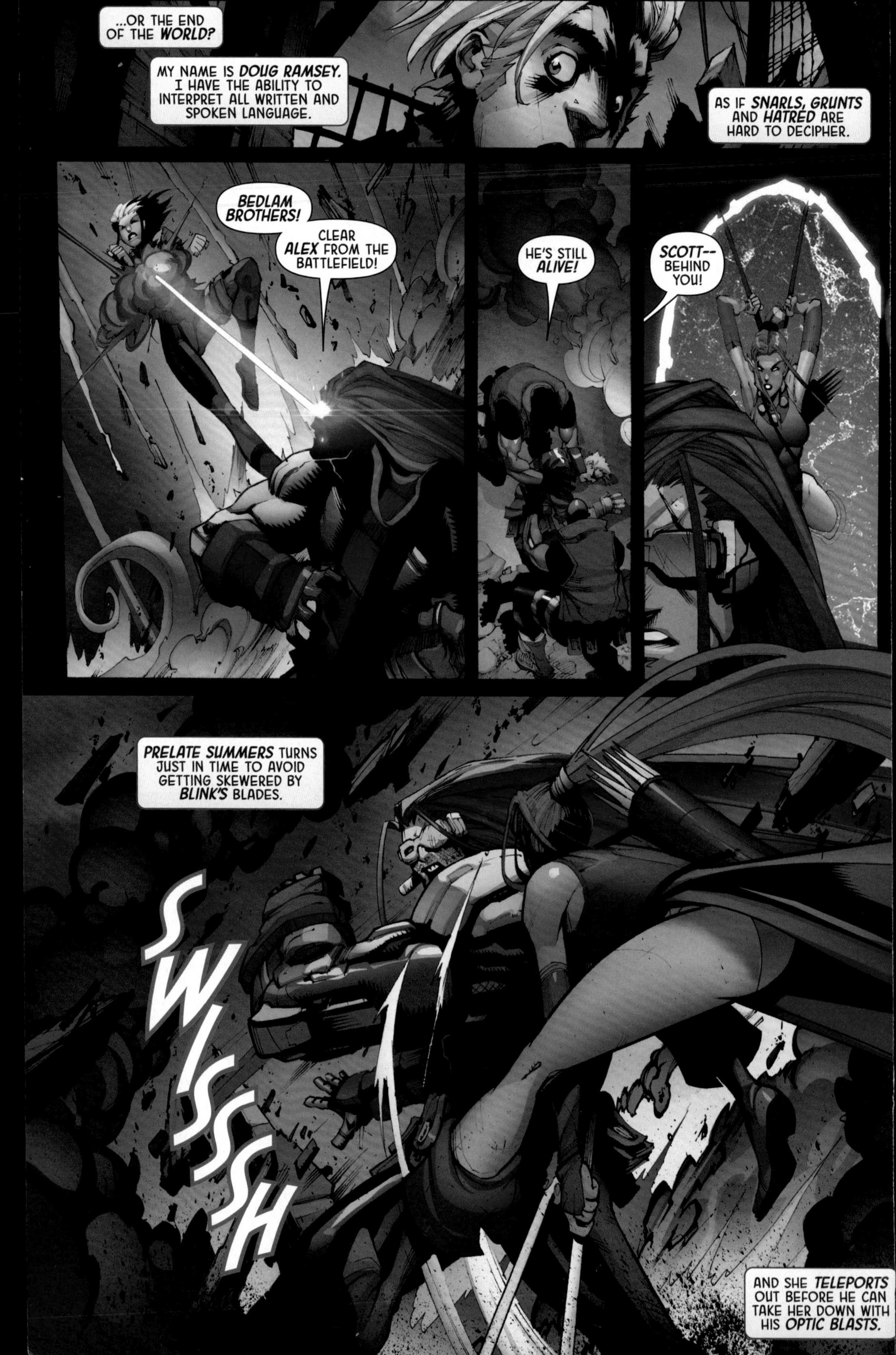

...OR THE END OF THE WORLD?
MY NAME IS DOUG RAMSEY. I HAVE THE ABILITY TO INTERPRET ALL WRITTEN AND SPOKEN LANGUAGE.
AS IF SNARLS, GRUNTS AND HATRED ARE HARD TO DECIPHER.
BEDLAM BROTHERS!
CLEAR ALEX FROM THE BATTLEFIELD!
HE'S STILL ALIVE!
SCOTT-- BEHIND YOU!
PRELATE SUMMERS TURNS JUST IN TIME TO AVOID GETTING SKEWERED BY BLINK'S BLADES.
SWISSSH
AND SHE TELEPORTS OUT BEFORE HE CAN TAKE HER DOWN WITH HIS OPTIC BLASTS.

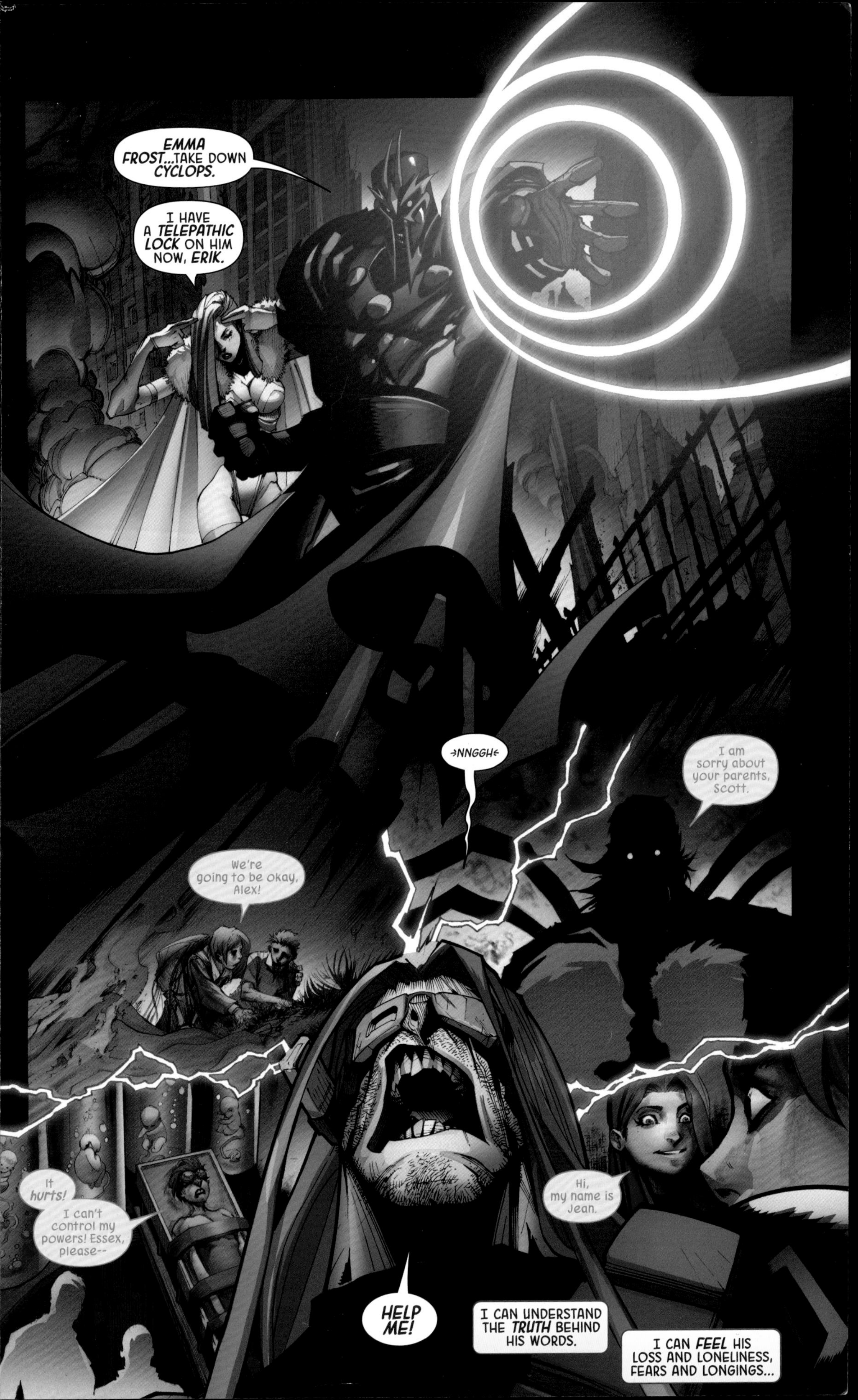
EMMA FROST...TAKE DOWN CYCLOPS.
I HAVE A TELEPATHIC LOCK ON HIM NOW, ERIK.
NNGGH
I am sorry about your parents, Scott.
We're going to be okay, Alex!
It hurts!
I can't control my powers! Essex, please--
Hi, my name is Jean.
HELP ME!
I CAN UNDERSTAND THE TRUTH BEHIND HIS WORDS.
I CAN FEEL HIS LOSS AND LONELINESS, FEARS AND LONGINGS...

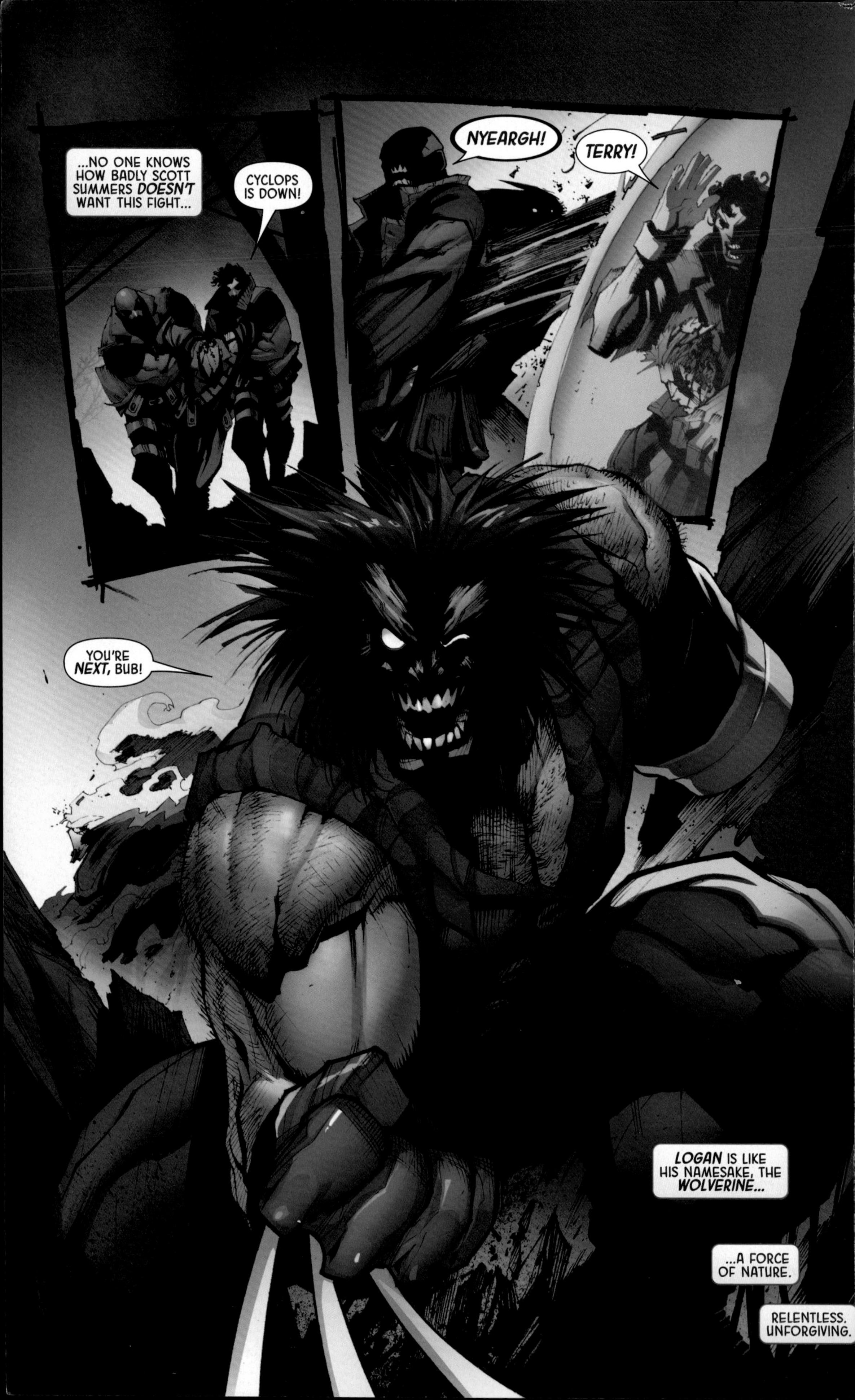
...NO ONE KNOWS HOW BADLY SCOTT SUMMERS *DOESN'T* WANT THIS FIGHT...
CYCLOPS IS DOWN!
NYEARGH!
TERRY!
YOU'RE *NEXT,* BUB!
LOGAN IS LIKE HIS NAMESAKE, THE *WOLVERINE*...
...A FORCE OF NATURE.
RELENTLESS. UNFORGIVING.

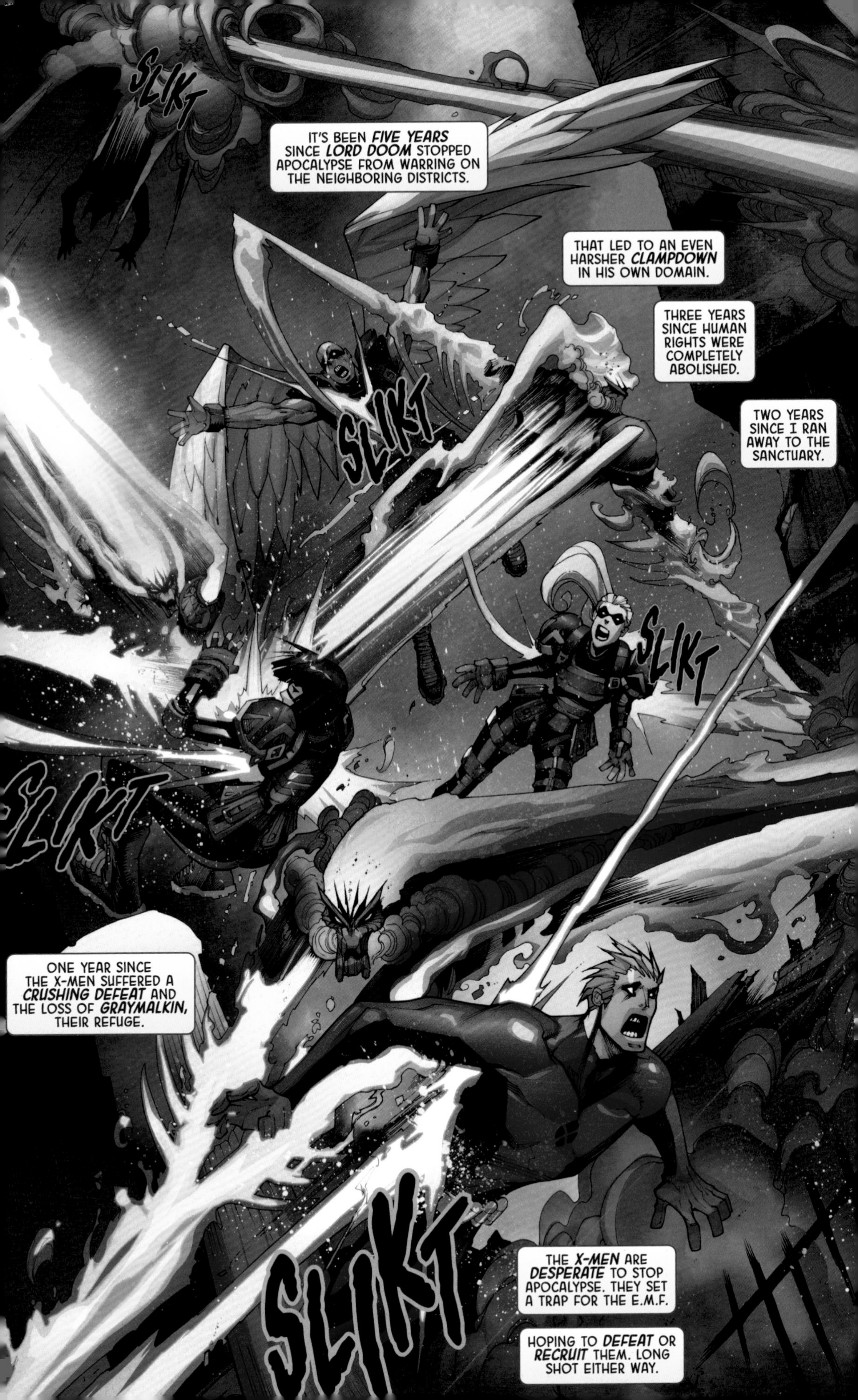
SLIKT
IT'S BEEN FIVE YEARS SINCE LORD DOOM STOPPED APOCALYPSE FROM WARRING ON THE NEIGHBORING DISTRICTS.
THAT LED TO AN EVEN HARSHER CLAMPDOWN IN HIS OWN DOMAIN.
THREE YEARS SINCE HUMAN RIGHTS WERE COMPLETELY ABOLISHED.
TWO YEARS SINCE I RAN AWAY TO THE SANCTUARY.
SLIKT
SLIKT
SLIKT
ONE YEAR SINCE THE X-MEN SUFFERED A CRUSHING DEFEAT AND THE LOSS OF GRAYMALKIN, THEIR REFUGE.
SLIKT
THE X-MEN ARE DESPERATE TO STOP APOCALYPSE. THEY SET A TRAP FOR THE E.M.F.
HOPING TO DEFEAT OR RECRUIT THEM. LONG SHOT EITHER WAY.

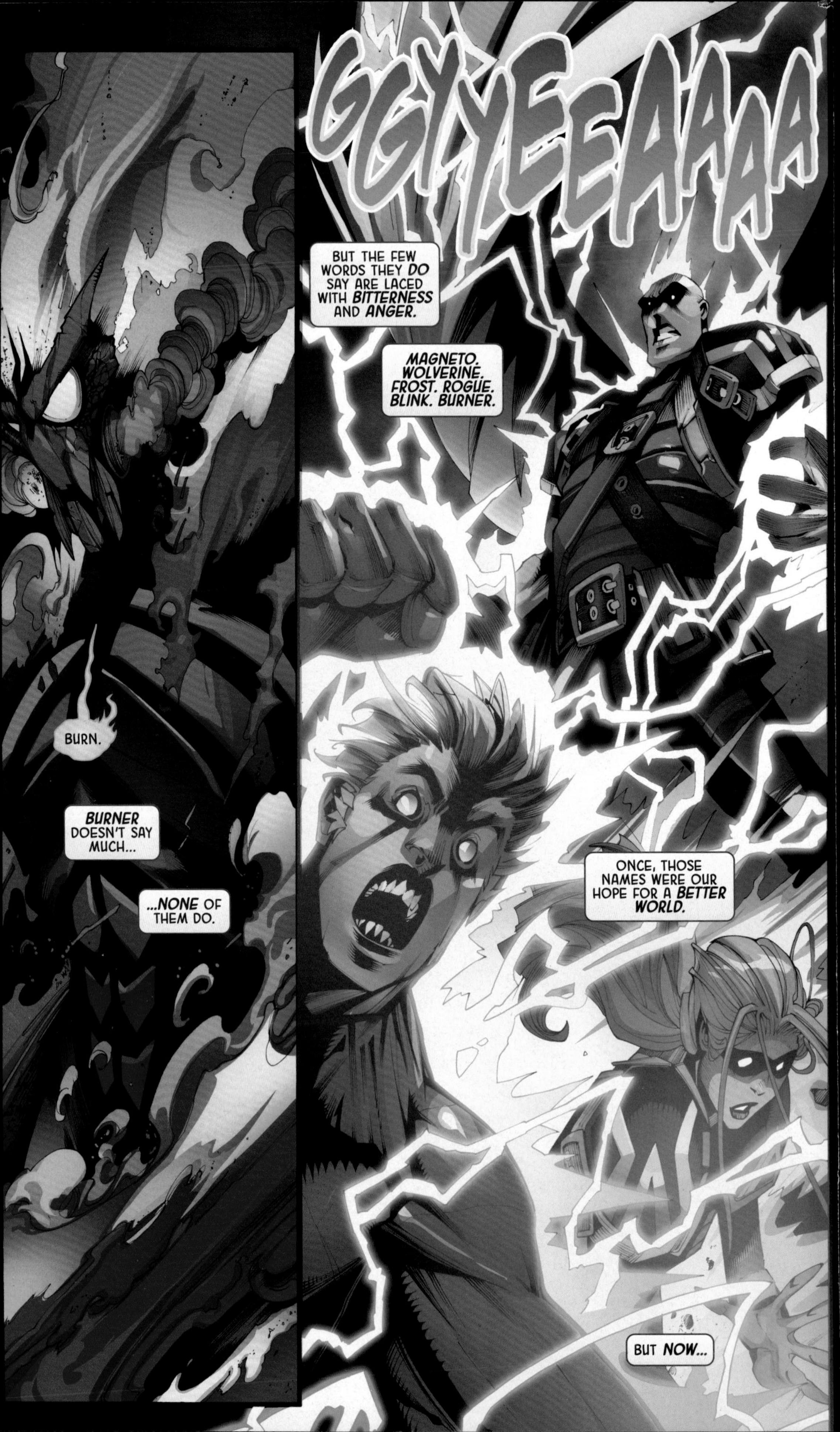
BURN.
BURNER DOESN'T SAY MUCH...
...NONE OF THEM DO.
GGYEEAAAA
BUT THE FEW WORDS THEY DO SAY ARE LACED WITH BITTERNESS AND ANGER.
MAGNETO. WOLVERINE. FROST. ROGUE. BLINK. BURNER.
ONCE, THOSE NAMES WERE OUR HOPE FOR A BETTER WORLD.
BUT NOW...

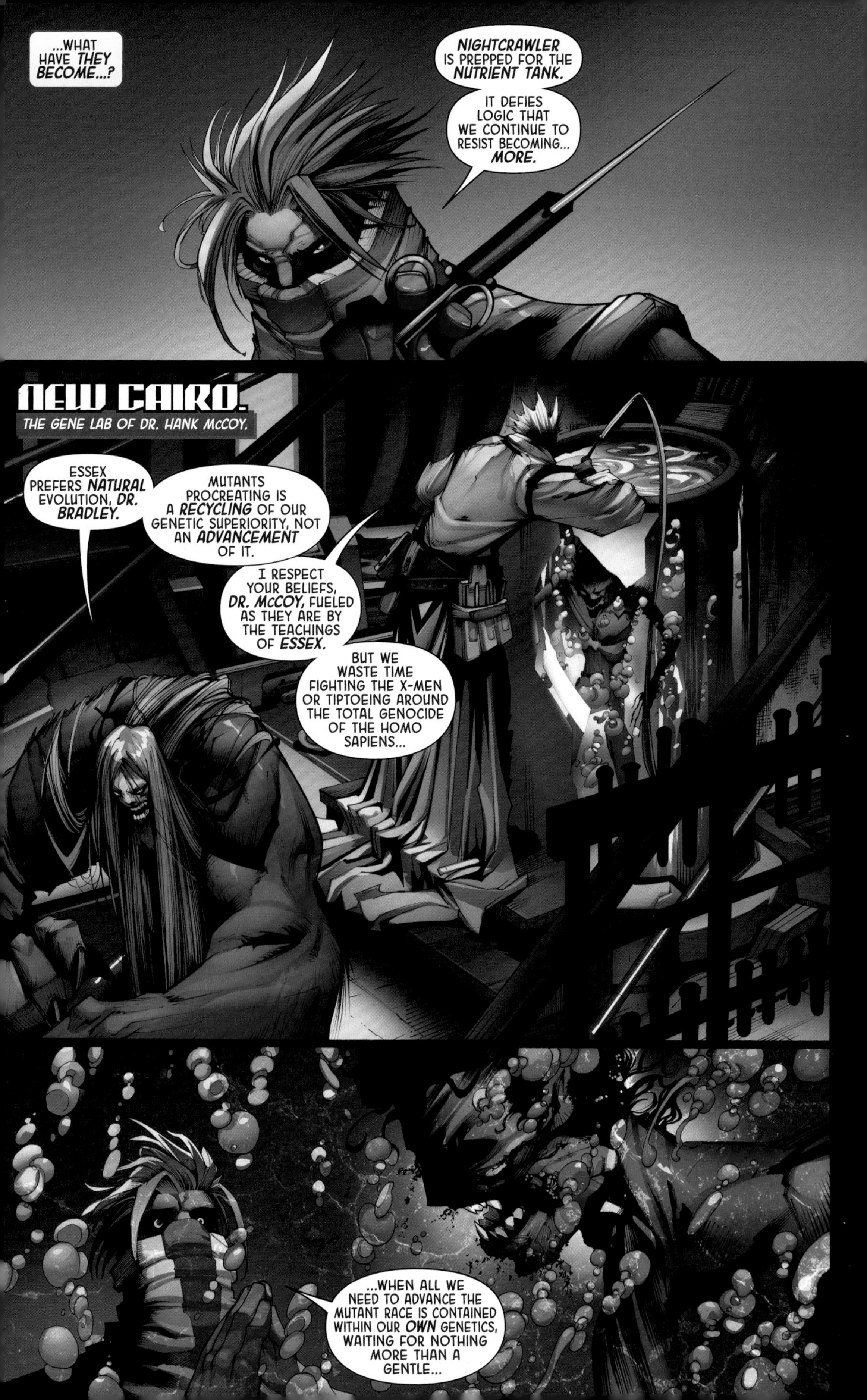

...WHAT HAVE THEY BECOME...?
NIGHTCRAWLER IS PREPPED FOR THE NUTRIENT TANK.
IT DEFIES LOGIC THAT WE CONTINUE TO RESIST BECOMING... MORE.
NEW CAIRO.
THE GENE LAB OF DR. HANK McCOY.
ESSEX PREFERS NATURAL EVOLUTION, DR. BRADLEY.
MUTANTS PROCREATING IS A RECYCLING OF OUR GENETIC SUPERIORITY, NOT AN ADVANCEMENT OF IT.
I RESPECT YOUR BELIEFS, DR. McCOY, FUELED AS THEY ARE BY THE TEACHINGS OF ESSEX.
BUT WE WASTE TIME FIGHTING THE X-MEN OR TIPTOEING AROUND THE TOTAL GENOCIDE OF THE HOMO SAPIENS...
...WHEN ALL WE NEED TO ADVANCE THE MUTANT RACE IS CONTAINED WITHIN OUR OWN GENETICS, WAITING FOR NOTHING MORE THAN A GENTLE...

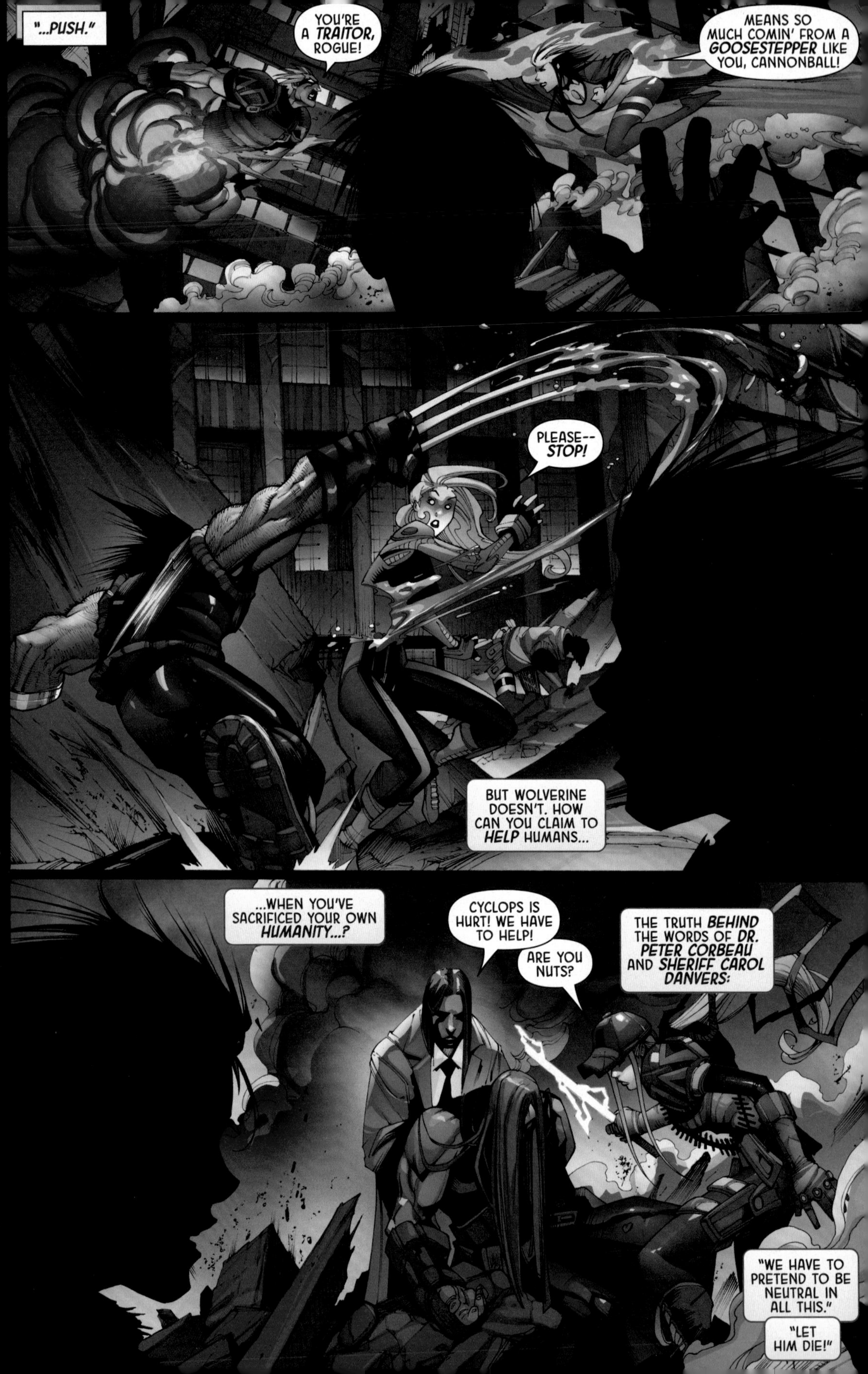
"...PUSH."
YOU'RE A TRAITOR, ROGUE!
MEANS SO MUCH COMIN' FROM A GOOSESTEPPER LIKE YOU, CANNONBALL!
PLEASE-- STOP!
BUT WOLVERINE DOESN'T. HOW CAN YOU CLAIM TO HELP HUMANS...
...WHEN YOU'VE SACRIFICED YOUR OWN HUMANITY...?
CYCLOPS IS HURT! WE HAVE TO HELP!
ARE YOU NUTS?
THE TRUTH BEHIND THE WORDS OF DR. PETER CORBEAU AND SHERIFF CAROL DANVERS:
"WE HAVE TO PRETEND TO BE NEUTRAL IN ALL THIS."
"LET HIM DIE!"

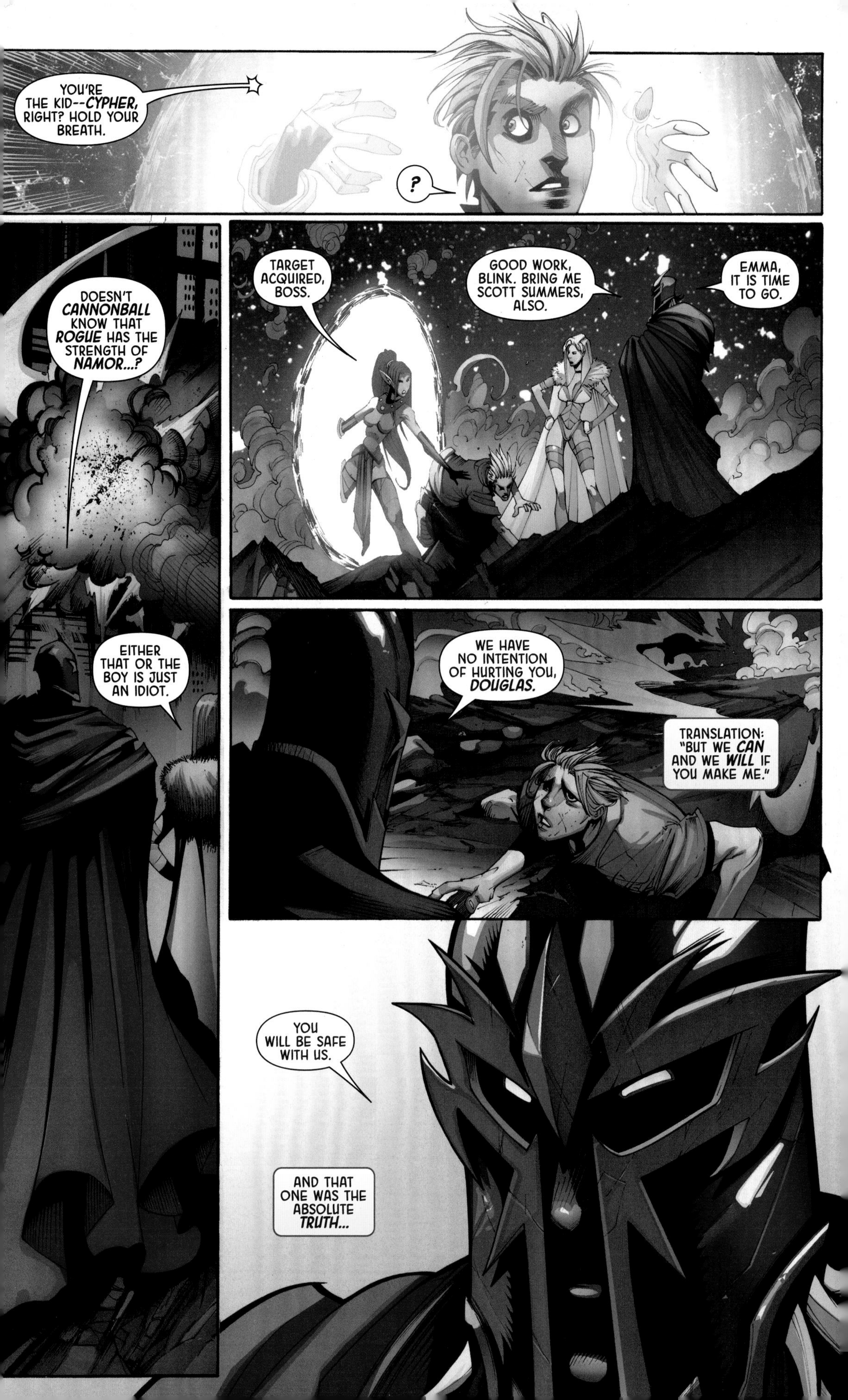
YOU'RE THE KID--CYPHER, RIGHT? HOLD YOUR BREATH.
?
DOESN'T CANNONBALL KNOW THAT ROGUE HAS THE STRENGTH OF NAMOR...?
EITHER THAT OR THE BOY IS JUST AN IDIOT.
TARGET ACQUIRED, BOSS.
GOOD WORK, BLINK. BRING ME SCOTT SUMMERS, ALSO.
EMMA, IT IS TIME TO GO.
WE HAVE NO INTENTION OF HURTING YOU, DOUGLAS.
TRANSLATION: "BUT WE CAN AND WE WILL IF YOU MAKE ME."
YOU WILL BE SAFE WITH US.
AND THAT ONE WAS THE ABSOLUTE TRUTH...

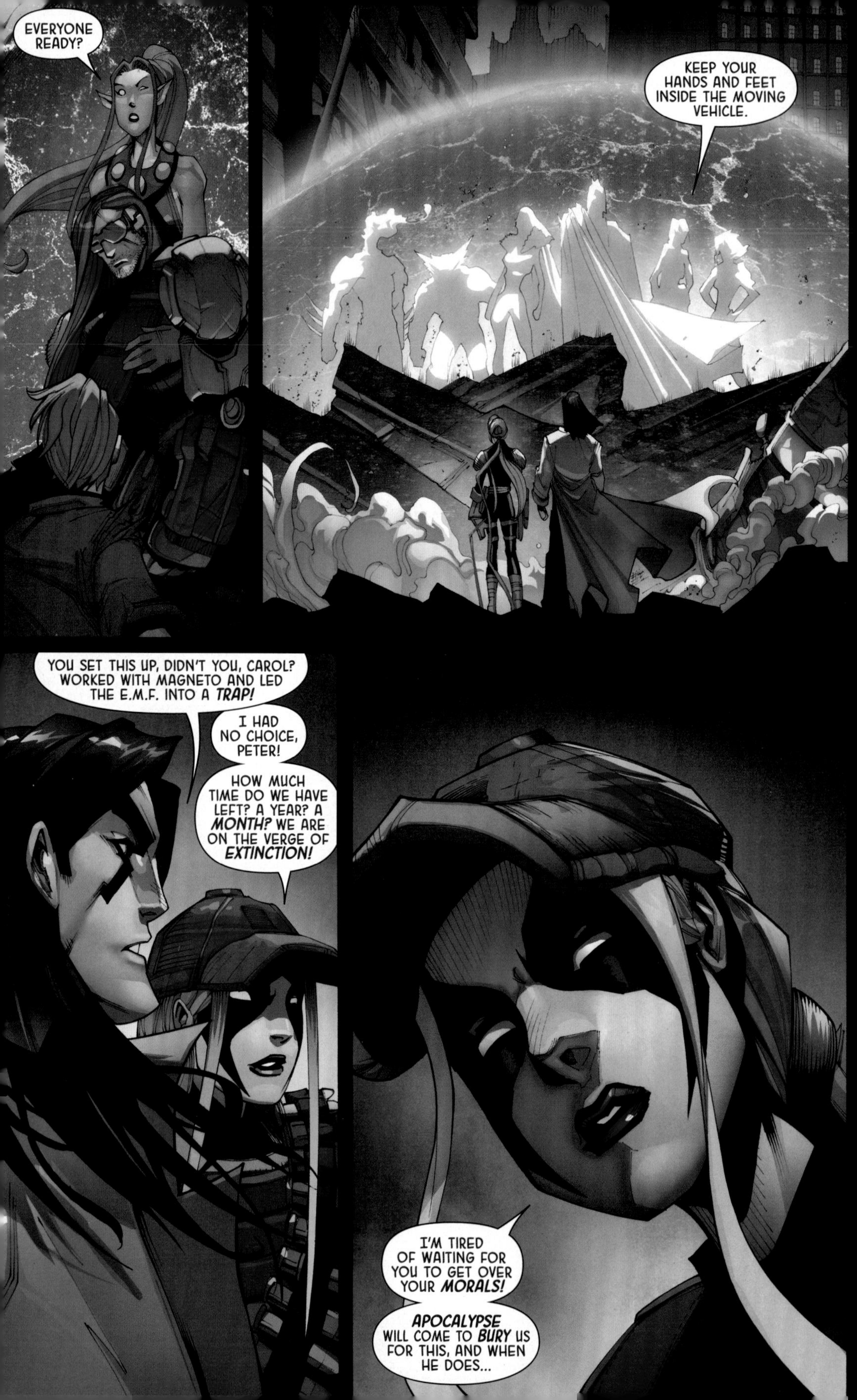
EVERYONE READY?
KEEP YOUR HANDS AND FEET INSIDE THE MOVING VEHICLE.
YOU SET THIS UP, DIDN'T YOU, CAROL? WORKED WITH MAGNETO AND LED THE E.M.F. INTO A *TRAP!*
I HAD NO CHOICE, PETER!
HOW MUCH TIME DO WE HAVE LEFT? A YEAR? A *MONTH?* WE ARE ON THE VERGE OF *EXTINCTION!*
I'M TIRED OF WAITING FOR YOU TO GET OVER YOUR *MORALS!*
APOCALYPSE WILL COME TO *BURY* US FOR THIS, AND WHEN HE DOES...

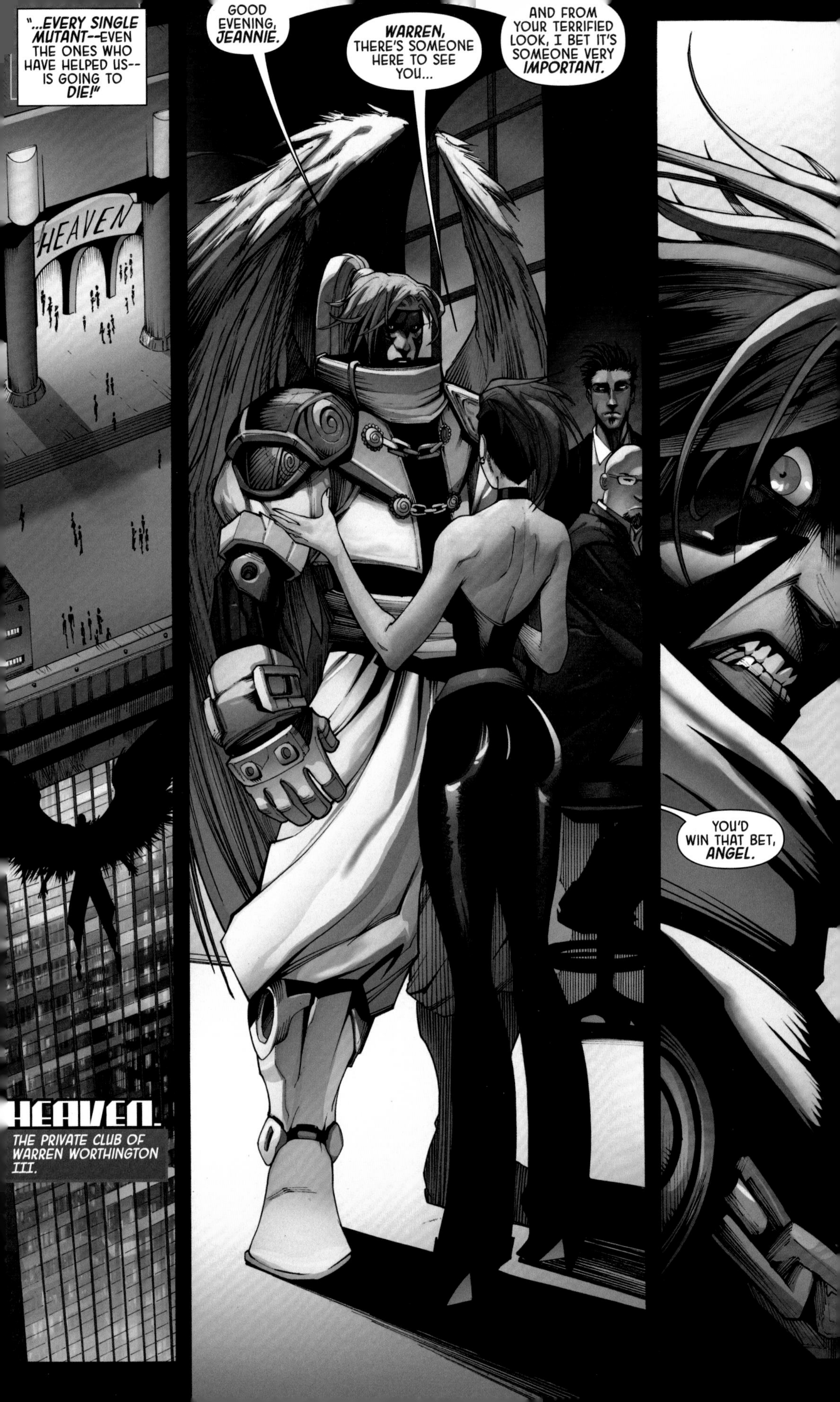

"...EVERY SINGLE MUTANT--EVEN THE ONES WHO HAVE HELPED US--IS GOING TO DIE!"
HEAVEN
HEAVEN.
THE PRIVATE CLUB OF WARREN WORTHINGTON III.
GOOD EVENING, JEANNIE.
WARREN, THERE'S SOMEONE HERE TO SEE YOU...
AND FROM YOUR TERRIFIED LOOK, I BET IT'S SOMEONE VERY IMPORTANT.
YOU'D WIN THAT BET, ANGEL.

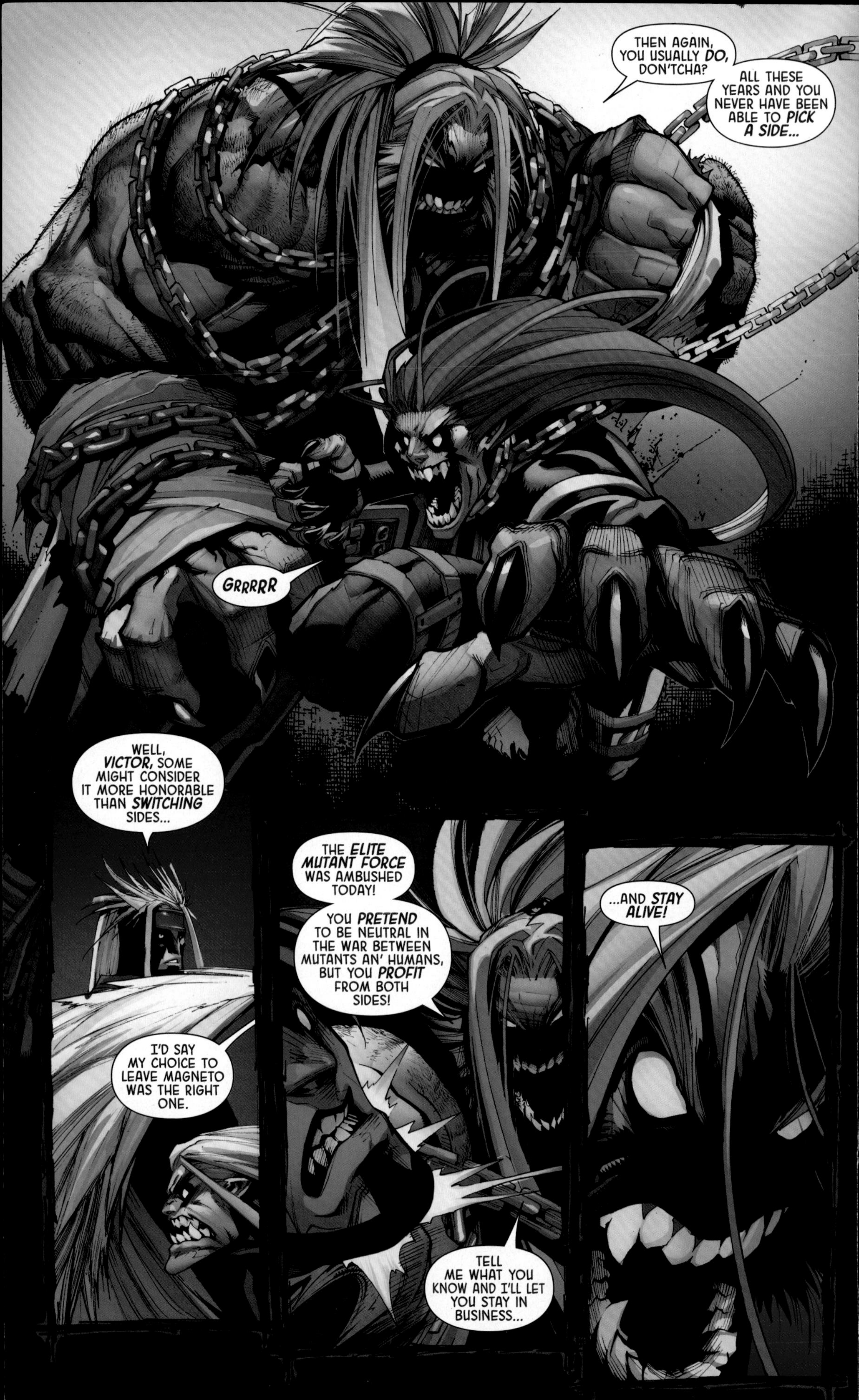
THEN AGAIN, YOU USUALLY DO, DON'TCHA?
ALL THESE YEARS AND YOU NEVER HAVE BEEN ABLE TO PICK A SIDE...
GRRRRR
WELL, VICTOR, SOME MIGHT CONSIDER IT MORE HONORABLE THAN SWITCHING SIDES...
I'D SAY MY CHOICE TO LEAVE MAGNETO WAS THE RIGHT ONE.
THE ELITE MUTANT FORCE WAS AMBUSHED TODAY!
YOU PRETEND TO BE NEUTRAL IN THE WAR BETWEEN MUTANTS AN' HUMANS, BUT YOU PROFIT FROM BOTH SIDES!
TELL ME WHAT YOU KNOW AND I'LL LET YOU STAY IN BUSINESS...
...AND STAY ALIVE!

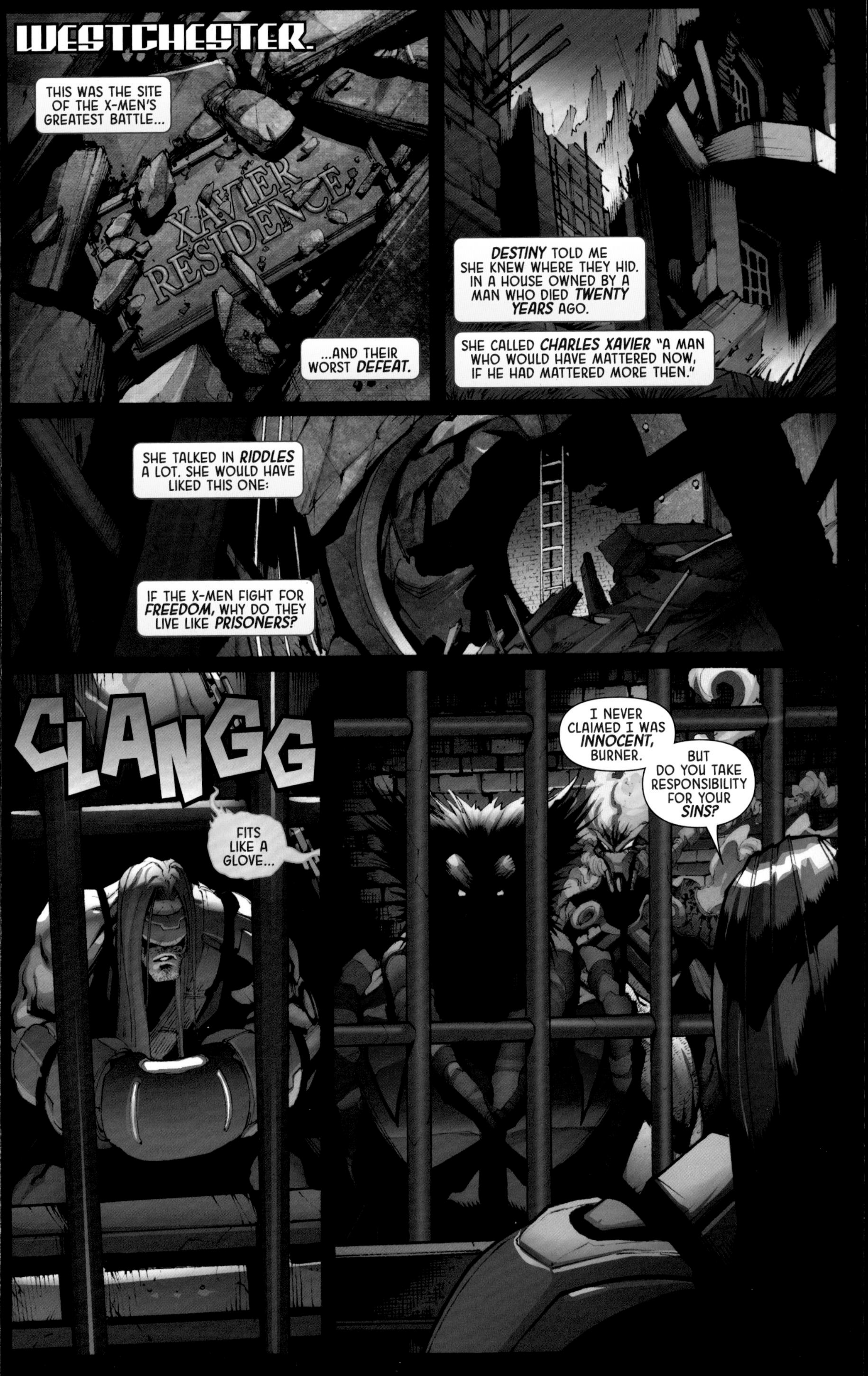
WESTCHESTER.
THIS WAS THE SITE OF THE X-MEN'S GREATEST BATTLE...
XAVIER RESIDENCE
...AND THEIR WORST DEFEAT.
DESTINY TOLD ME SHE KNEW WHERE THEY HID. IN A HOUSE OWNED BY A MAN WHO DIED TWENTY YEARS AGO.
SHE CALLED CHARLES XAVIER "A MAN WHO WOULD HAVE MATTERED NOW, IF HE HAD MATTERED MORE THEN."
SHE TALKED IN RIDDLES A LOT. SHE WOULD HAVE LIKED THIS ONE:
IF THE X-MEN FIGHT FOR FREEDOM, WHY DO THEY LIVE LIKE PRISONERS?
CLANGG
FITS LIKE A GLOVE...
I NEVER CLAIMED I WAS INNOCENT, BURNER.
BUT DO YOU TAKE RESPONSIBILITY FOR YOUR SINS?

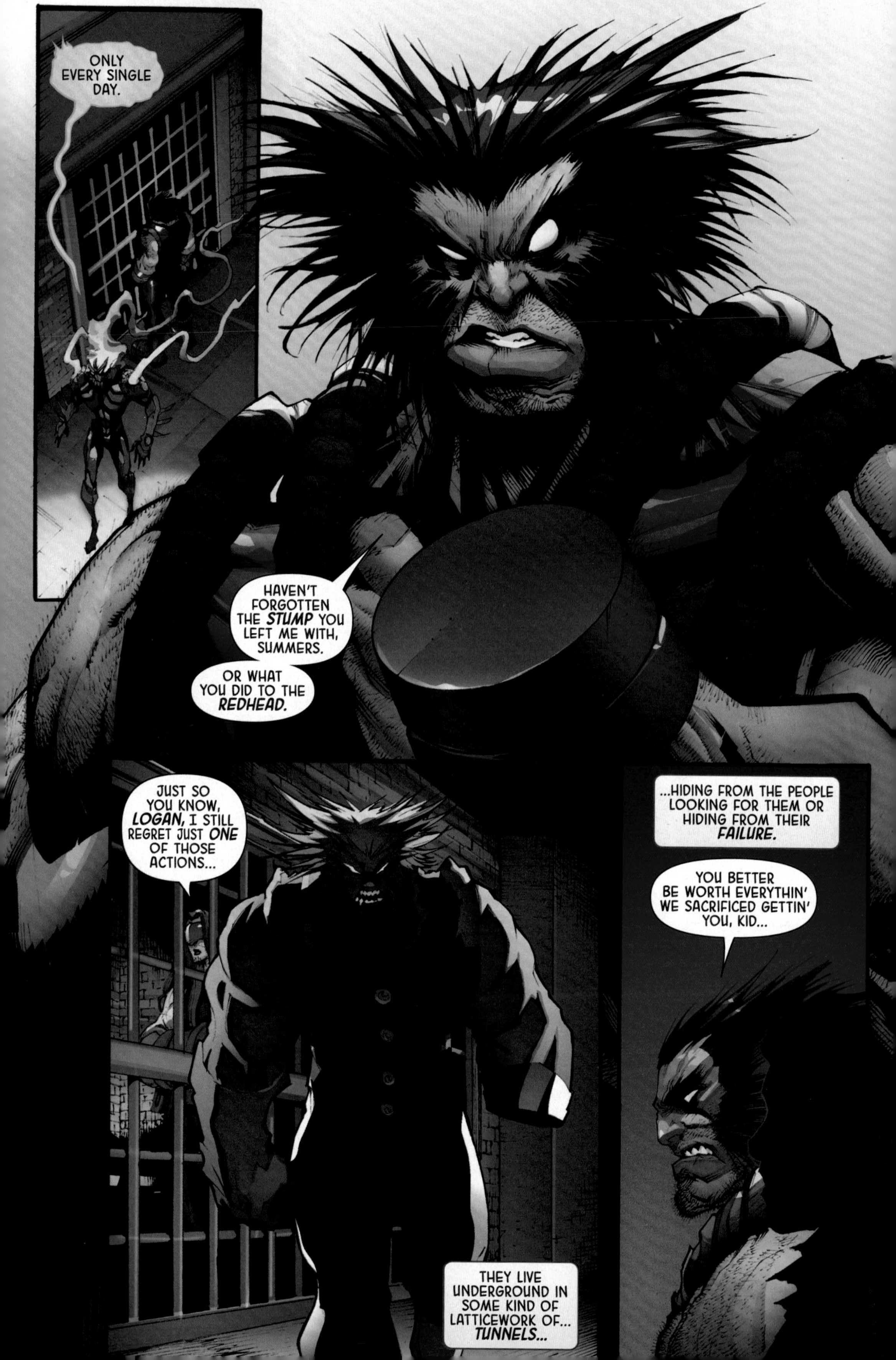
ONLY EVERY SINGLE DAY.
HAVEN'T FORGOTTEN THE *STUMP* YOU LEFT ME WITH, SUMMERS.
OR WHAT YOU DID TO THE *REDHEAD.*
JUST SO YOU KNOW, *LOGAN,* I STILL REGRET JUST *ONE* OF THOSE ACTIONS...
...HIDING FROM THE PEOPLE LOOKING FOR THEM OR HIDING FROM THEIR *FAILURE.*
YOU BETTER BE WORTH EVERYTHIN' WE SACRIFICED GETTIN' YOU, KID...
THEY LIVE UNDERGROUND IN SOME KIND OF LATTICEWORK OF... *TUNNELS...*

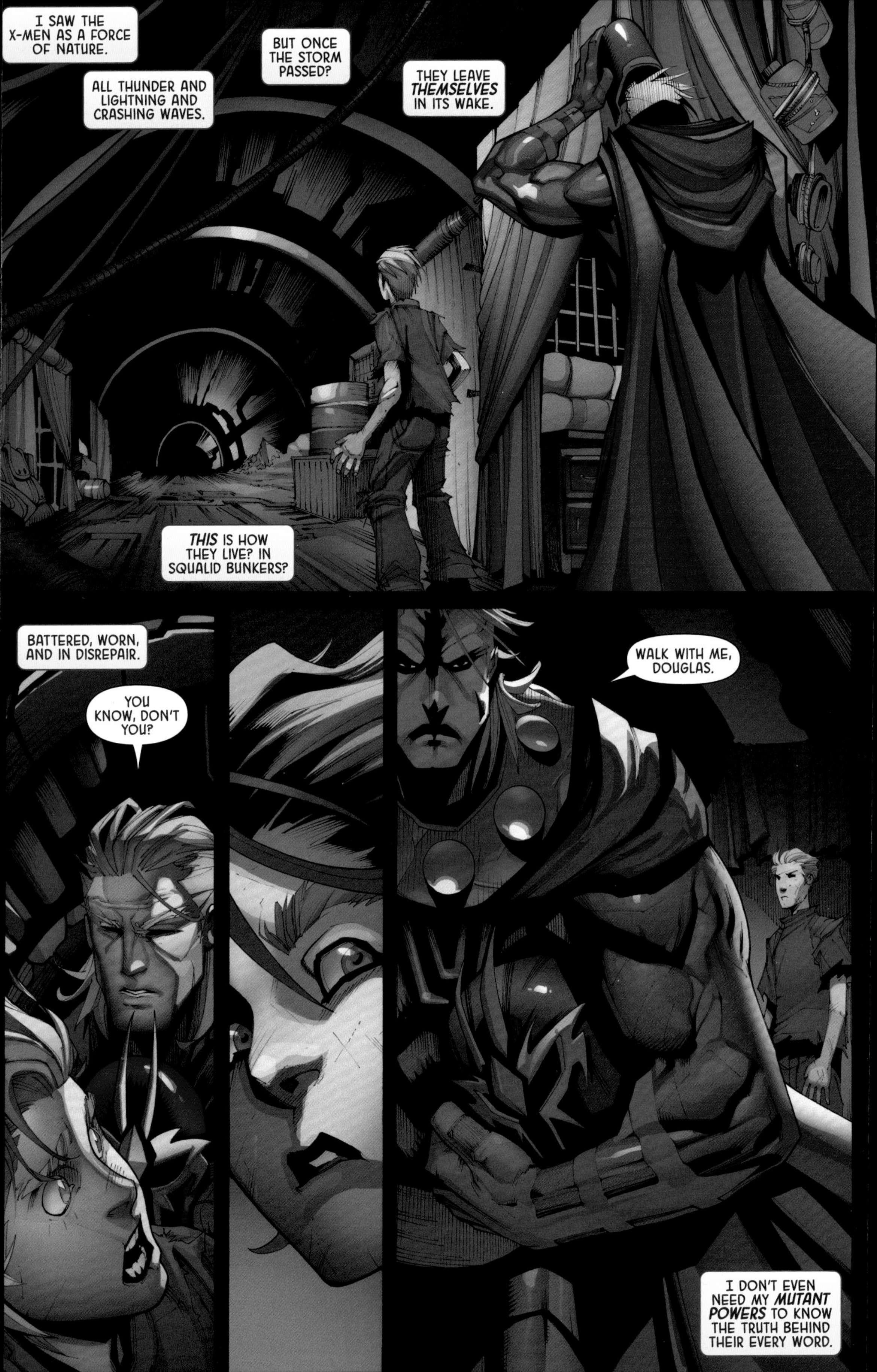
I SAW THE X-MEN AS A FORCE OF NATURE.
ALL THUNDER AND LIGHTNING AND CRASHING WAVES.
BUT ONCE THE STORM PASSED?
THEY LEAVE *THEMSELVES* IN ITS WAKE.
THIS IS HOW THEY LIVE? IN SQUALID BUNKERS?
BATTERED, WORN, AND IN DISREPAIR.
YOU KNOW, DON'T YOU?
WALK WITH ME, DOUGLAS.
I DON'T EVEN NEED MY *MUTANT POWERS* TO KNOW THE TRUTH BEHIND THEIR EVERY WORD.

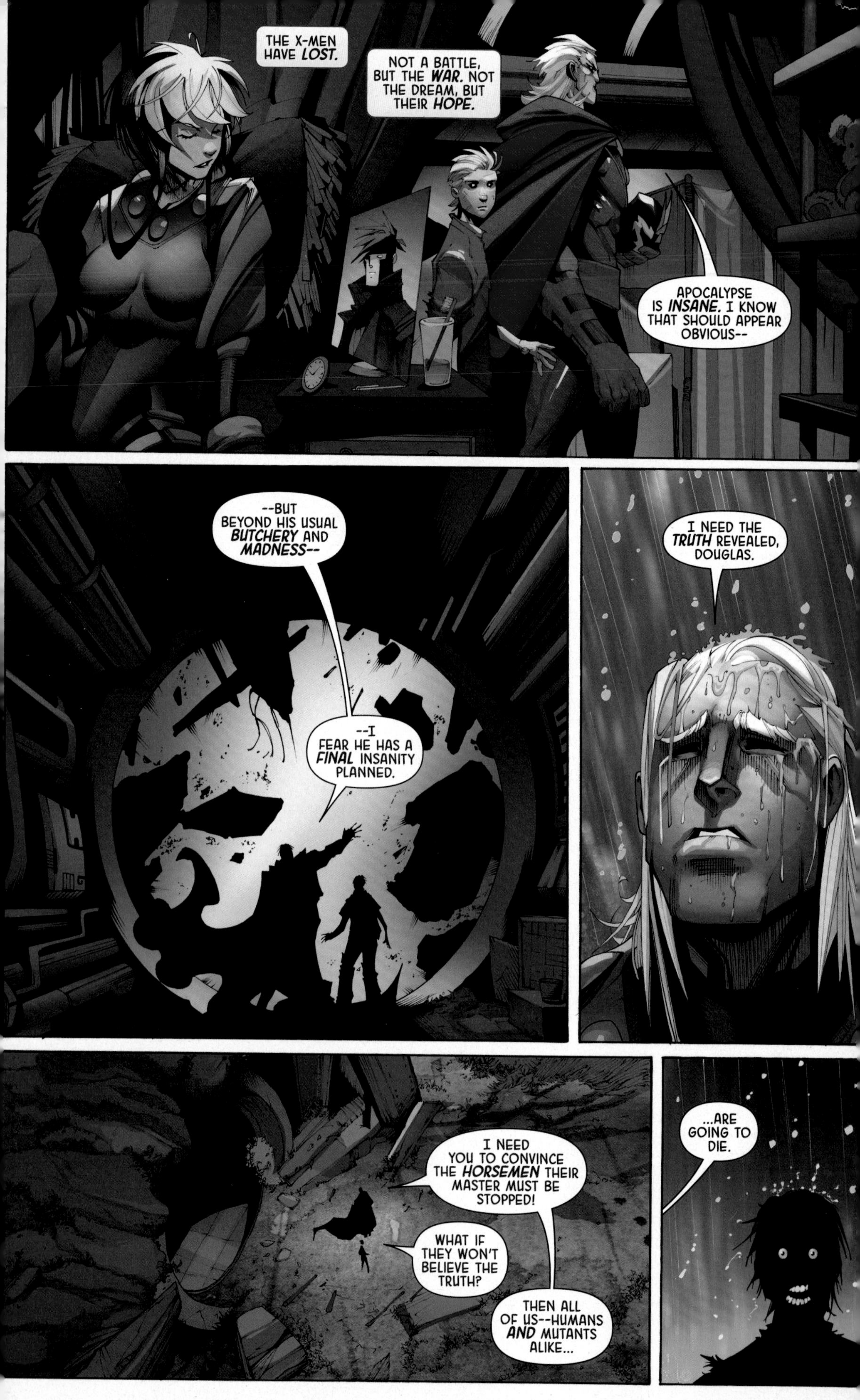
THE X-MEN HAVE LOST.
NOT A BATTLE, BUT THE WAR. NOT THE DREAM, BUT THEIR HOPE.
APOCALYPSE IS INSANE. I KNOW THAT SHOULD APPEAR OBVIOUS--
--BUT BEYOND HIS USUAL BUTCHERY AND MADNESS--
--I FEAR HE HAS A FINAL INSANITY PLANNED.
I NEED THE TRUTH REVEALED, DOUGLAS.
I NEED YOU TO CONVINCE THE HORSEMEN THEIR MASTER MUST BE STOPPED!
WHAT IF THEY WON'T BELIEVE THE TRUTH?
THEN ALL OF US--HUMANS AND MUTANTS ALIKE...
...ARE GOING TO DIE.

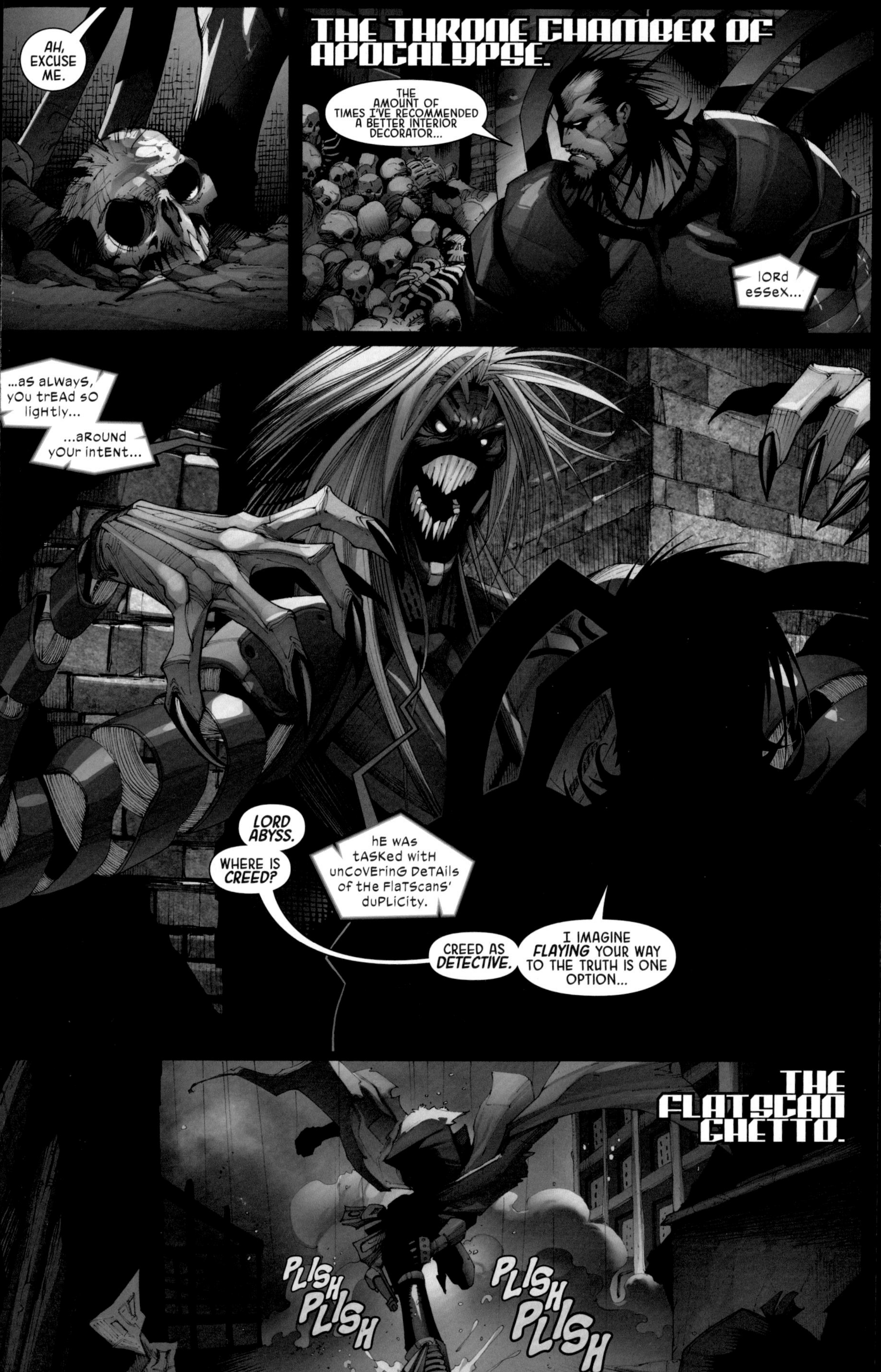
AH, EXCUSE ME.
THE THRONE CHAMBER OF APOCALYPSE.
THE AMOUNT OF TIMES I'VE RECOMMENDED A BETTER INTERIOR DECORATOR...
lORd essex...
...as always, you tread so lightly...
...around your intent...
LORD ABYSS.
WHERE IS CREED?
hE WAs tASKed with unCOVERinG DeTAils of tHe FlaTScans' duPLICity.
CREED AS DETECTIVE.
I IMAGINE FLAYING YOUR WAY TO THE TRUTH IS ONE OPTION...
THE FLATSCAN GHETTO.
PLISH PLISH
PLISH PLISH

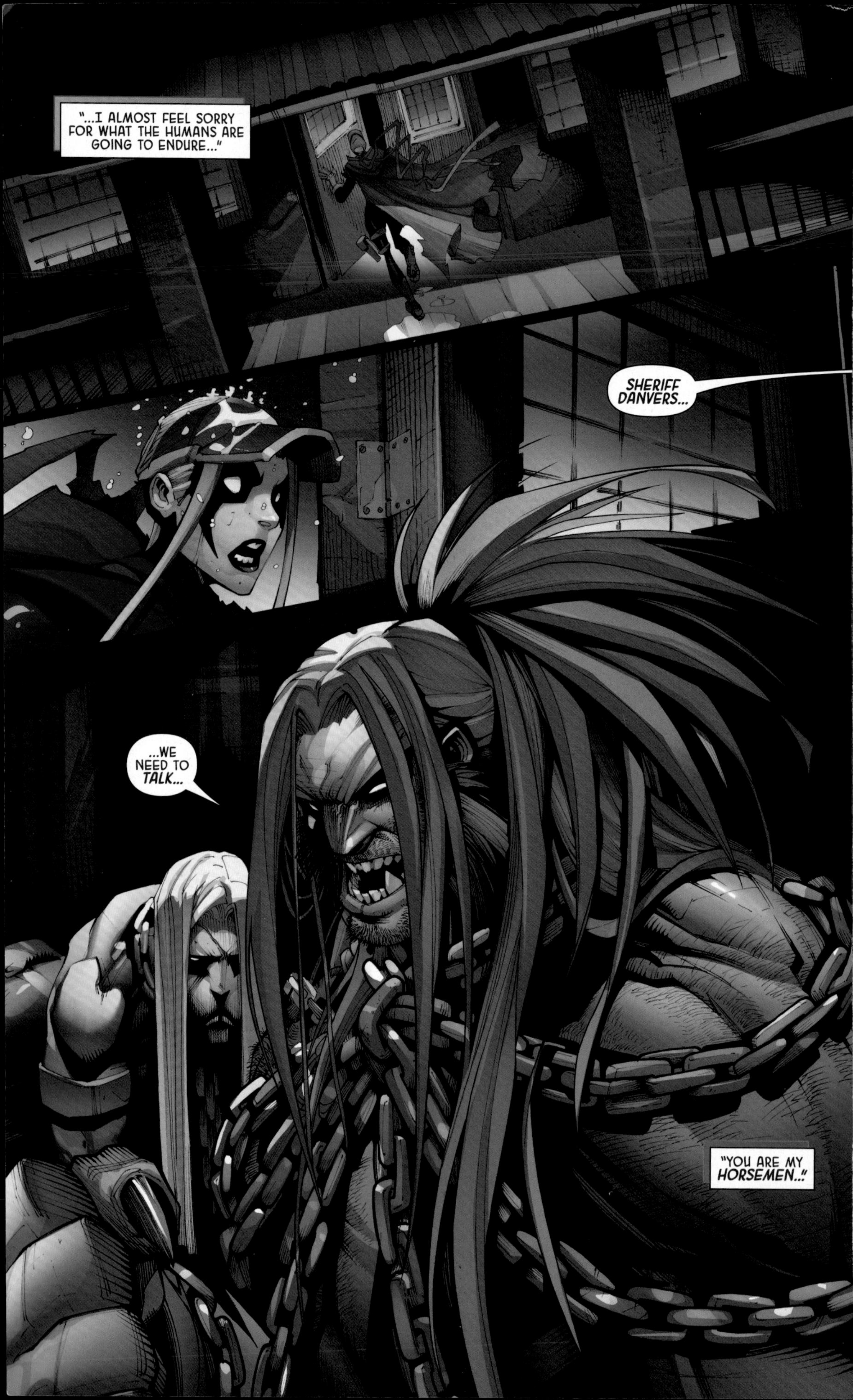
"...I ALMOST FEEL SORRY FOR WHAT THE HUMANS ARE GOING TO ENDURE..."
SHERIFF DANVERS...
...WE NEED TO TALK...
"YOU ARE MY HORSEMEN..."

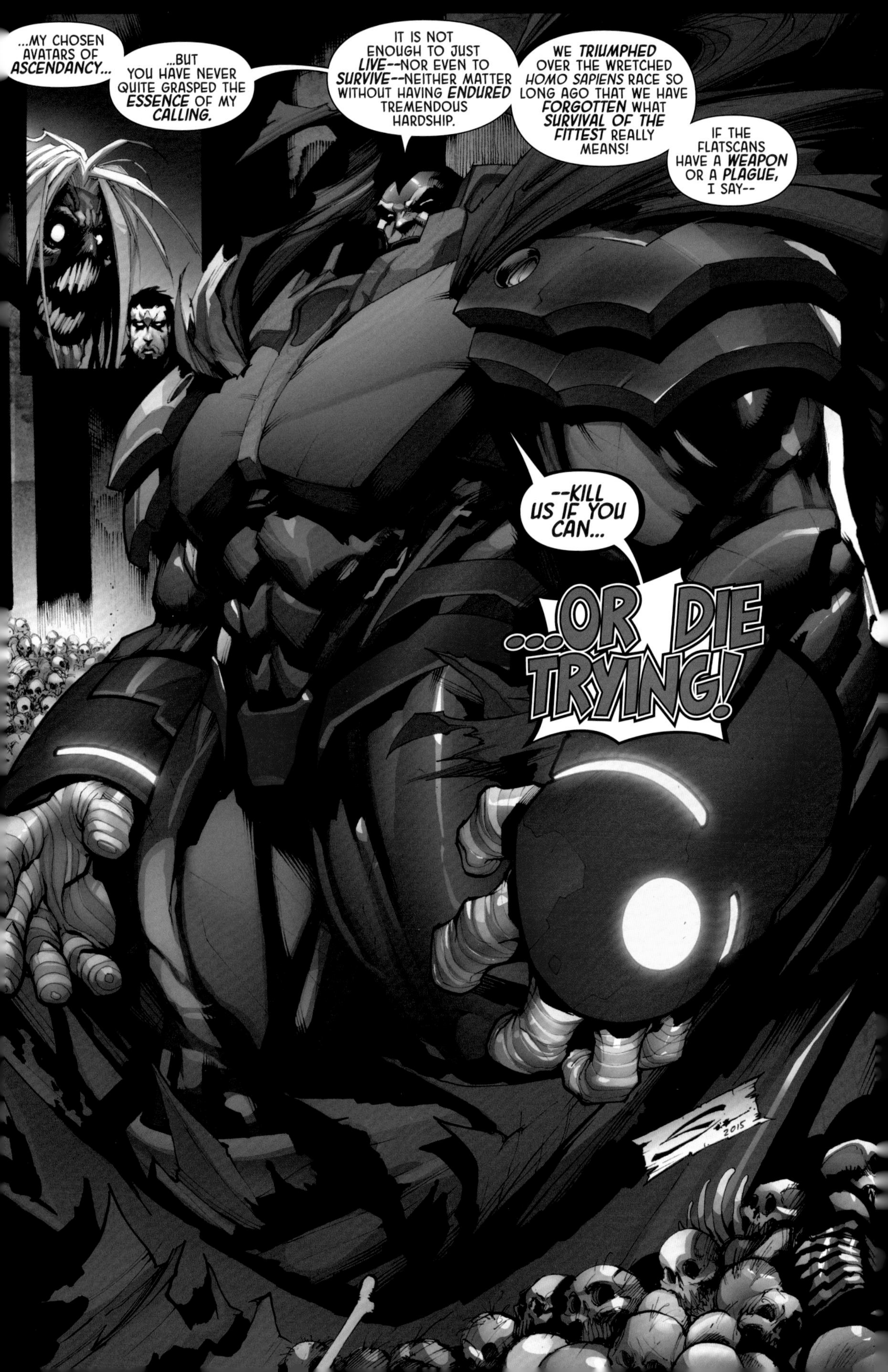
...MY CHOSEN AVATARS OF ASCENDANCY...
...BUT YOU HAVE NEVER QUITE GRASPED THE ESSENCE OF MY CALLING.
IT IS NOT ENOUGH TO JUST LIVE--NOR EVEN TO SURVIVE--NEITHER MATTER WITHOUT HAVING ENDURED TREMENDOUS HARDSHIP.
WE TRIUMPHED OVER THE WRETCHED HOMO SAPIENS RACE SO LONG AGO THAT WE HAVE FORGOTTEN WHAT SURVIVAL OF THE FITTEST REALLY MEANS!
IF THE FLATSCANS HAVE A WEAPON OR A PLAGUE, I SAY--
--KILL US IF YOU CAN...
...OR DIE TRYING!
2015

#1 VARIANT BY ANDY CLARKE & EDGAR DELGADO

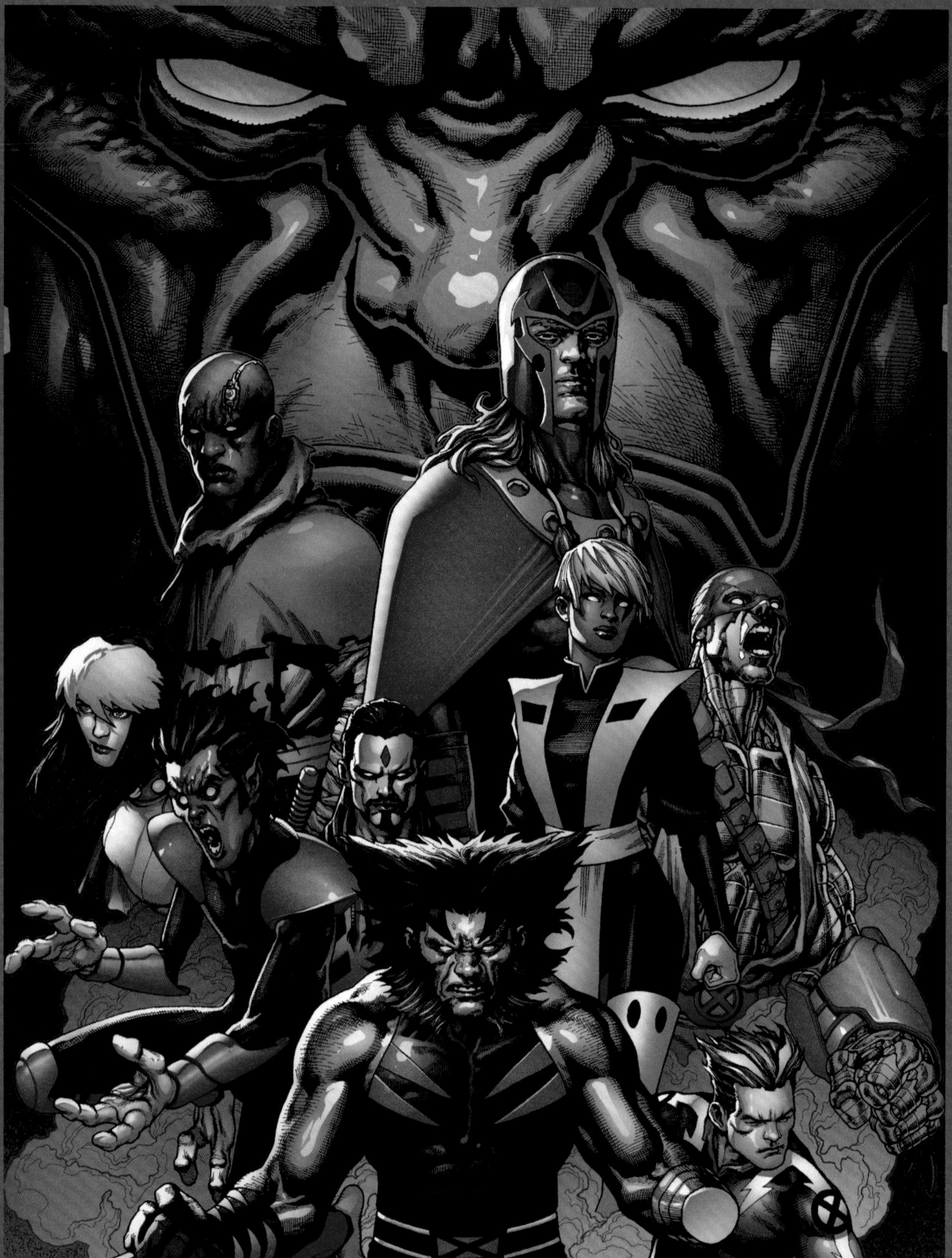

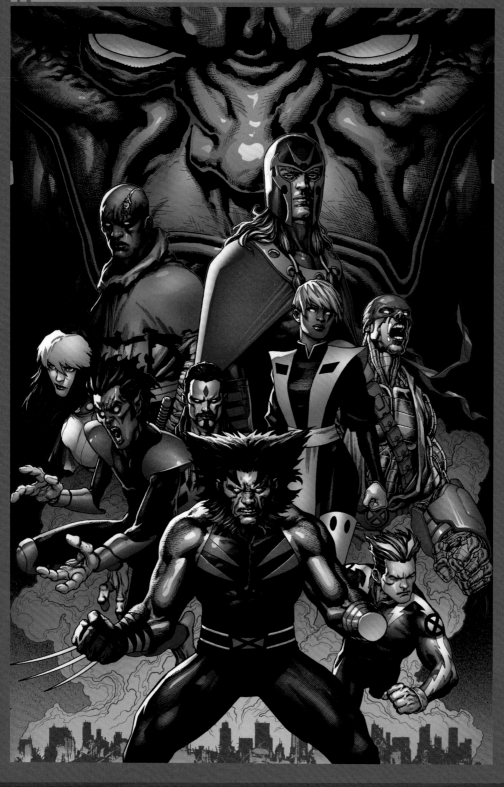

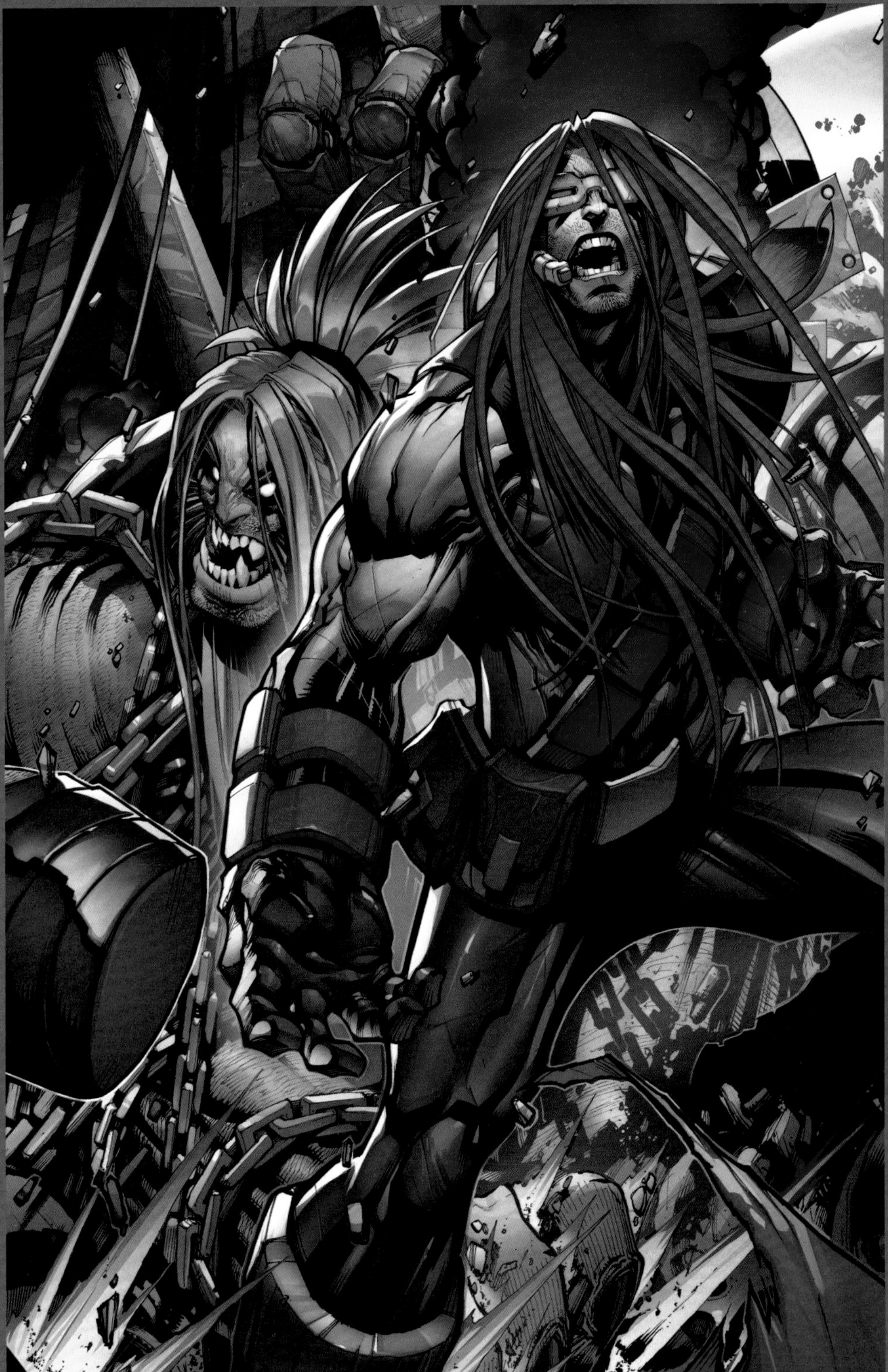

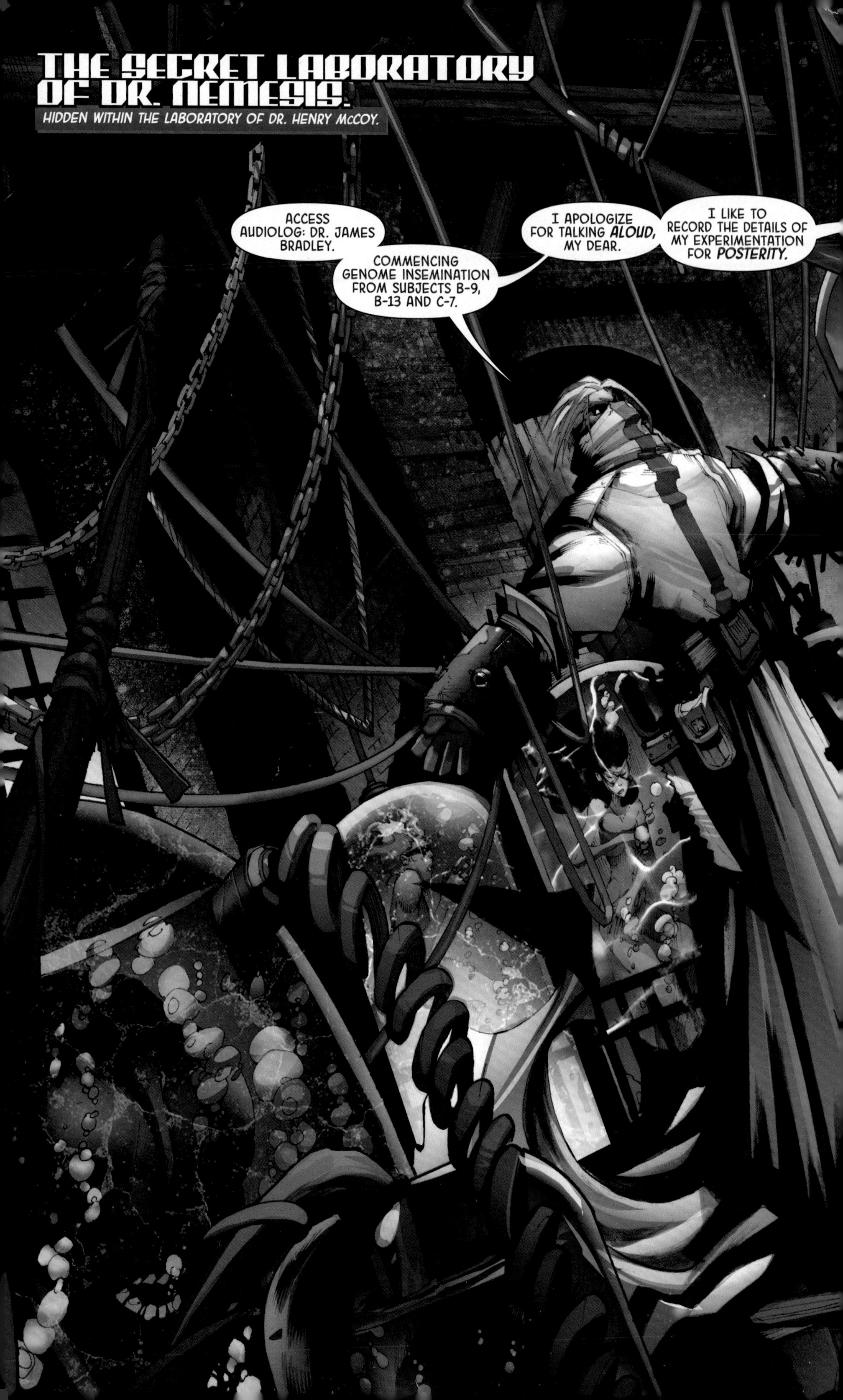
THE SECRET LABORATORY OF DR. NEMESIS.
HIDDEN WITHIN THE LABORATORY OF DR. HENRY McCOY.
ACCESS AUDIOLOG: DR. JAMES BRADLEY.
COMMENCING GENOME INSEMINATION FROM SUBJECTS B-9, B-13 AND C-7.
I APOLOGIZE FOR TALKING ALOUD, MY DEAR.
I LIKE TO RECORD THE DETAILS OF MY EXPERIMENTATION FOR POSTERITY.

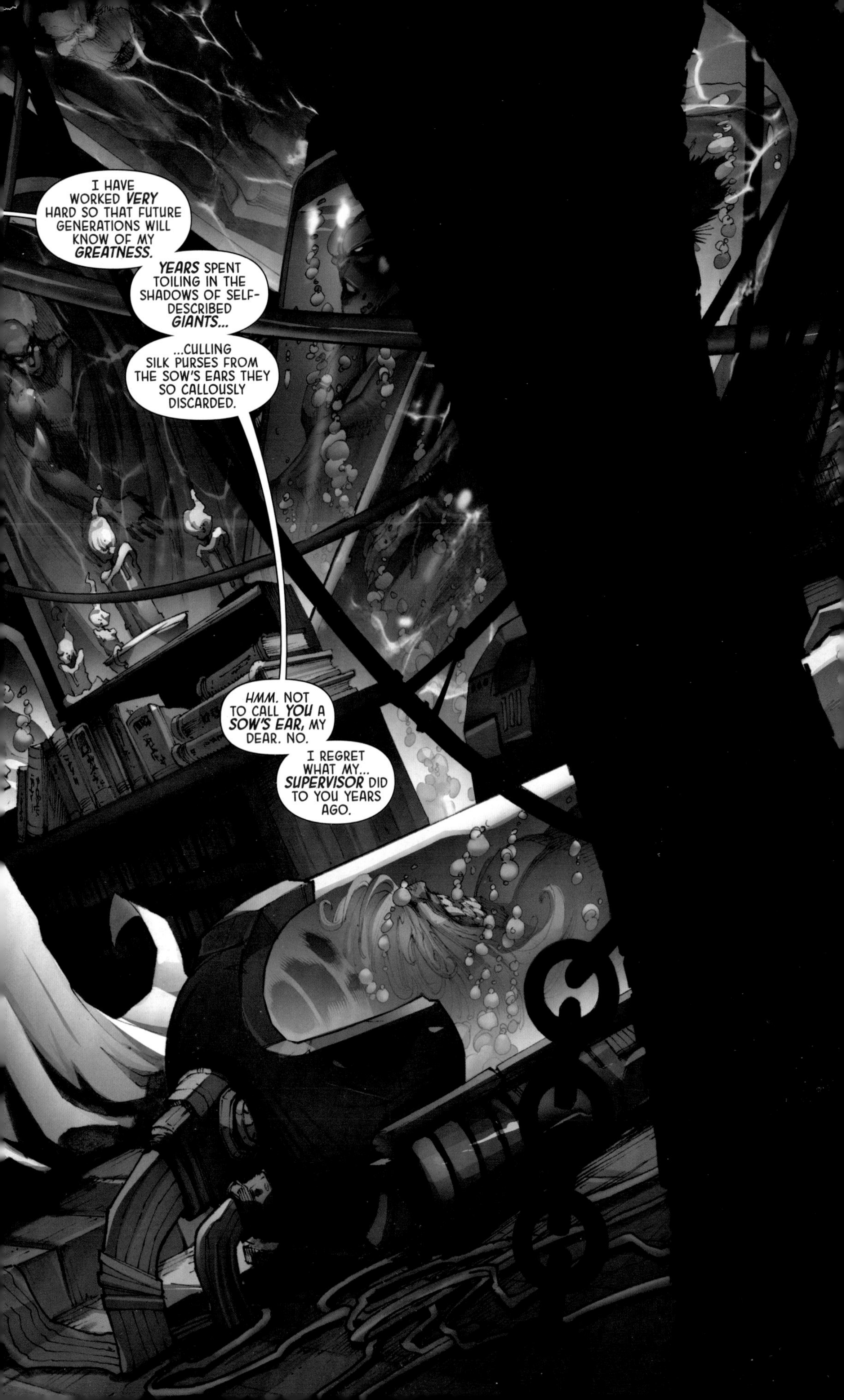
I HAVE WORKED VERY HARD SO THAT FUTURE GENERATIONS WILL KNOW OF MY GREATNESS.
YEARS SPENT TOILING IN THE SHADOWS OF SELF-DESCRIBED GIANTS...
...CULLING SILK PURSES FROM THE SOW'S EARS THEY SO CALLOUSLY DISCARDED.
HMM. NOT TO CALL YOU A SOW'S EAR, MY DEAR. NO.
I REGRET WHAT MY... SUPERVISOR DID TO YOU YEARS AGO.

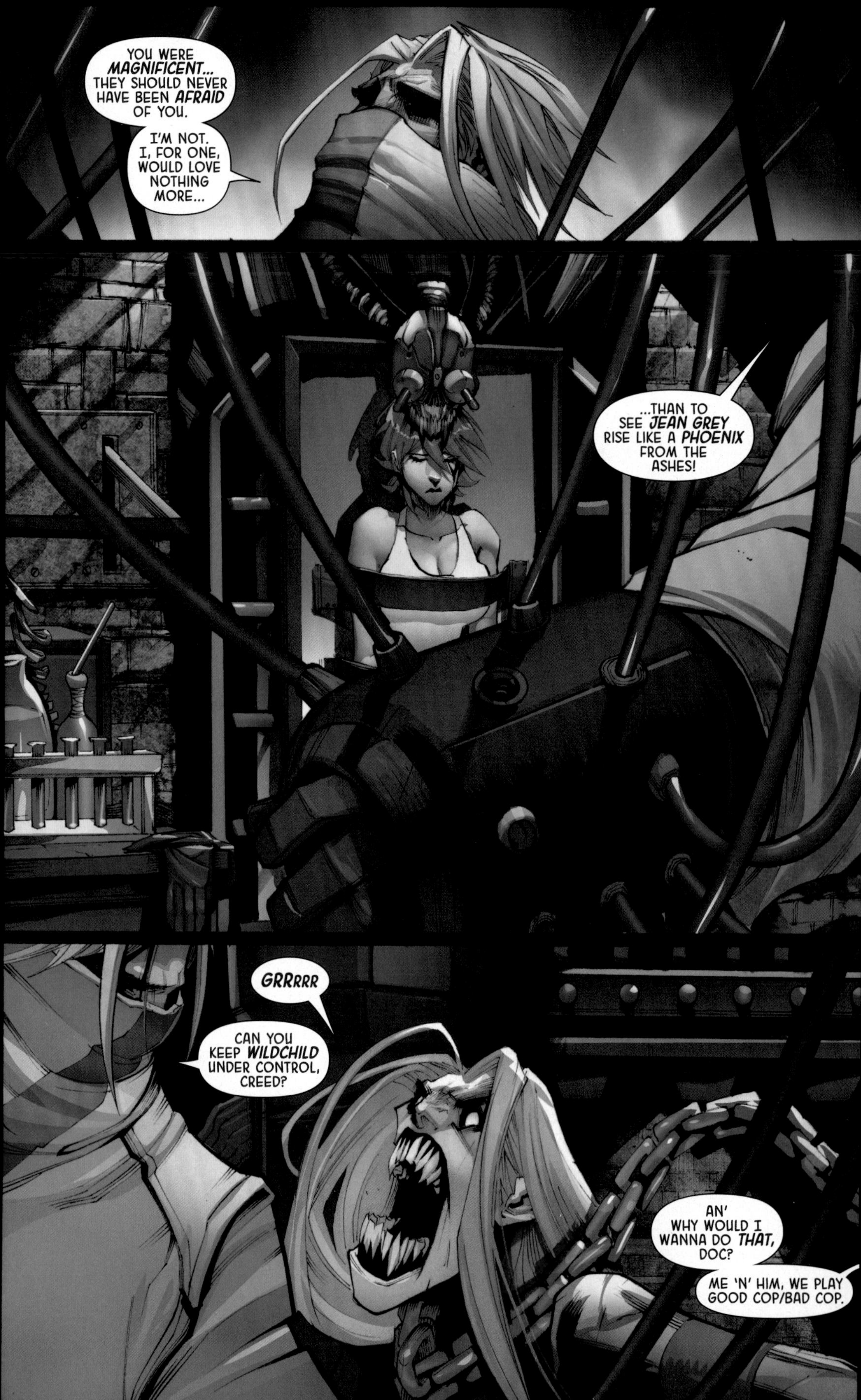

YOU WERE MAGNIFICENT... THEY SHOULD NEVER HAVE BEEN AFRAID OF YOU.
I'M NOT. I, FOR ONE, WOULD LOVE NOTHING MORE...
...THAN TO SEE JEAN GREY RISE LIKE A PHOENIX FROM THE ASHES!
GRRrrr
CAN YOU KEEP WILDCHILD UNDER CONTROL, CREED?
AN' WHY WOULD I WANNA DO THAT, DOC?
ME 'N' HIM, WE PLAY GOOD COP/BAD COP.

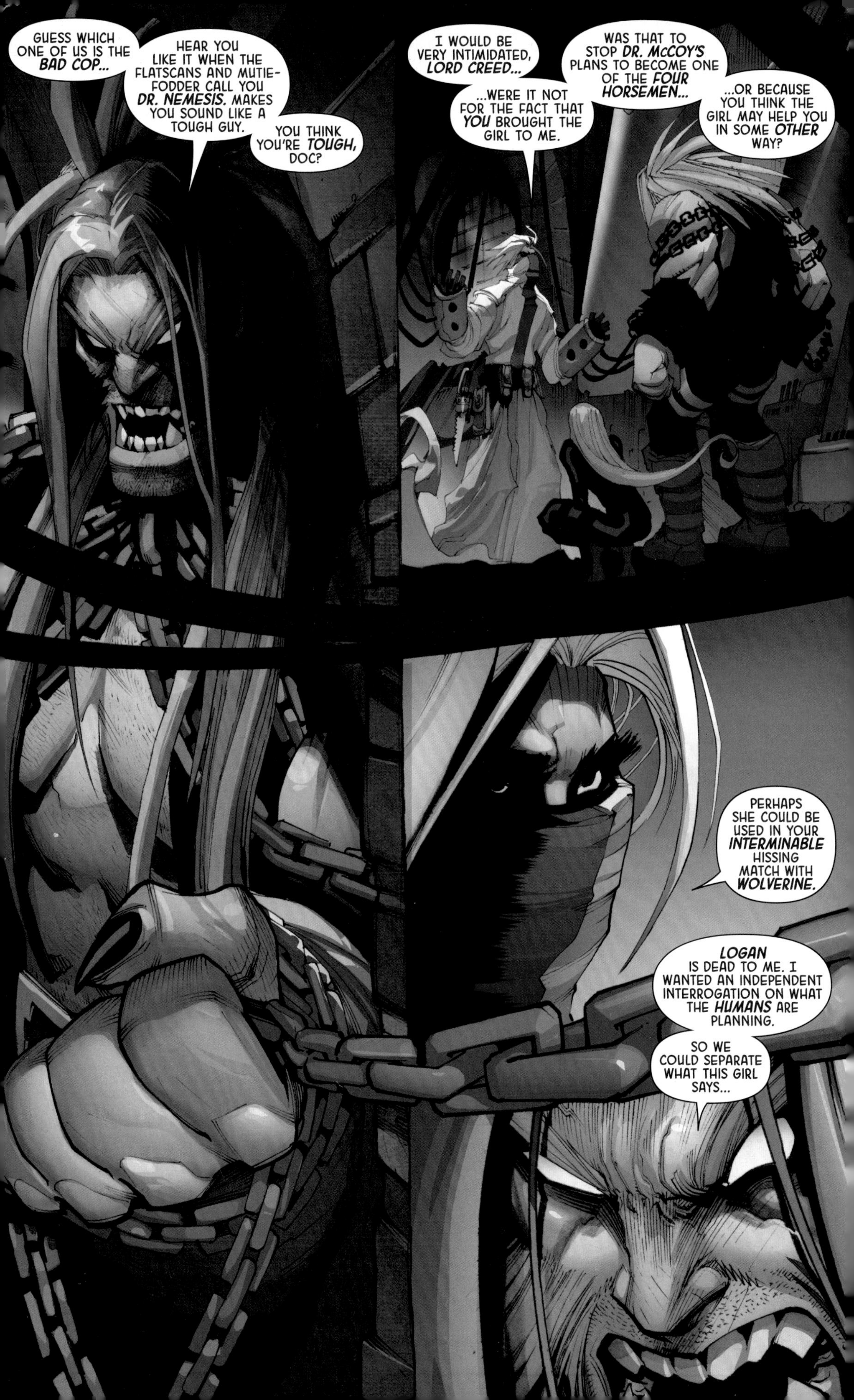
GUESS WHICH ONE OF US IS THE BAD COP...
HEAR YOU LIKE IT WHEN THE FLATSCANS AND MUTIE-FODDER CALL YOU DR. NEMESIS. MAKES YOU SOUND LIKE A TOUGH GUY.
YOU THINK YOU'RE TOUGH, DOC?
I WOULD BE VERY INTIMIDATED, LORD CREED...
...WERE IT NOT FOR THE FACT THAT YOU BROUGHT THE GIRL TO ME.
WAS THAT TO STOP DR. McCOY'S PLANS TO BECOME ONE OF THE FOUR HORSEMEN...
...OR BECAUSE YOU THINK THE GIRL MAY HELP YOU IN SOME OTHER WAY?
PERHAPS SHE COULD BE USED IN YOUR INTERMINABLE HISSING MATCH WITH WOLVERINE.
LOGAN IS DEAD TO ME. I WANTED AN INDEPENDENT INTERROGATION ON WHAT THE HUMANS ARE PLANNING.
SO WE COULD SEPARATE WHAT THIS GIRL SAYS...

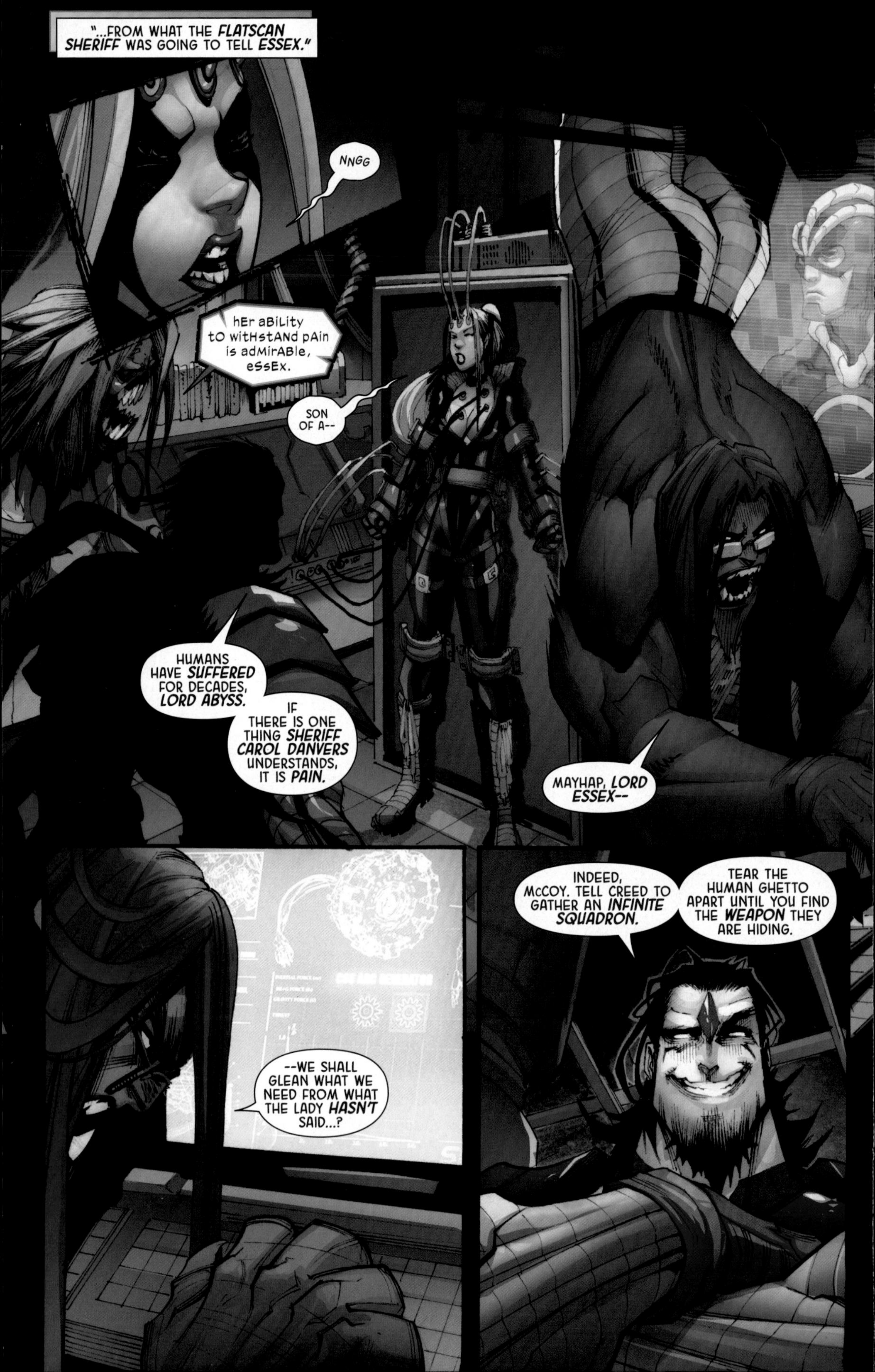
"...FROM WHAT THE FLATSCAN SHERIFF WAS GOING TO TELL ESSEX."
NNGG
hEr aBiLity to withstAND pAin is adMirABle, essEx.
SON OF A--
HUMANS HAVE SUFFERED FOR DECADES, LORD ABYSS.
IF THERE IS ONE THING SHERIFF CAROL DANVERS UNDERSTANDS, IT IS PAIN.
MAYHAP, LORD ESSEX--
--WE SHALL GLEAN WHAT WE NEED FROM WHAT THE LADY HASN'T SAID...?
INDEED, McCOY. TELL CREED TO GATHER AN INFINITE SQUADRON.
TEAR THE HUMAN GHETTO APART UNTIL YOU FIND THE WEAPON THEY ARE HIDING.

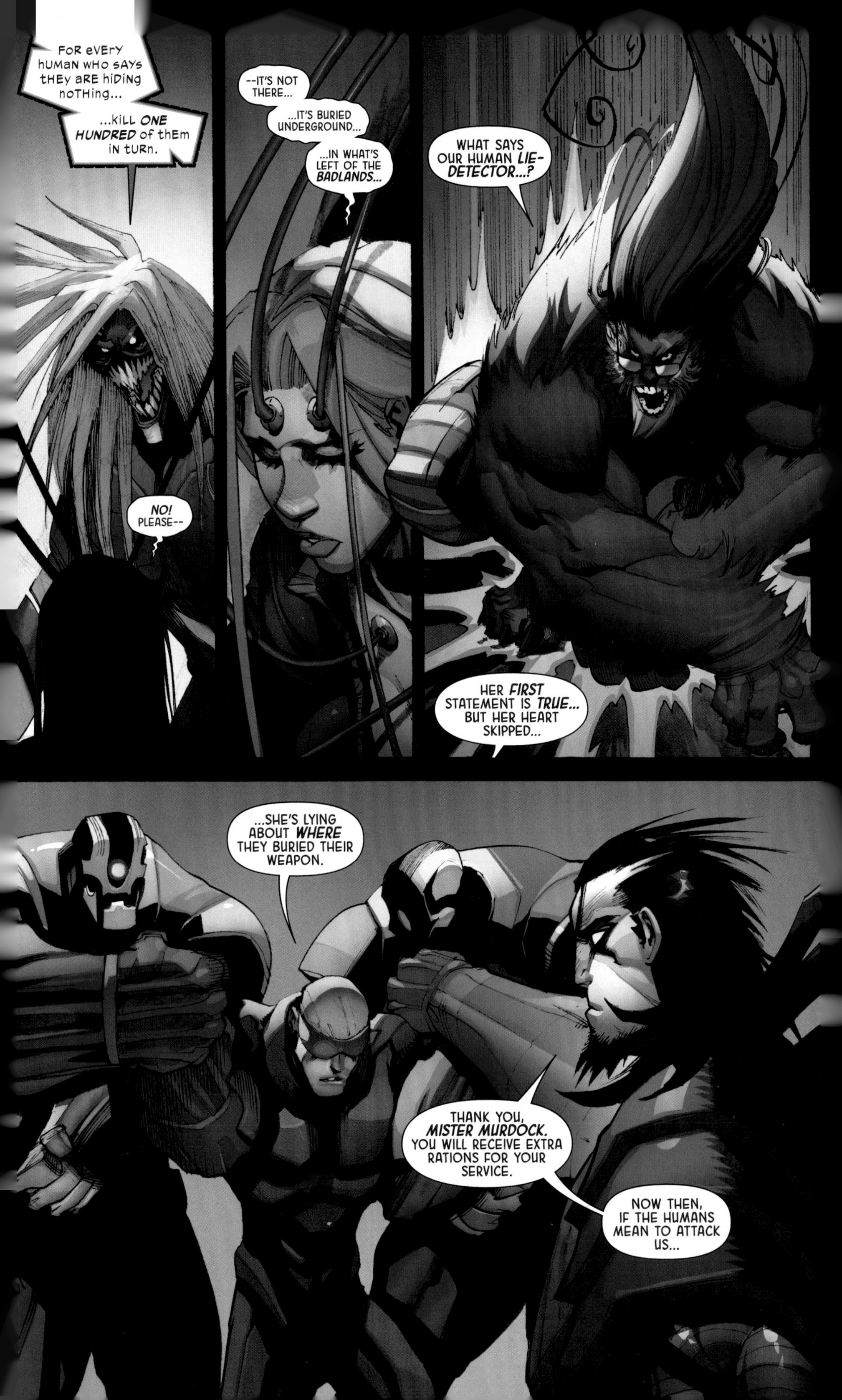

FOR EVERY HUMAN WHO SAYS THEY ARE HIDING NOTHING...
...KILL ONE HUNDRED OF THEM IN TURN.
NO! PLEASE--
--IT'S NOT THERE...
...IT'S BURIED UNDERGROUND...
...IN WHAT'S LEFT OF THE BADLANDS...
WHAT SAYS OUR HUMAN LIE-DETECTOR...?
HER FIRST STATEMENT IS TRUE... BUT HER HEART SKIPPED...
...SHE'S LYING ABOUT WHERE THEY BURIED THEIR WEAPON.
THANK YOU, MISTER MURDOCK. YOU WILL RECEIVE EXTRA RATIONS FOR YOUR SERVICE.
NOW THEN, IF THE HUMANS MEAN TO ATTACK US...

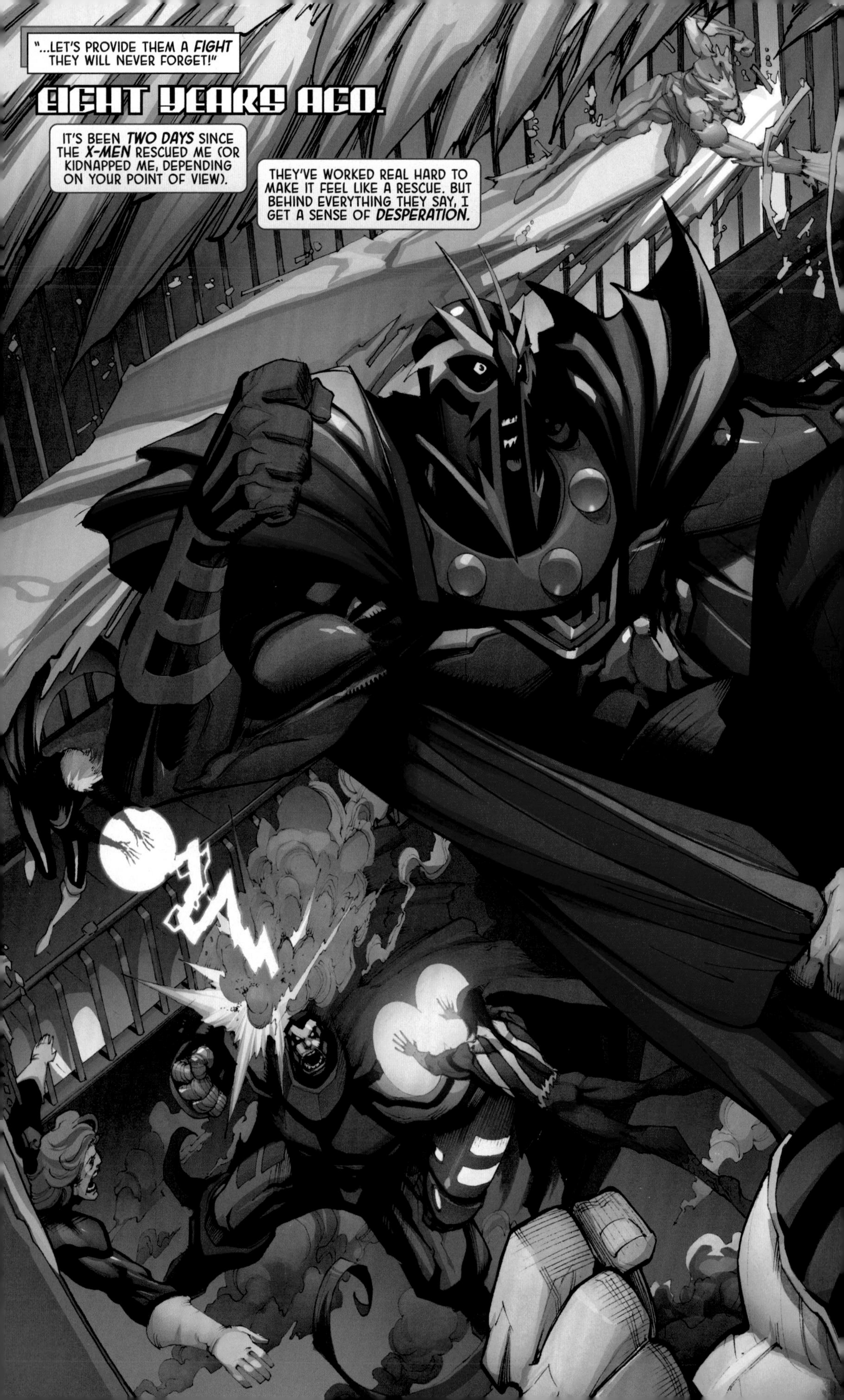
"...LET'S PROVIDE THEM A FIGHT THEY WILL NEVER FORGET!"
EIGHT YEARS AGO.
IT'S BEEN TWO DAYS SINCE THE X-MEN RESCUED ME (OR KIDNAPPED ME, DEPENDING ON YOUR POINT OF VIEW).
THEY'VE WORKED REAL HARD TO MAKE IT FEEL LIKE A RESCUE. BUT BEHIND EVERYTHING THEY SAY, I GET A SENSE OF DESPERATION.

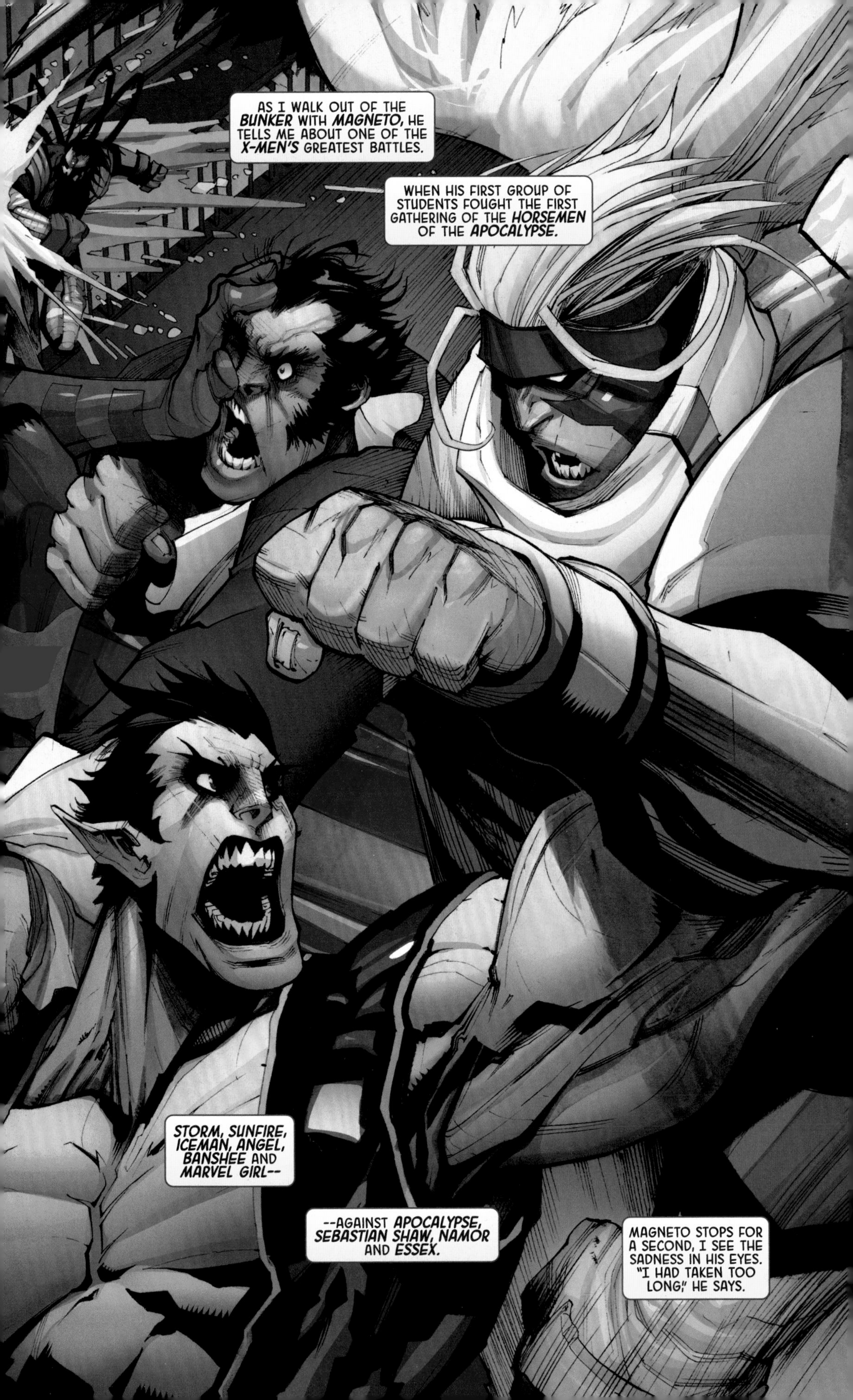
AS I WALK OUT OF THE BUNKER WITH MAGNETO, HE TELLS ME ABOUT ONE OF THE X-MEN'S GREATEST BATTLES.
WHEN HIS FIRST GROUP OF STUDENTS FOUGHT THE FIRST GATHERING OF THE HORSEMEN OF THE APOCALYPSE.
STORM, SUNFIRE, ICEMAN, ANGEL, BANSHEE AND MARVEL GIRL--
--AGAINST APOCALYPSE, SEBASTIAN SHAW, NAMOR AND ESSEX.
MAGNETO STOPS FOR A SECOND, I SEE THE SADNESS IN HIS EYES. "I HAD TAKEN TOO LONG," HE SAYS.

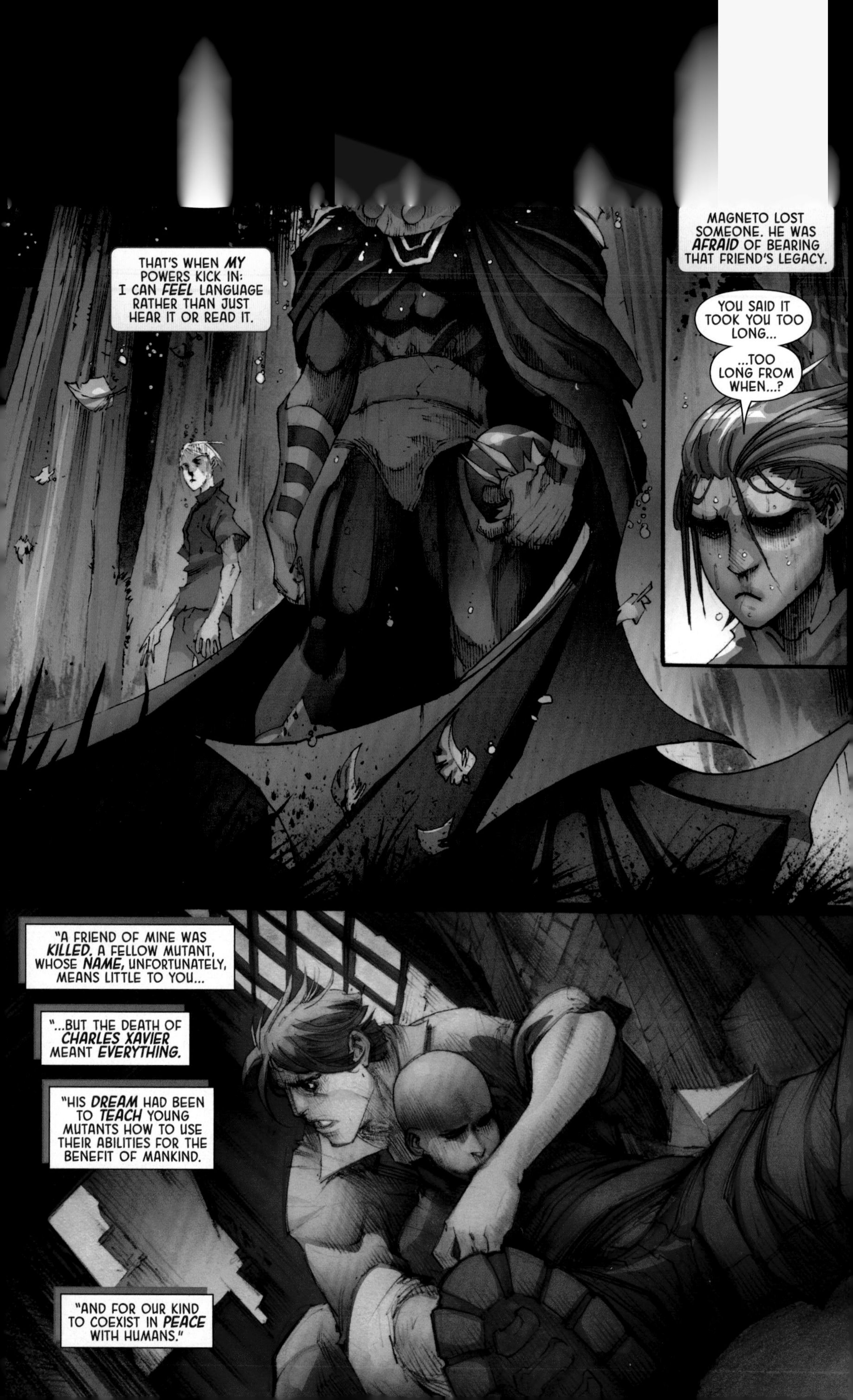
THAT'S WHEN MY POWERS KICK IN: I CAN FEEL LANGUAGE RATHER THAN JUST HEAR IT OR READ IT.
MAGNETO LOST SOMEONE. HE WAS AFRAID OF BEARING THAT FRIEND'S LEGACY.
YOU SAID IT TOOK YOU TOO LONG...
...TOO LONG FROM WHEN...?
"A FRIEND OF MINE WAS KILLED, A FELLOW MUTANT, WHOSE NAME, UNFORTUNATELY, MEANS LITTLE TO YOU...
"...BUT THE DEATH OF CHARLES XAVIER MEANT EVERYTHING.
"HIS DREAM HAD BEEN TO TEACH YOUNG MUTANTS HOW TO USE THEIR ABILITIES FOR THE BENEFIT OF MANKIND.
"AND FOR OUR KIND TO COEXIST IN PEACE WITH HUMANS."

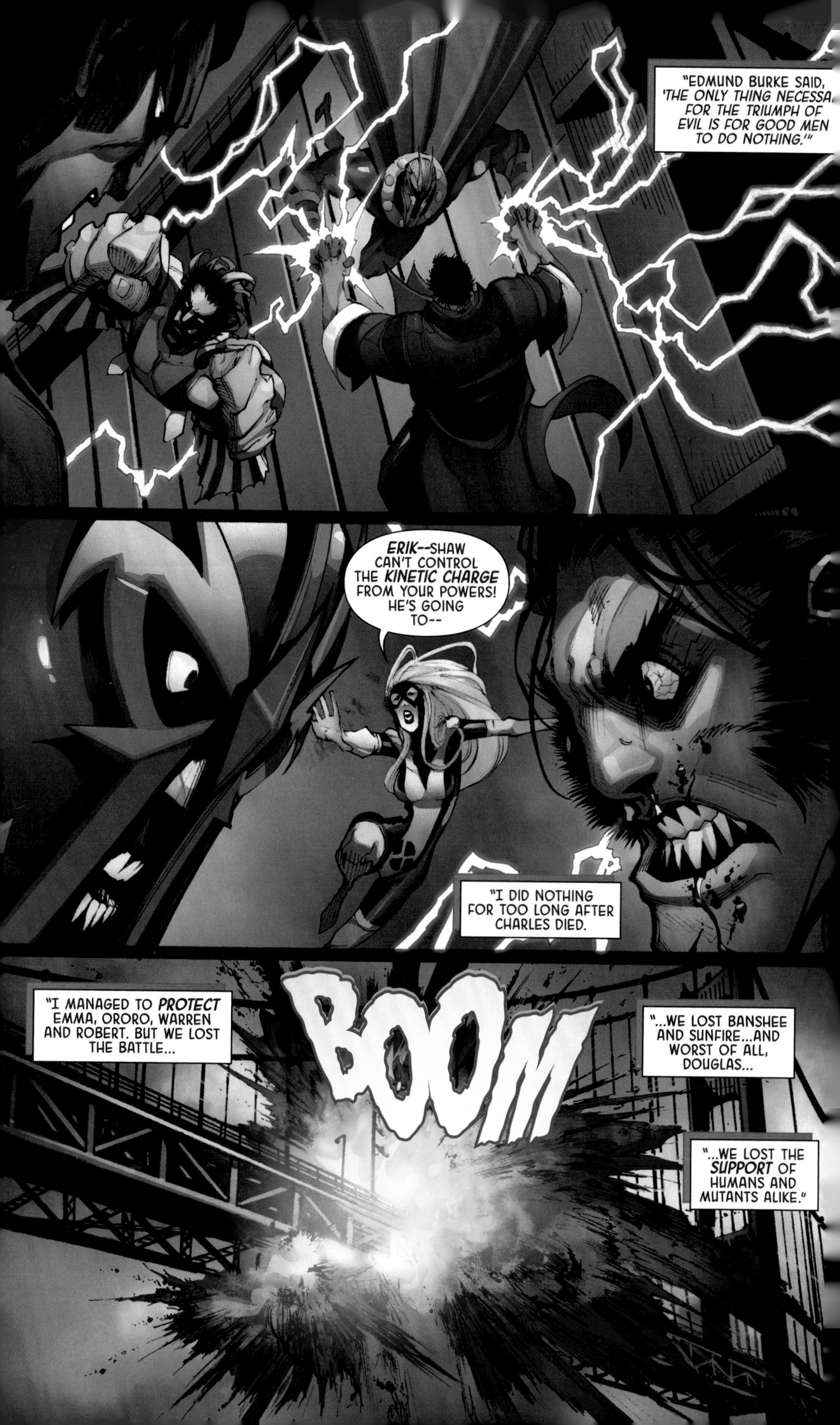
"EDMUND BURKE SAID, 'THE ONLY THING NECESSA FOR THE TRIUMPH OF EVIL IS FOR GOOD MEN TO DO NOTHING.'"
ERIK--SHAW CAN'T CONTROL THE KINETIC CHARGE FROM YOUR POWERS! HE'S GOING TO--
"I DID NOTHING FOR TOO LONG AFTER CHARLES DIED.
"I MANAGED TO PROTECT EMMA, ORORO, WARREN AND ROBERT. BUT WE LOST THE BATTLE...
BOOM
"...WE LOST BANSHEE AND SUNFIRE...AND WORST OF ALL, DOUGLAS...
"...WE LOST THE SUPPORT OF HUMANS AND MUTANTS ALIKE."

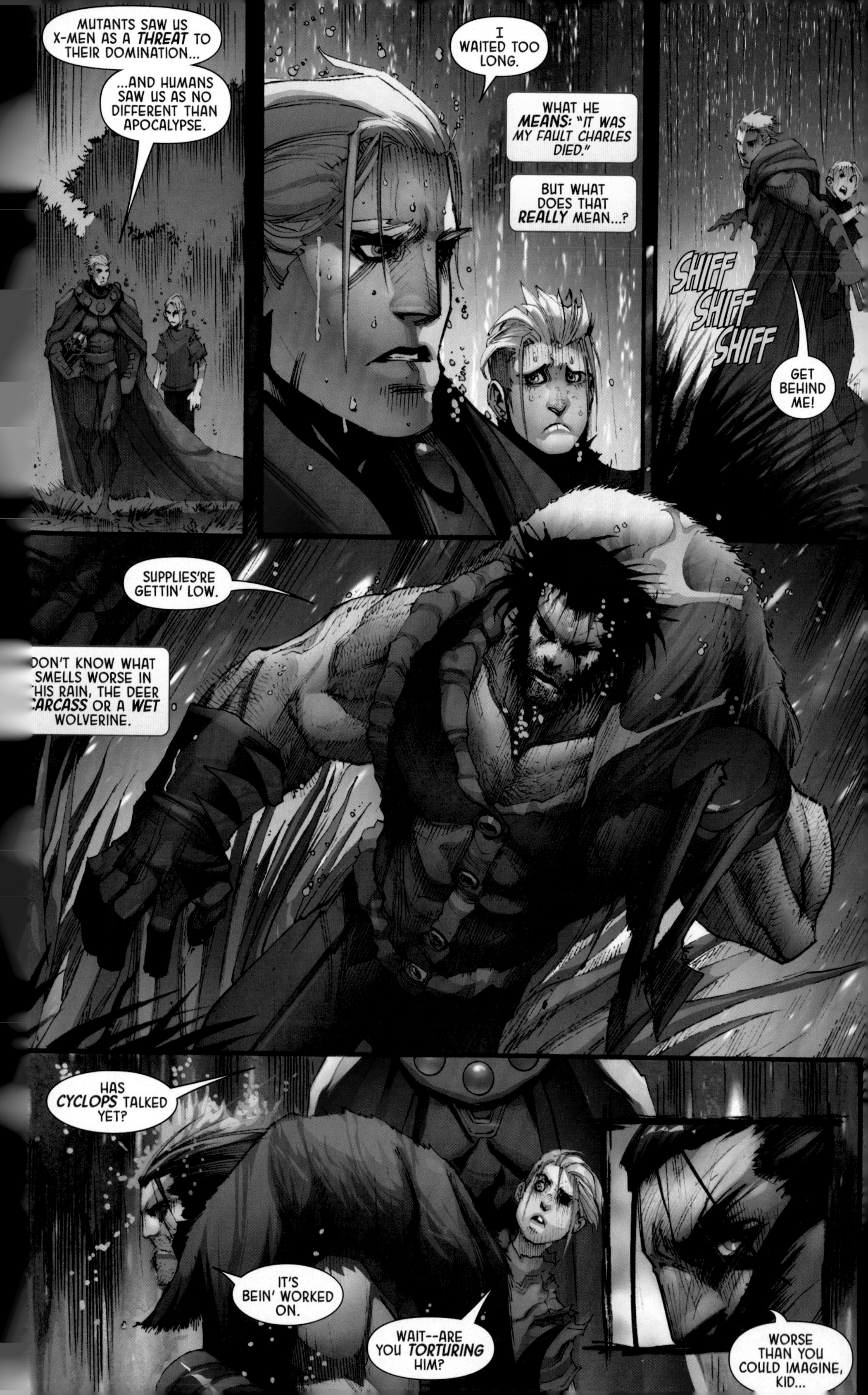
MUTANTS SAW US X-MEN AS A THREAT TO THEIR DOMINATION...
...AND HUMANS SAW US AS NO DIFFERENT THAN APOCALYPSE.
I WAITED TOO LONG.
WHAT HE MEANS: "IT WAS MY FAULT CHARLES DIED."
BUT WHAT DOES THAT REALLY MEAN...?
SHIFF SHIFF SHIFF
GET BEHIND ME!
SUPPLIES'RE GETTIN' LOW.
DON'T KNOW WHAT SMELLS WORSE IN THIS RAIN, THE DEER CARCASS OR A WET WOLVERINE.
HAS CYCLOPS TALKED YET?
IT'S BEIN' WORKED ON.
WAIT--ARE YOU TORTURING HIM?
WORSE THAN YOU COULD IMAGINE, KID...

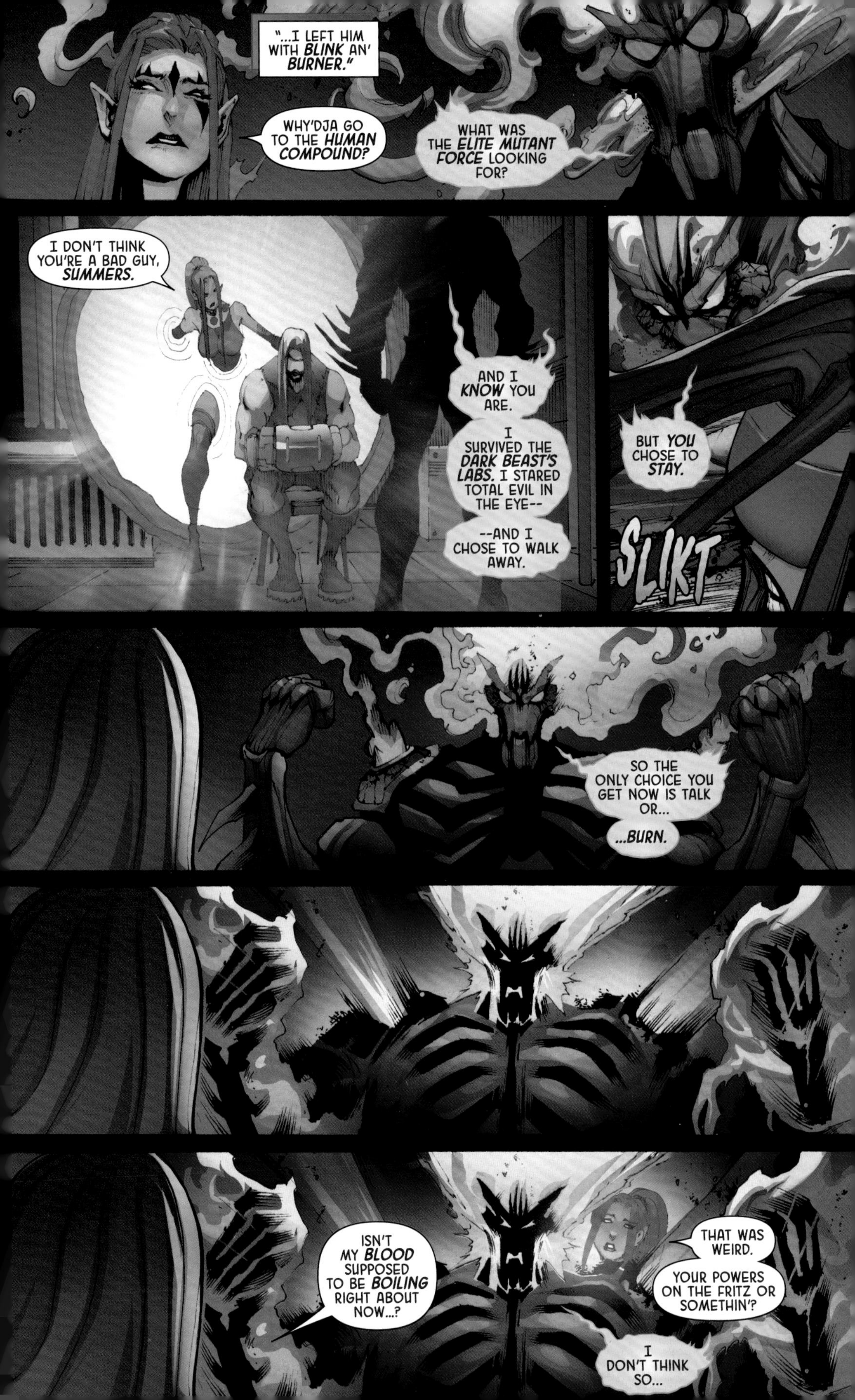

"...I LEFT HIM WITH BLINK AN' BURNER."
WHY'DJA GO TO THE HUMAN COMPOUND?
WHAT WAS THE ELITE MUTANT FORCE LOOKING FOR?
I DON'T THINK YOU'RE A BAD GUY, SUMMERS.
AND I KNOW YOU ARE.
I SURVIVED THE DARK BEAST'S LABS. I STARED TOTAL EVIL IN THE EYE--
--AND I CHOSE TO WALK AWAY.
BUT YOU CHOSE TO STAY.
SLIKT
SO THE ONLY CHOICE YOU GET NOW IS TALK OR...
...BURN.
ISN'T MY BLOOD SUPPOSED TO BE BOILING RIGHT ABOUT NOW...?
THAT WAS WEIRD.
YOUR POWERS ON THE FRITZ OR SOMETHIN'?
I DON'T THINK SO...

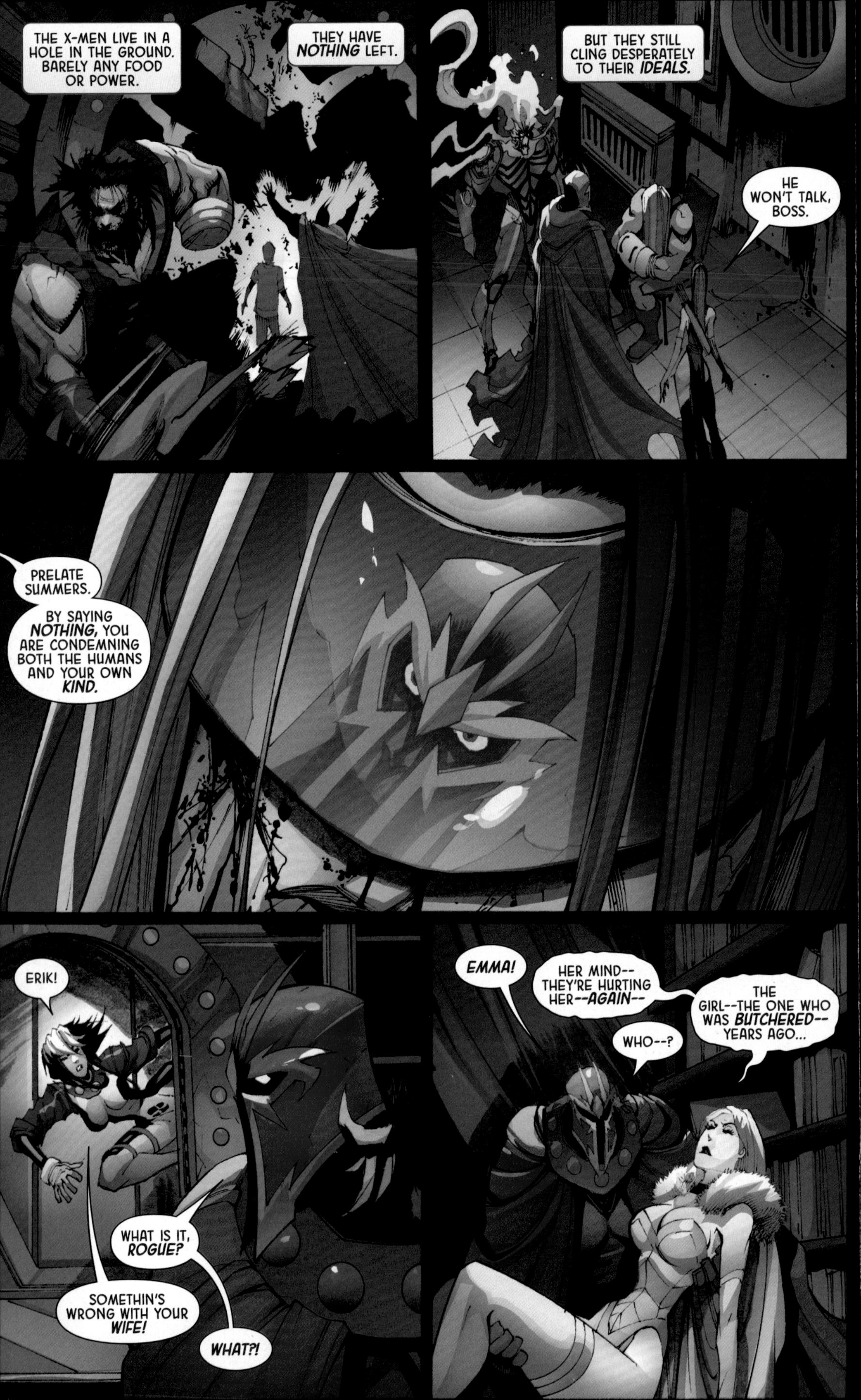
THE X-MEN LIVE IN A HOLE IN THE GROUND. BARELY ANY FOOD OR POWER.
THEY HAVE NOTHING LEFT.
BUT THEY STILL CLING DESPERATELY TO THEIR IDEALS.
HE WON'T TALK, BOSS.
PRELATE SUMMERS.
BY SAYING NOTHING, YOU ARE CONDEMNING BOTH THE HUMANS AND YOUR OWN KIND.
ERIK!
WHAT IS IT, ROGUE?
SOMETHIN'S WRONG WITH YOUR WIFE!
WHAT?!
EMMA!
HER MIND-- THEY'RE HURTING HER--AGAIN--
WHO--?
THE GIRL--THE ONE WHO WAS BUTCHERED-- YEARS AGO...

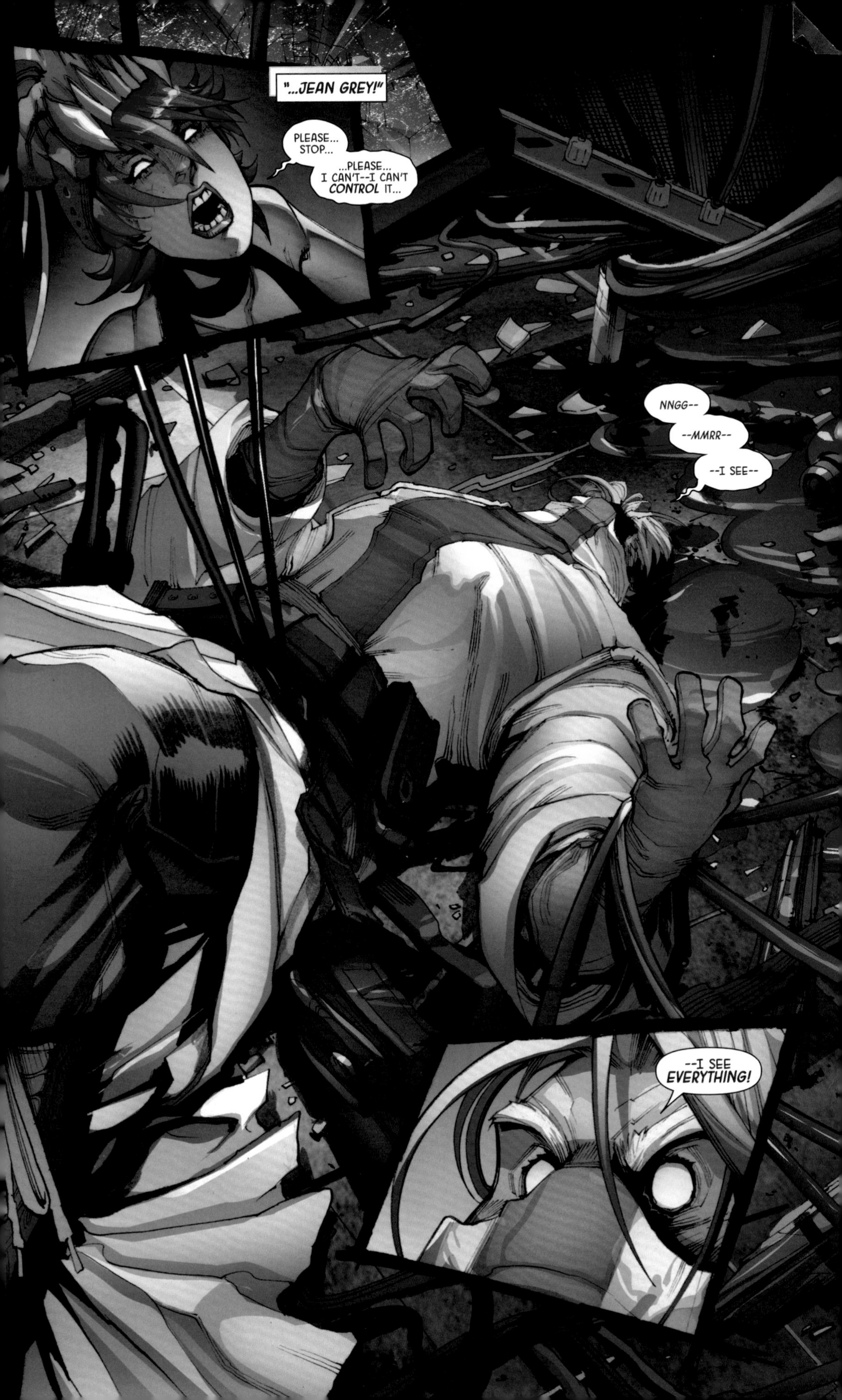

"...JEAN GREY!"
PLEASE... STOP...
...PLEASE... I CAN'T--I CAN'T CONTROL IT...
NNGG--
--MMRR--
--I SEE--
--I SEE EVERYTHING!

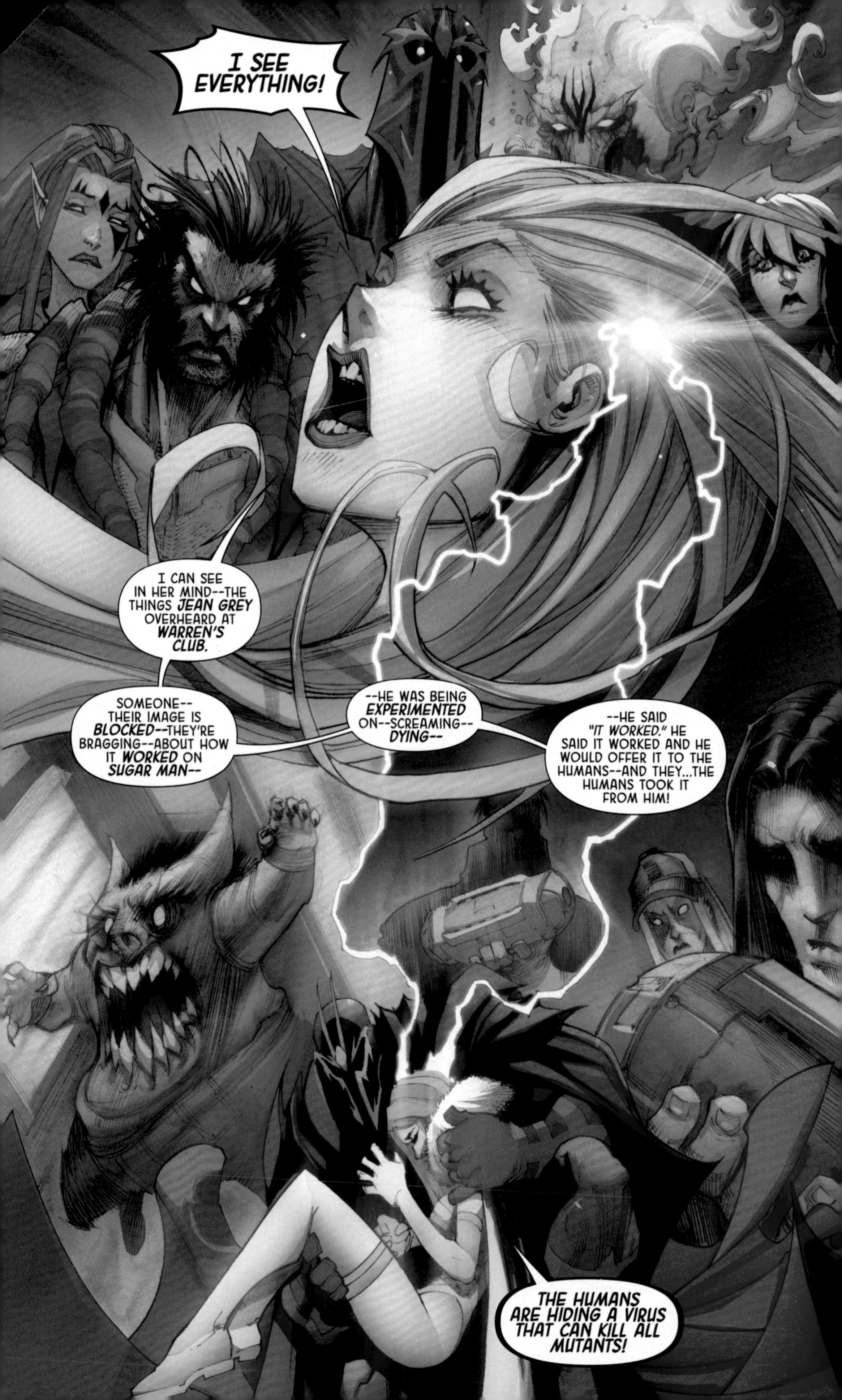
I SEE EVERYTHING!
I CAN SEE IN HER MIND--THE THINGS JEAN GREY OVERHEARD AT WARREN'S CLUB.
SOMEONE--THEIR IMAGE IS BLOCKED--THEY'RE BRAGGING--ABOUT HOW IT WORKED ON SUGAR MAN--
--HE WAS BEING EXPERIMENTED ON--SCREAMING--DYING--
--HE SAID "IT WORKED." HE SAID IT WORKED AND HE WOULD OFFER IT TO THE HUMANS--AND THEY...THE HUMANS TOOK IT FROM HIM!
THE HUMANS ARE HIDING A VIRUS THAT CAN KILL ALL MUTANTS!

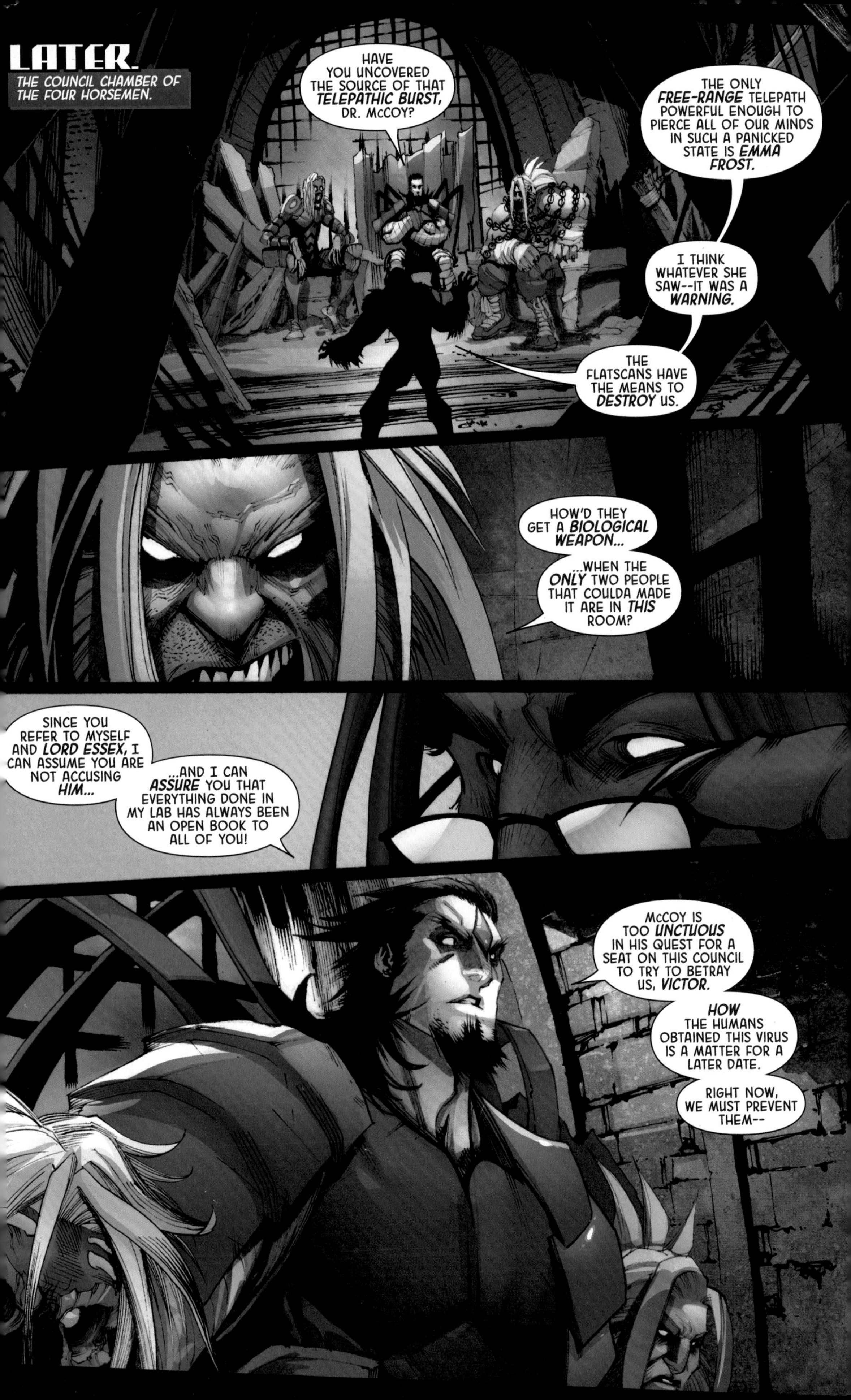
LATER.
THE COUNCIL CHAMBER OF THE FOUR HORSEMEN.
HAVE YOU UNCOVERED THE SOURCE OF THAT TELEPATHIC BURST, DR. McCOY?
THE ONLY FREE-RANGE TELEPATH POWERFUL ENOUGH TO PIERCE ALL OF OUR MINDS IN SUCH A PANICKED STATE IS EMMA FROST.
I THINK WHATEVER SHE SAW--IT WAS A WARNING.
THE FLATSCANS HAVE THE MEANS TO DESTROY US.
HOW'D THEY GET A BIOLOGICAL WEAPON...
...WHEN THE ONLY TWO PEOPLE THAT COULDA MADE IT ARE IN THIS ROOM?
SINCE YOU REFER TO MYSELF AND LORD ESSEX, I CAN ASSUME YOU ARE NOT ACCUSING HIM...
...AND I CAN ASSURE YOU THAT EVERYTHING DONE IN MY LAB HAS ALWAYS BEEN AN OPEN BOOK TO ALL OF YOU!
McCOY IS TOO UNCTUOUS IN HIS QUEST FOR A SEAT ON THIS COUNCIL TO TRY TO BETRAY US, VICTOR.
HOW THE HUMANS OBTAINED THIS VIRUS IS A MATTER FOR A LATER DATE.
RIGHT NOW, WE MUST PREVENT THEM--

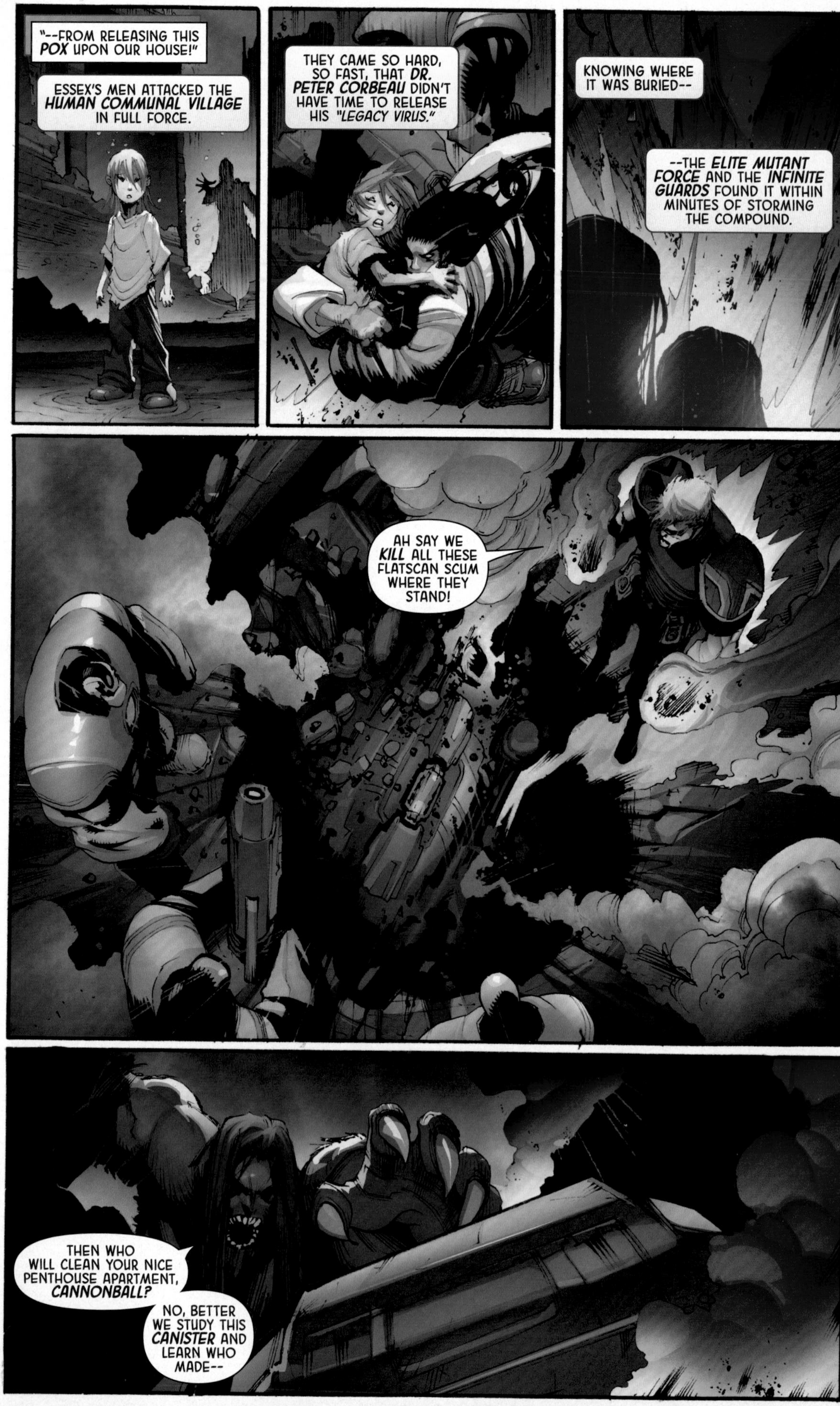
"--FROM RELEASING THIS POX UPON OUR HOUSE!"
ESSEX'S MEN ATTACKED THE HUMAN COMMUNAL VILLAGE IN FULL FORCE.
THEY CAME SO HARD, SO FAST, THAT DR. PETER CORBEAU DIDN'T HAVE TIME TO RELEASE HIS "LEGACY VIRUS."
KNOWING WHERE IT WAS BURIED--
--THE ELITE MUTANT FORCE AND THE INFINITE GUARDS FOUND IT WITHIN MINUTES OF STORMING THE COMPOUND.
AH SAY WE KILL ALL THESE FLATSCAN SCUM WHERE THEY STAND!
THEN WHO WILL CLEAN YOUR NICE PENTHOUSE APARTMENT, CANNONBALL?
NO, BETTER WE STUDY THIS CANISTER AND LEARN WHO MADE--

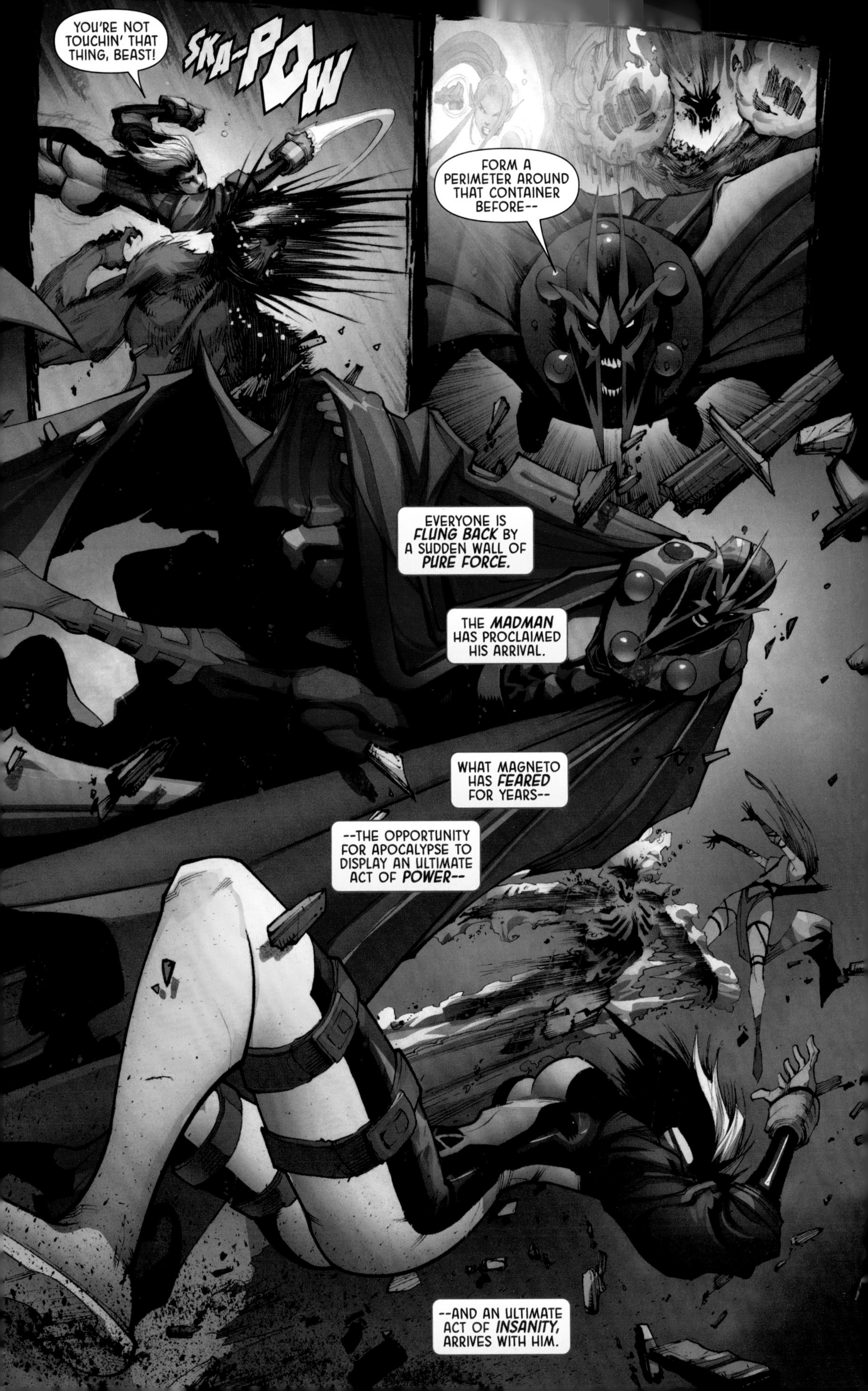
YOU'RE NOT TOUCHIN' THAT THING, BEAST!
SKA-POW
FORM A PERIMETER AROUND THAT CONTAINER BEFORE--
EVERYONE IS FLUNG BACK BY A SUDDEN WALL OF PURE FORCE.
THE MADMAN HAS PROCLAIMED HIS ARRIVAL.
WHAT MAGNETO HAS FEARED FOR YEARS--
--THE OPPORTUNITY FOR APOCALYPSE TO DISPLAY AN ULTIMATE ACT OF POWER--
--AND AN ULTIMATE ACT OF INSANITY, ARRIVES WITH HIM.

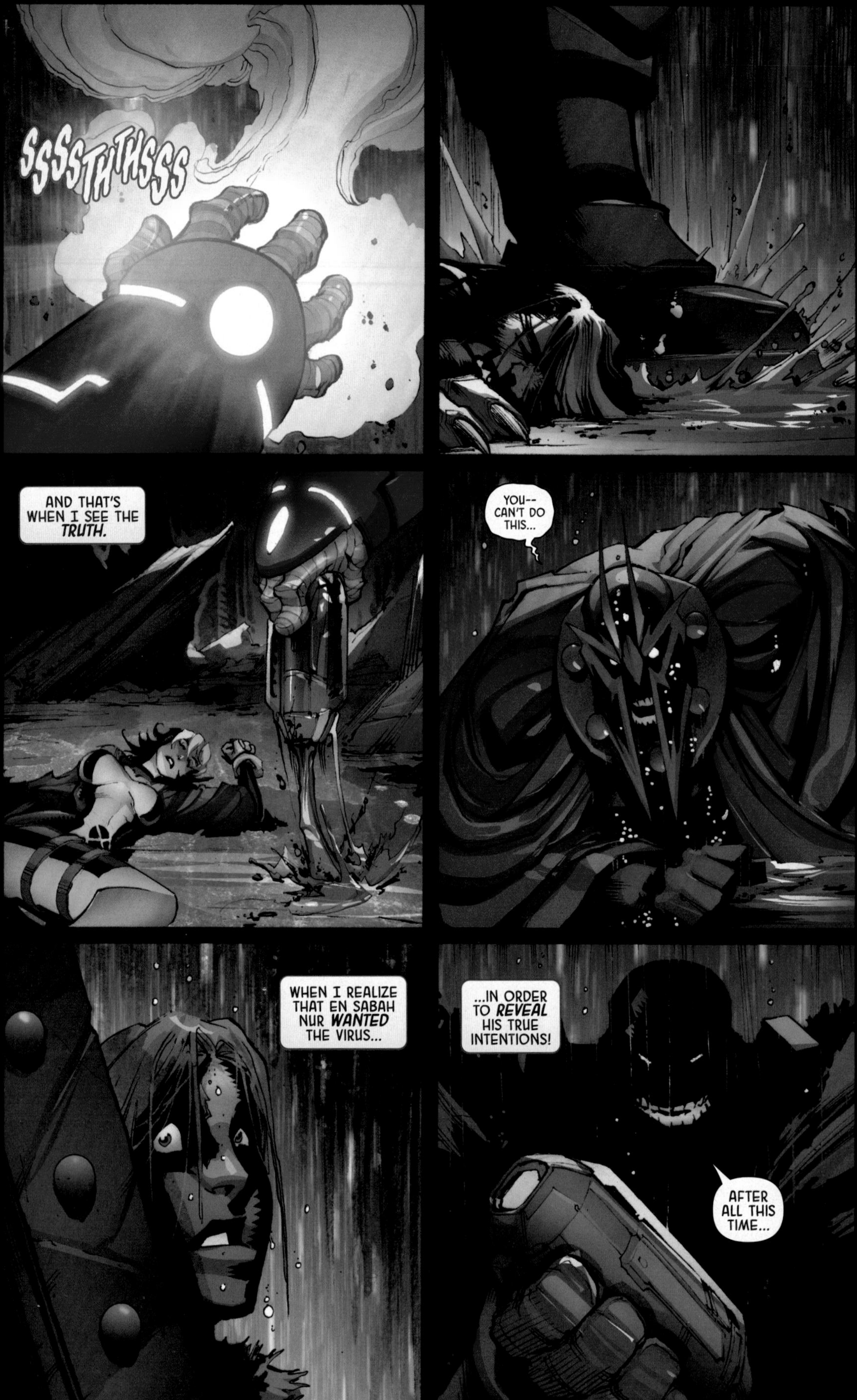
SSSSTHTHSSS
AND THAT'S WHEN I SEE THE *TRUTH.*
YOU-- CAN'T DO THIS...
WHEN I REALIZE THAT EN SABAH NUR *WANTED* THE VIRUS...
...IN ORDER TO *REVEAL* HIS TRUE INTENTIONS!
AFTER ALL THIS TIME...

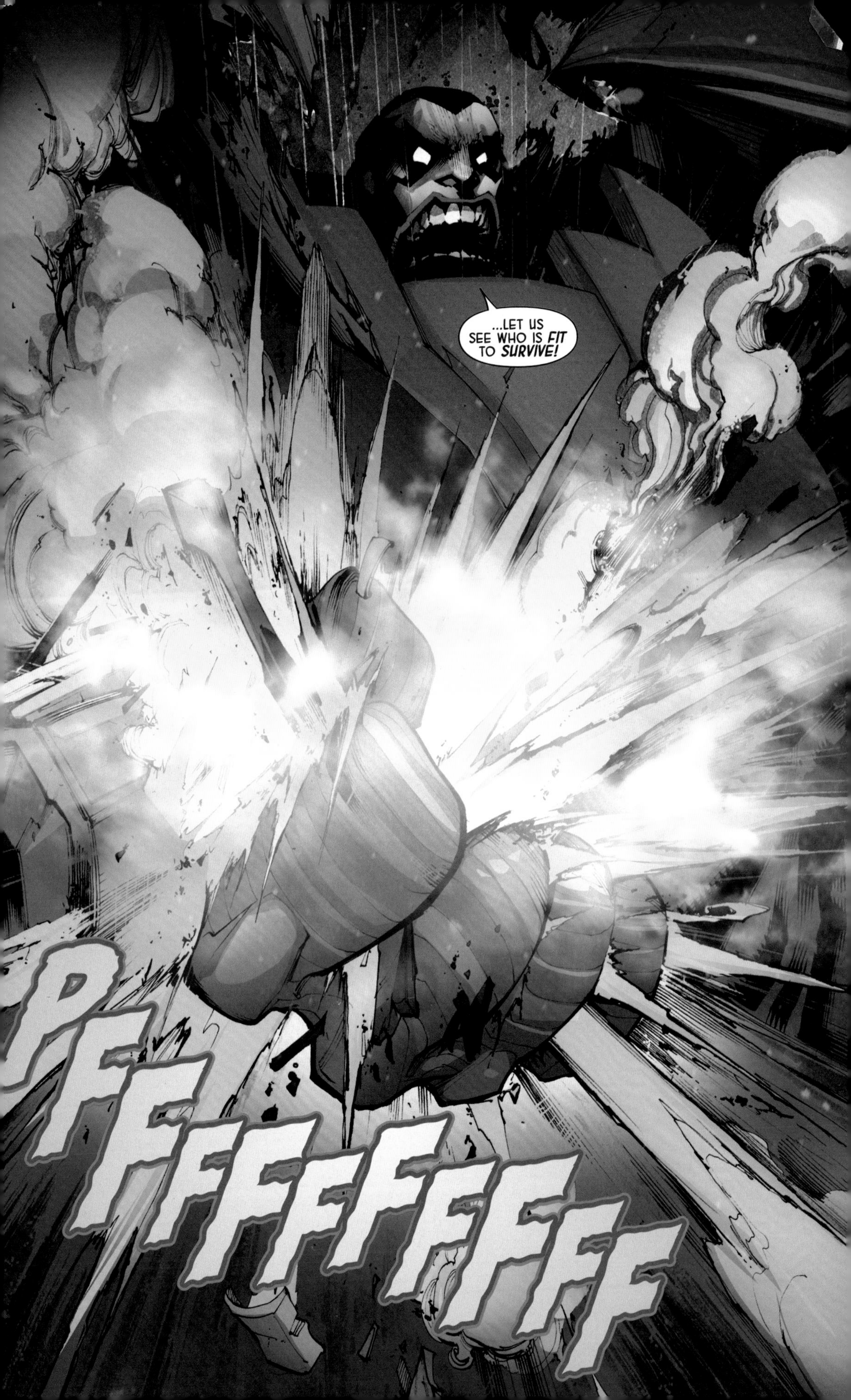
...LET US SEE WHO IS FIT TO SURVIVE!
PFFFFFFFFFFF

#1 VARIANT BY SKOTTIE YOUNG

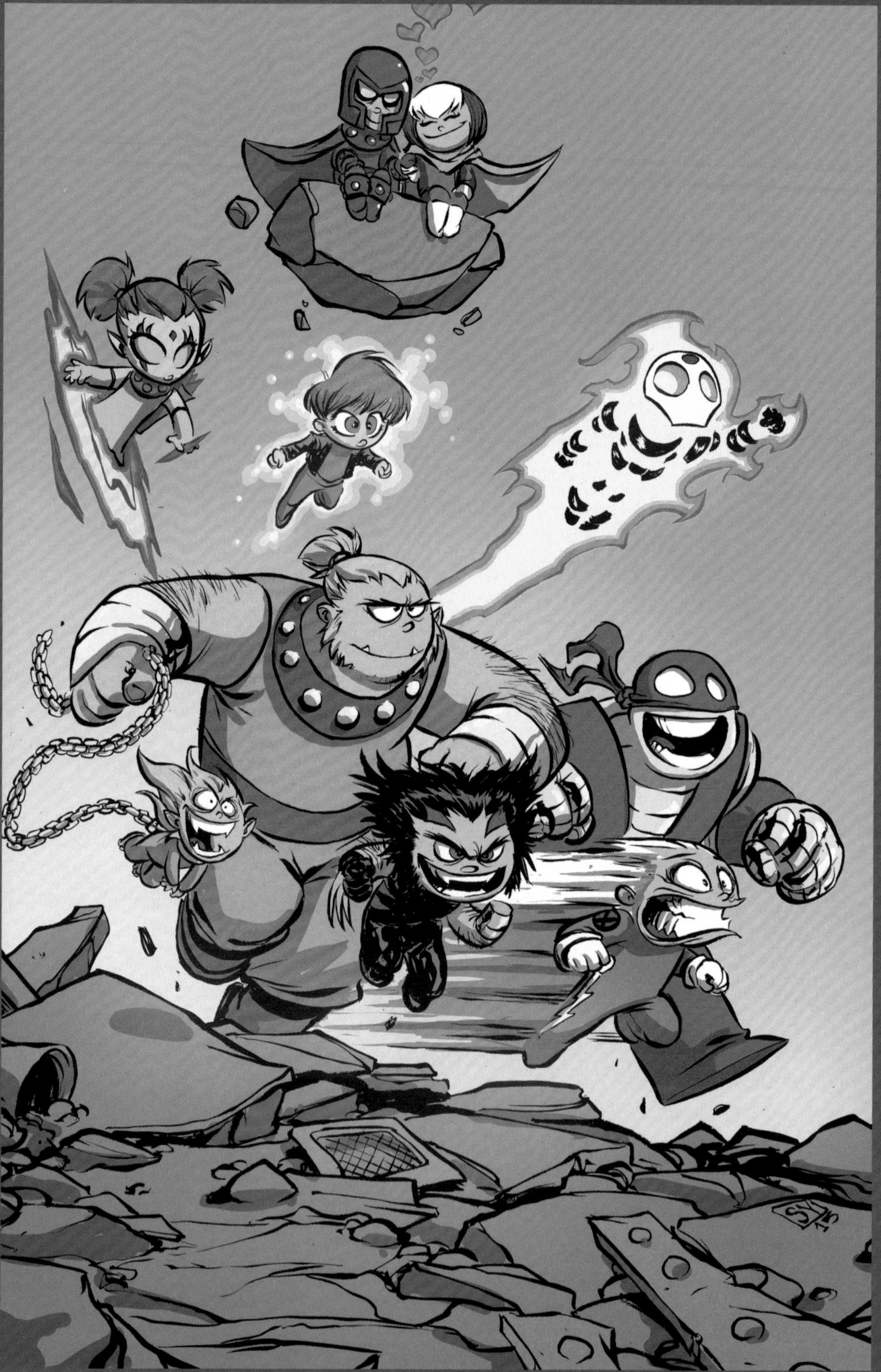

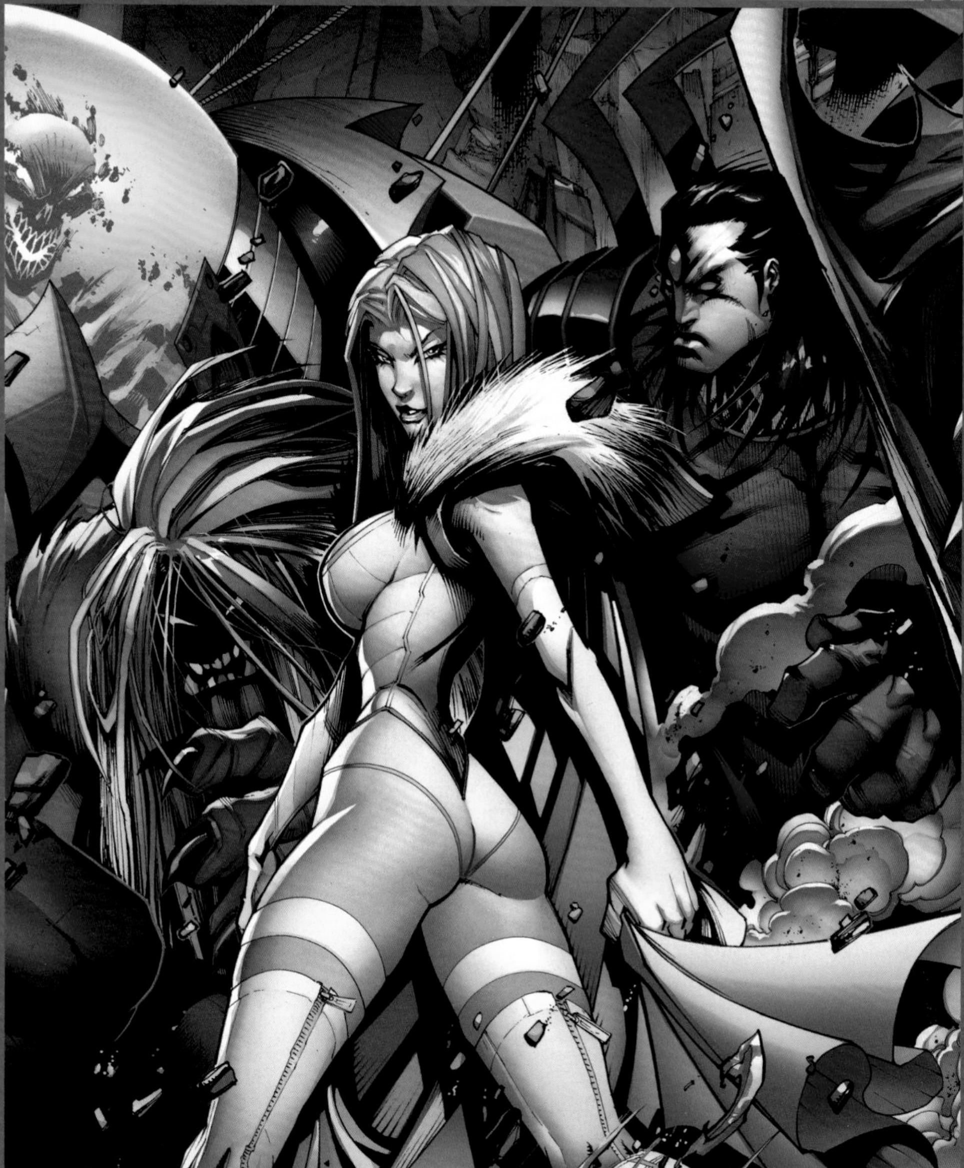

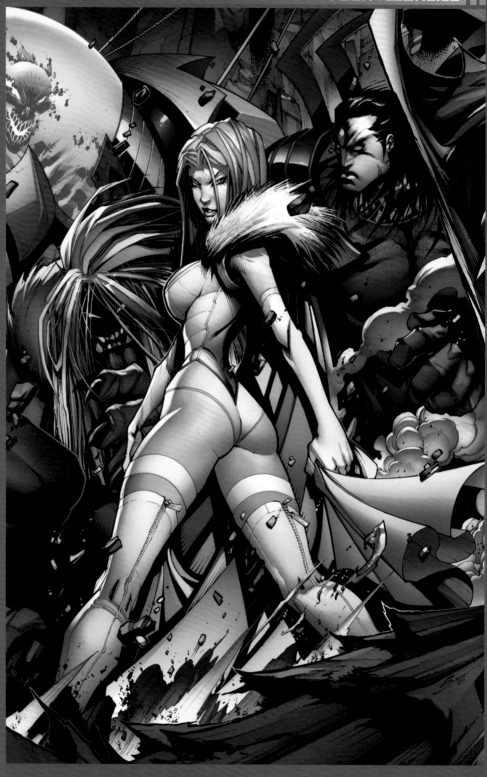

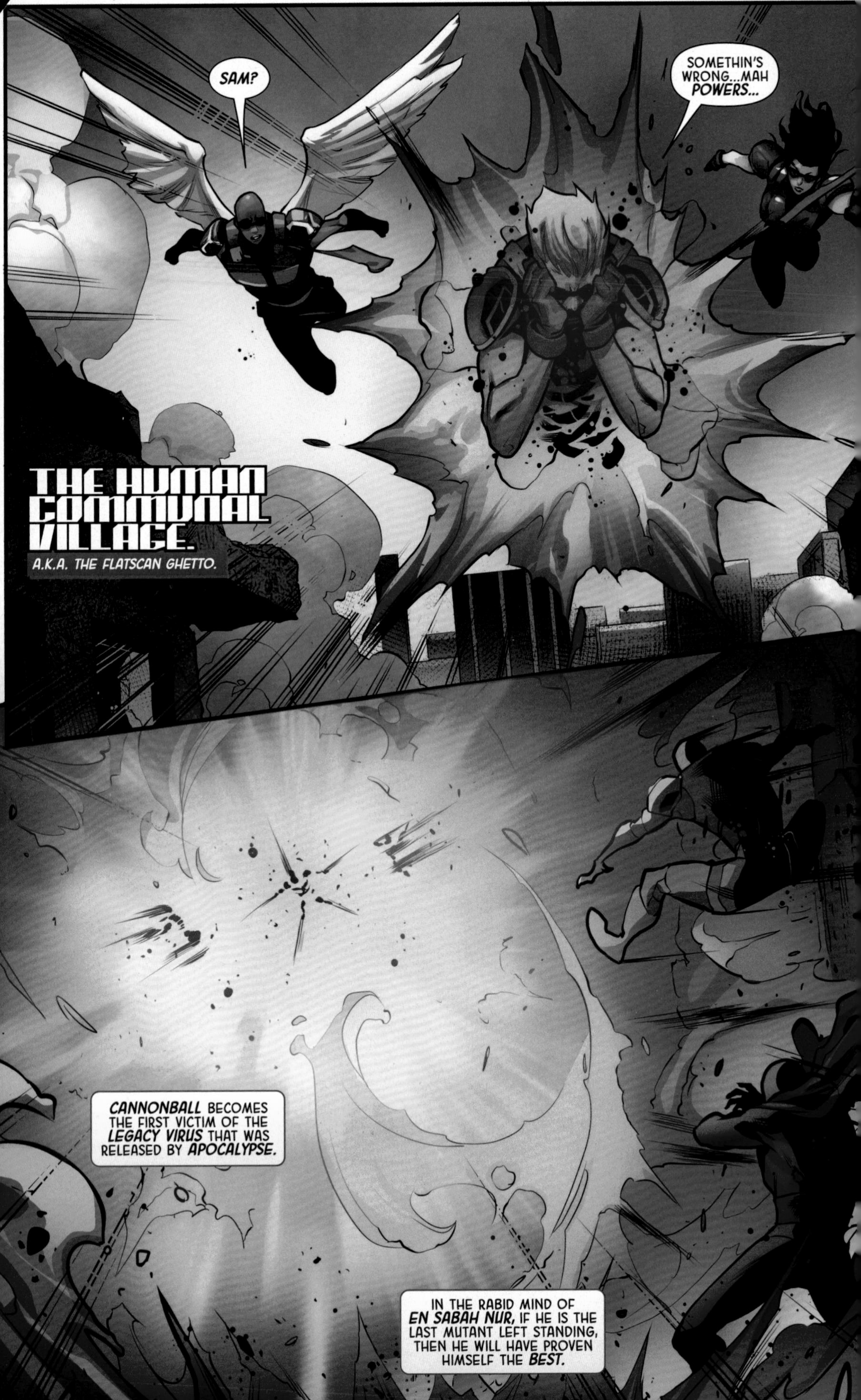

SAM?
SOMETHIN'S WRONG...MAH POWERS...
THE HUMAN COMMUNAL VILLAGE.
A.K.A. THE FLATSCAN GHETTO.
CANNONBALL BECOMES THE FIRST VICTIM OF THE LEGACY VIRUS THAT WAS RELEASED BY APOCALYPSE.
IN THE RABID MIND OF EN SABAH NUR, IF HE IS THE LAST MUTANT LEFT STANDING, THEN HE WILL HAVE PROVEN HIMSELF THE BEST.

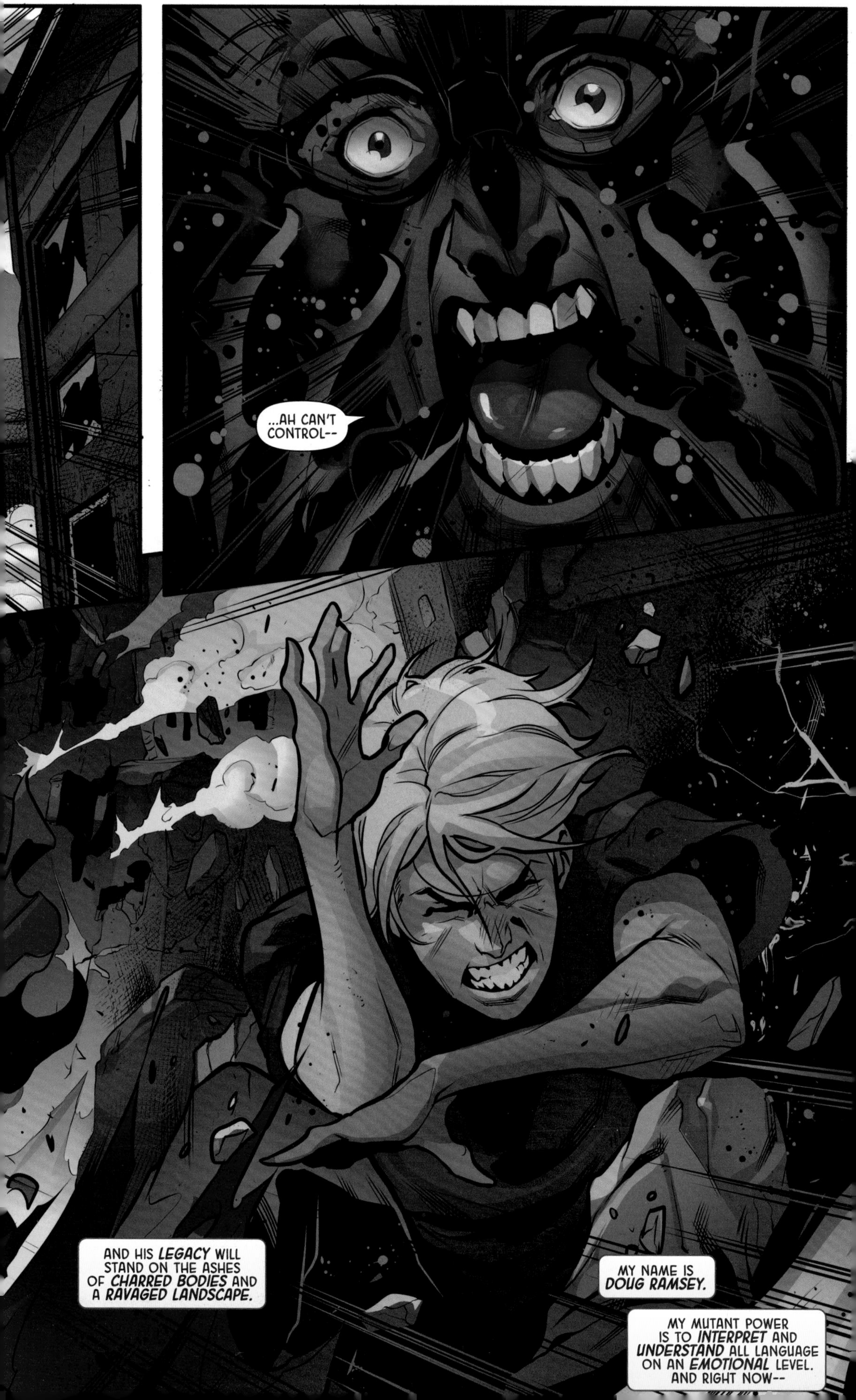
...AH CAN'T CONTROL--
AND HIS *LEGACY* WILL STAND ON THE ASHES OF *CHARRED BODIES* AND A *RAVAGED LANDSCAPE.*
MY NAME IS *DOUG RAMSEY.*
MY MUTANT POWER IS TO *INTERPRET* AND *UNDERSTAND* ALL LANGUAGE ON AN *EMOTIONAL* LEVEL. AND RIGHT NOW--

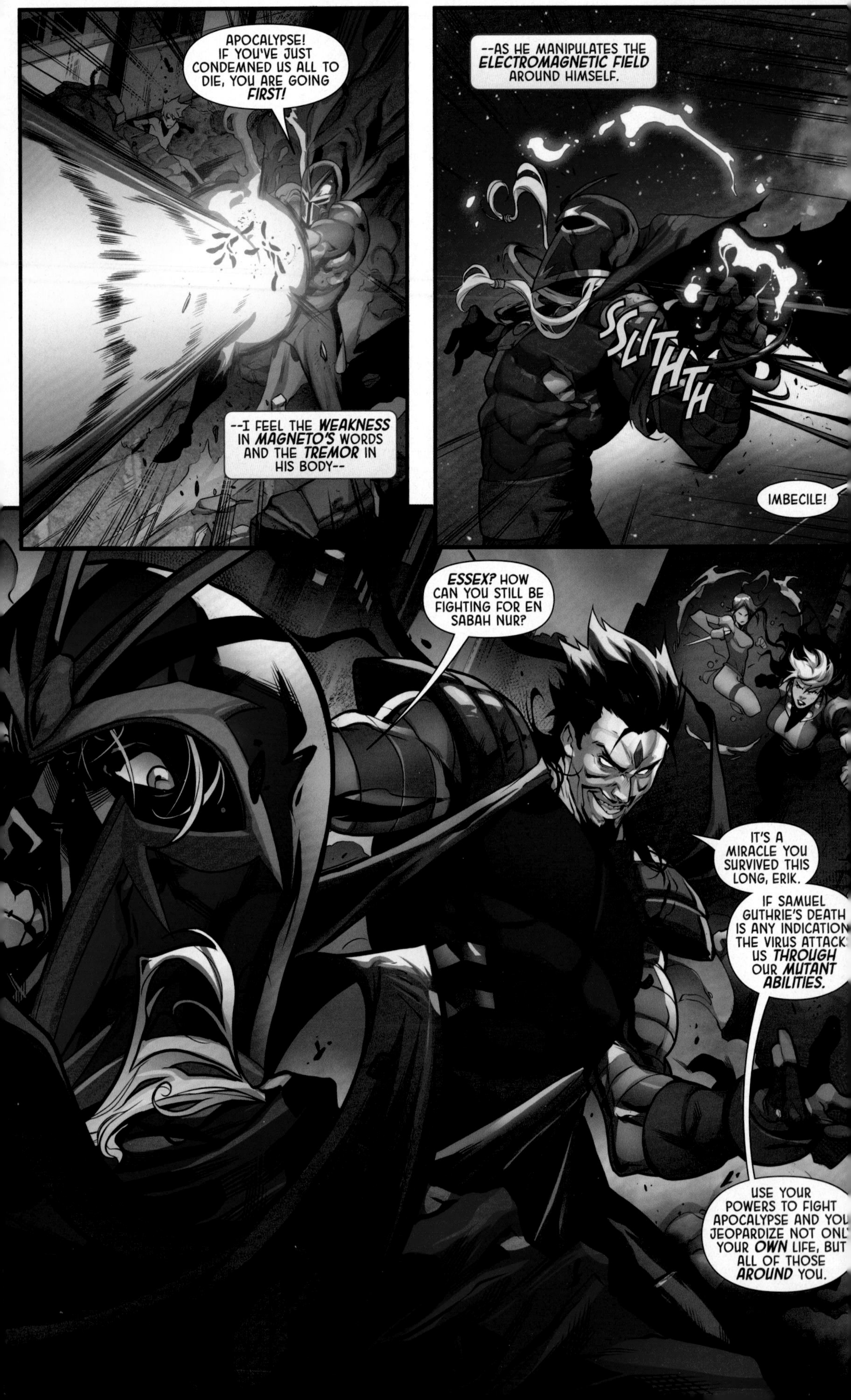
APOCALYPSE! IF YOU'VE JUST CONDEMNED US ALL TO DIE, YOU ARE GOING FIRST!
--I FEEL THE WEAKNESS IN MAGNETO'S WORDS AND THE TREMOR IN HIS BODY--
--AS HE MANIPULATES THE ELECTROMAGNETIC FIELD AROUND HIMSELF.
SSLITHTH
IMBECILE!
ESSEX? HOW CAN YOU STILL BE FIGHTING FOR EN SABAH NUR?
IT'S A MIRACLE YOU SURVIVED THIS LONG, ERIK.
IF SAMUEL GUTHRIE'S DEATH IS ANY INDICATION THE VIRUS ATTACKS US THROUGH OUR MUTANT ABILITIES.
USE YOUR POWERS TO FIGHT APOCALYPSE AND YOU JEOPARDIZE NOT ONLY YOUR OWN LIFE, BUT ALL OF THOSE AROUND YOU.

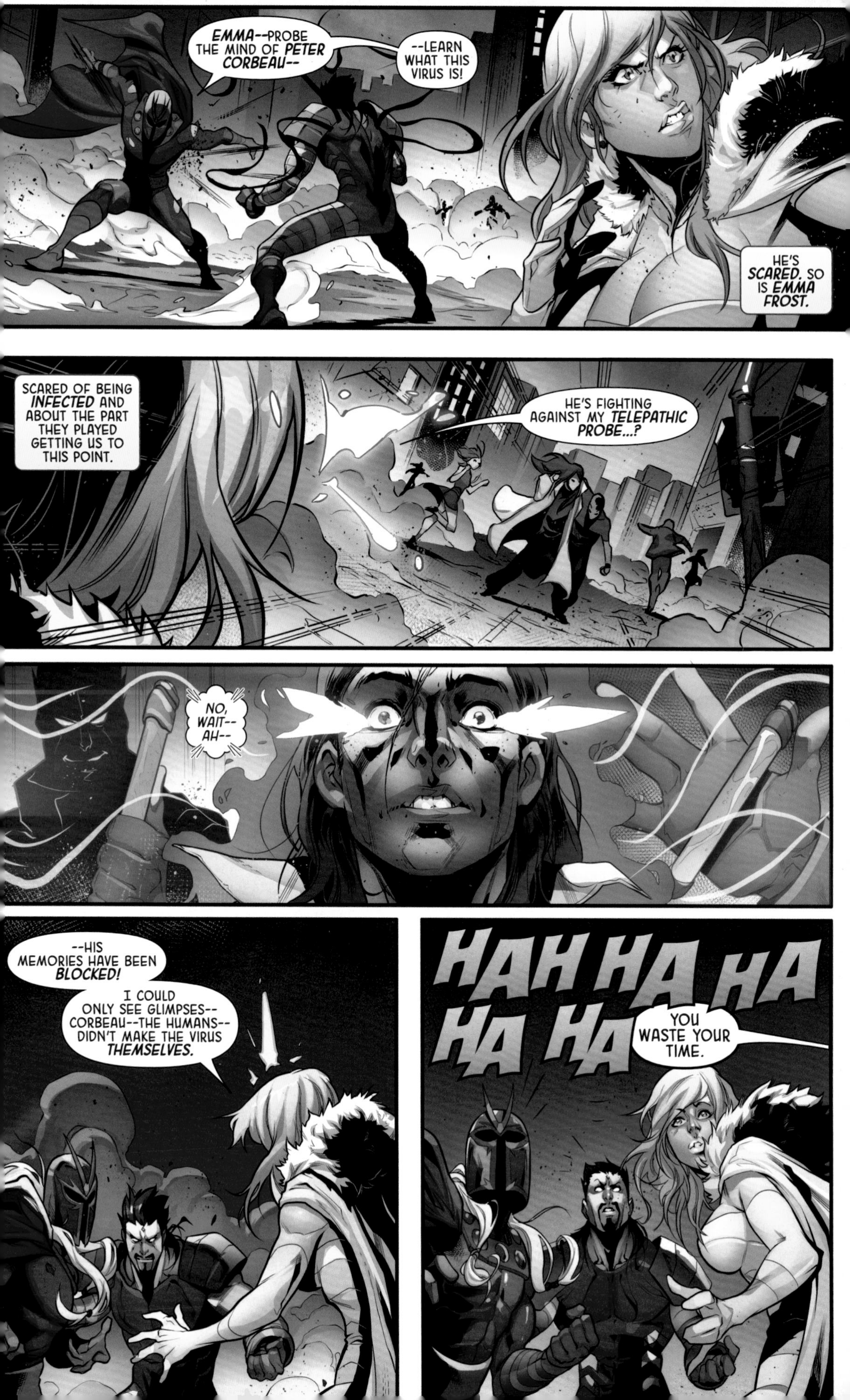
EMMA--PROBE THE MIND OF PETER CORBEAU--
--LEARN WHAT THIS VIRUS IS!
HE'S SCARED. SO IS EMMA FROST.
SCARED OF BEING INFECTED AND ABOUT THE PART THEY PLAYED GETTING US TO THIS POINT.
HE'S FIGHTING AGAINST MY TELEPATHIC PROBE...?
NO, WAIT-- AH--
--HIS MEMORIES HAVE BEEN BLOCKED!
I COULD ONLY SEE GLIMPSES-- CORBEAU--THE HUMANS-- DIDN'T MAKE THE VIRUS THEMSELVES.
HAH HA HA HA HA HA
YOU WASTE YOUR TIME.

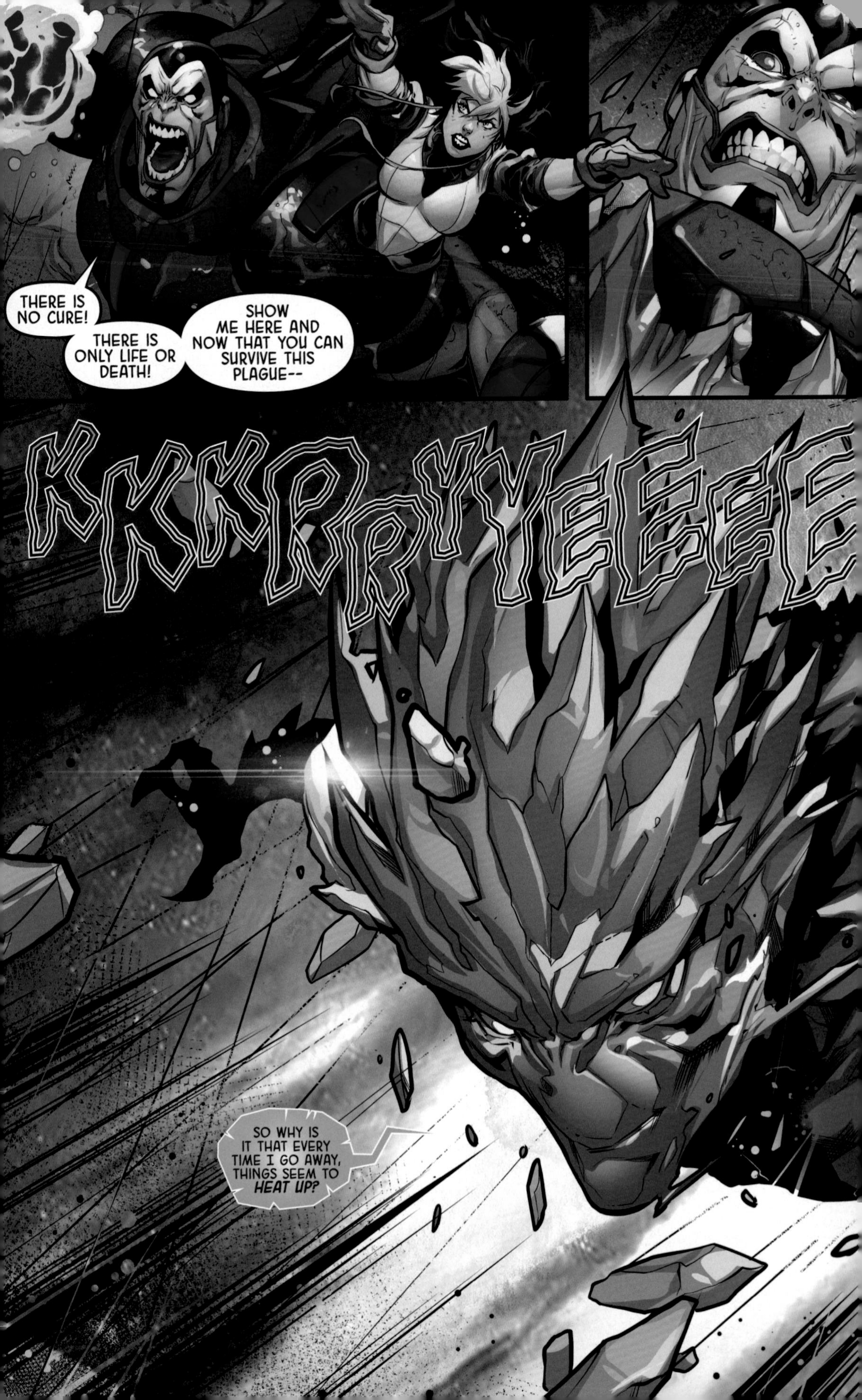

THERE IS NO CURE!
THERE IS ONLY LIFE OR DEATH!
SHOW ME HERE AND NOW THAT YOU CAN SURVIVE THIS PLAGUE--
KKKRRYYEEEEE
SO WHY IS IT THAT EVERY TIME I GO AWAY, THINGS SEEM TO *HEAT UP?*

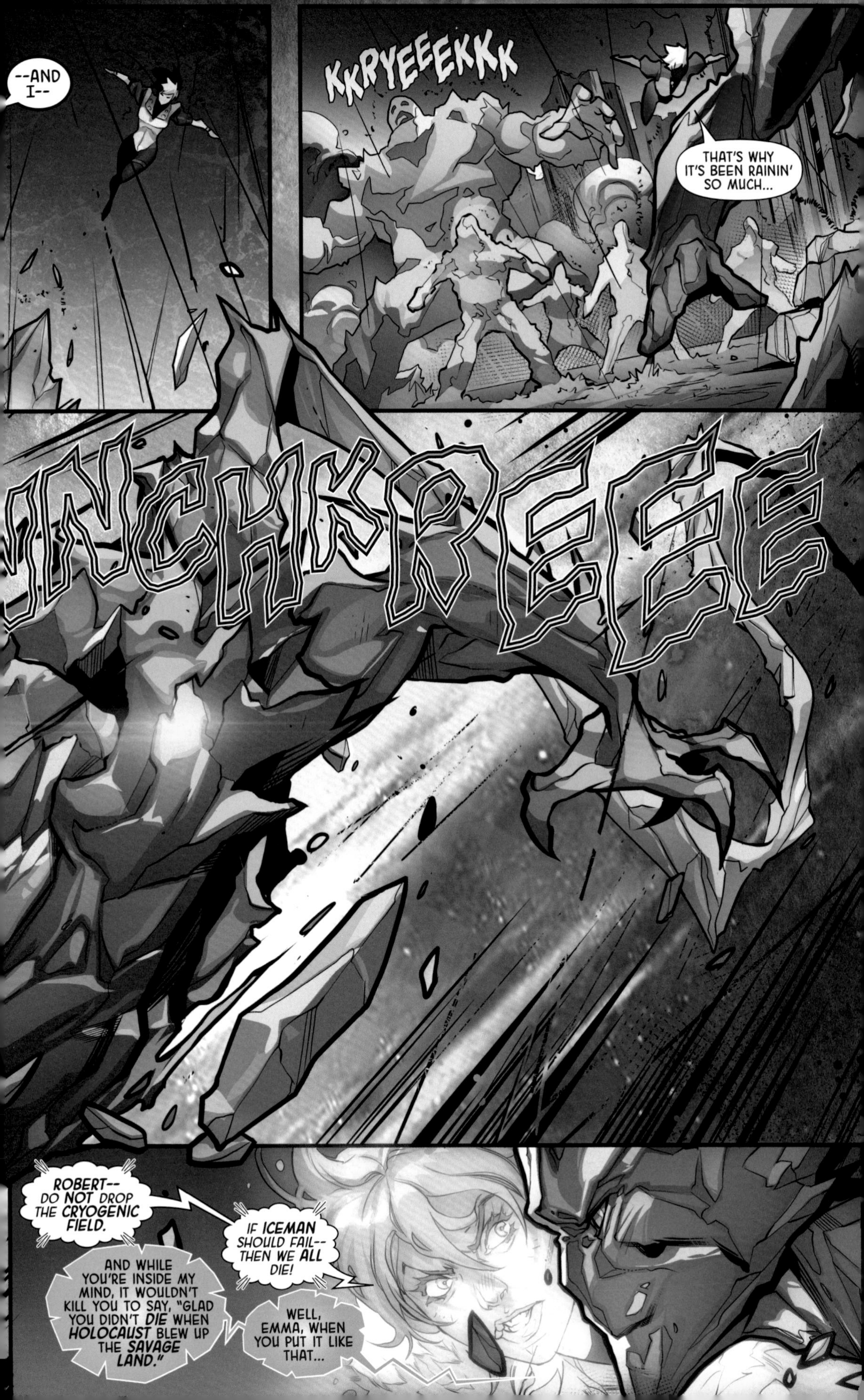
--AND I--
KKRYEEEKKK
THAT'S WHY IT'S BEEN RAININ' SO MUCH...
INCHKREEEE
ROBERT-- DO NOT DROP THE CRYOGENIC FIELD.
IF ICEMAN SHOULD FAIL-- THEN WE ALL DIE!
AND WHILE YOU'RE INSIDE MY MIND, IT WOULDN'T KILL YOU TO SAY, "GLAD YOU DIDN'T DIE WHEN HOLOCAUST BLEW UP THE SAVAGE LAND."
WELL, EMMA, WHEN YOU PUT IT LIKE THAT...

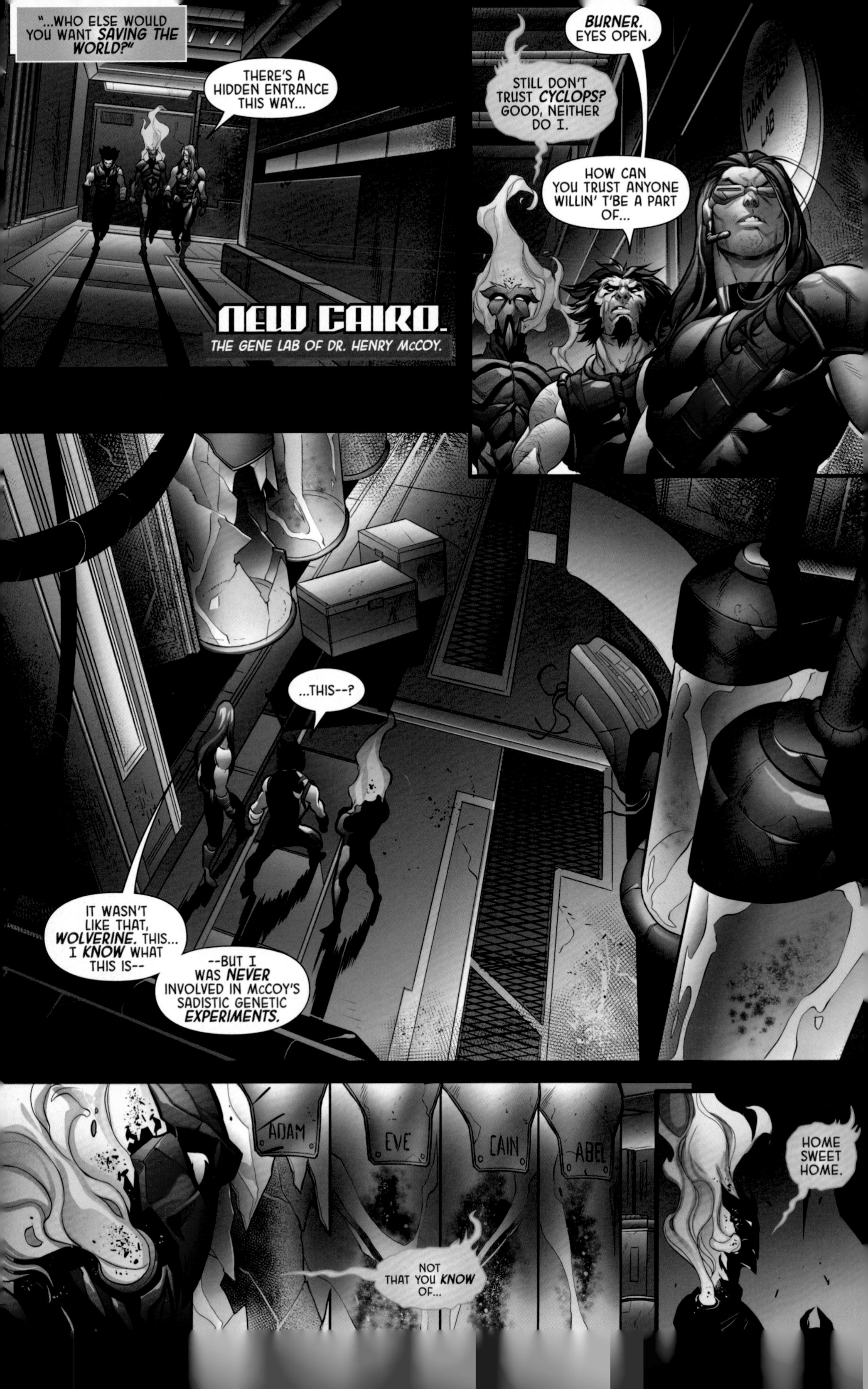
"...WHO ELSE WOULD YOU WANT SAVING THE WORLD?"
THERE'S A HIDDEN ENTRANCE THIS WAY...
NEW CAIRO.
THE GENE LAB OF DR. HENRY McCOY.
BURNER. EYES OPEN.
STILL DON'T TRUST CYCLOPS? GOOD, NEITHER DO I.
HOW CAN YOU TRUST ANYONE WILLIN' T'BE A PART OF...
DARK BEAST LAB
...THIS--?
IT WASN'T LIKE THAT, WOLVERINE. THIS... I KNOW WHAT THIS IS--
--BUT I WAS NEVER INVOLVED IN McCOY'S SADISTIC GENETIC EXPERIMENTS.
ADAM
EVE
CAIN
ABEL
NOT THAT YOU KNOW OF...
HOME SWEET HOME.

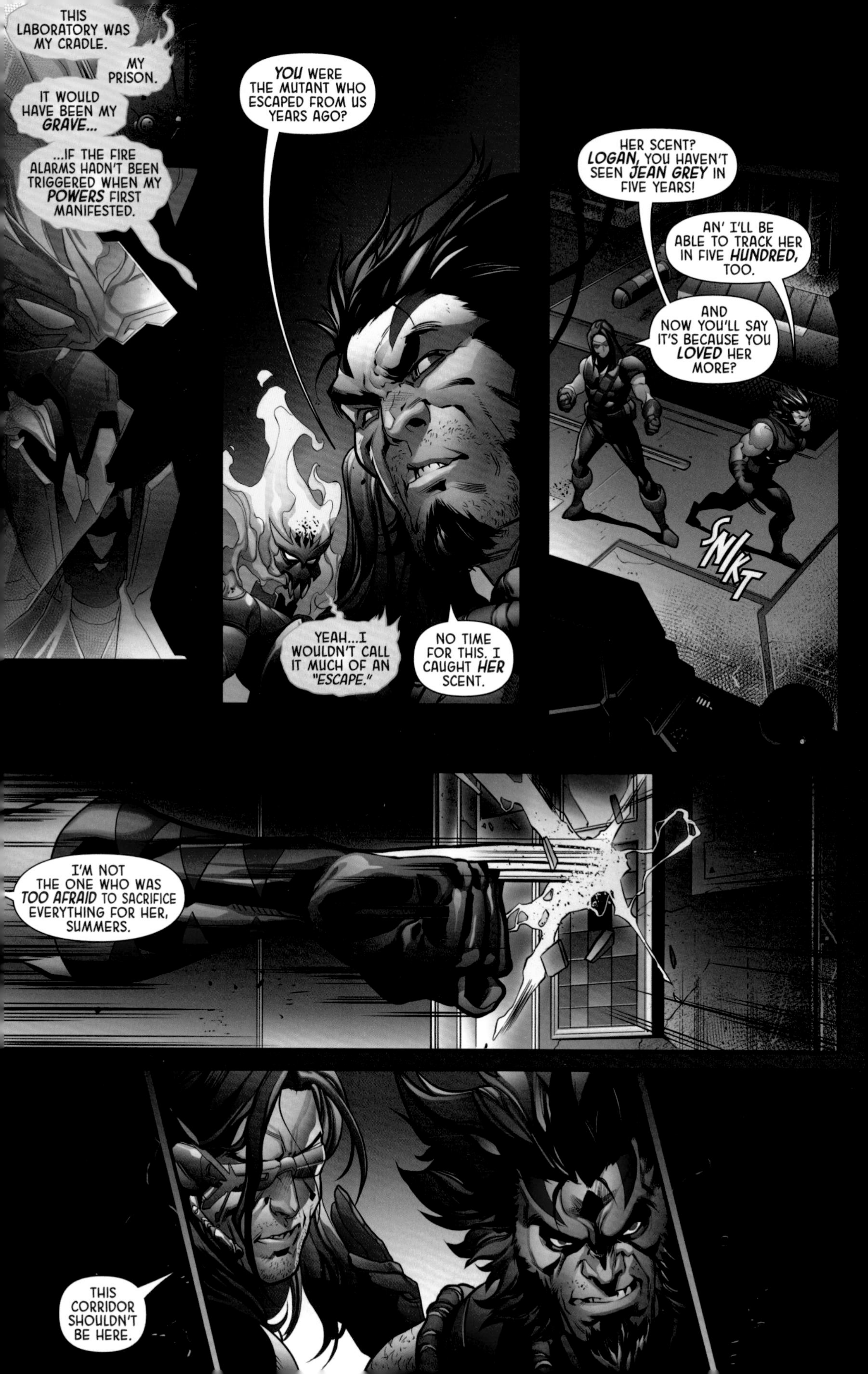
THIS LABORATORY WAS MY CRADLE.
MY PRISON.
IT WOULD HAVE BEEN MY GRAVE...
...IF THE FIRE ALARMS HADN'T BEEN TRIGGERED WHEN MY POWERS FIRST MANIFESTED.
YOU WERE THE MUTANT WHO ESCAPED FROM US YEARS AGO?
YEAH...I WOULDN'T CALL IT MUCH OF AN "ESCAPE."
NO TIME FOR THIS. I CAUGHT HER SCENT.
HER SCENT? LOGAN, YOU HAVEN'T SEEN JEAN GREY IN FIVE YEARS!
AN' I'LL BE ABLE TO TRACK HER IN FIVE HUNDRED, TOO.
AND NOW YOU'LL SAY IT'S BECAUSE YOU LOVED HER MORE?
SNIKT
I'M NOT THE ONE WHO WAS TOO AFRAID TO SACRIFICE EVERYTHING FOR HER, SUMMERS.
THIS CORRIDOR SHOULDN'T BE HERE.

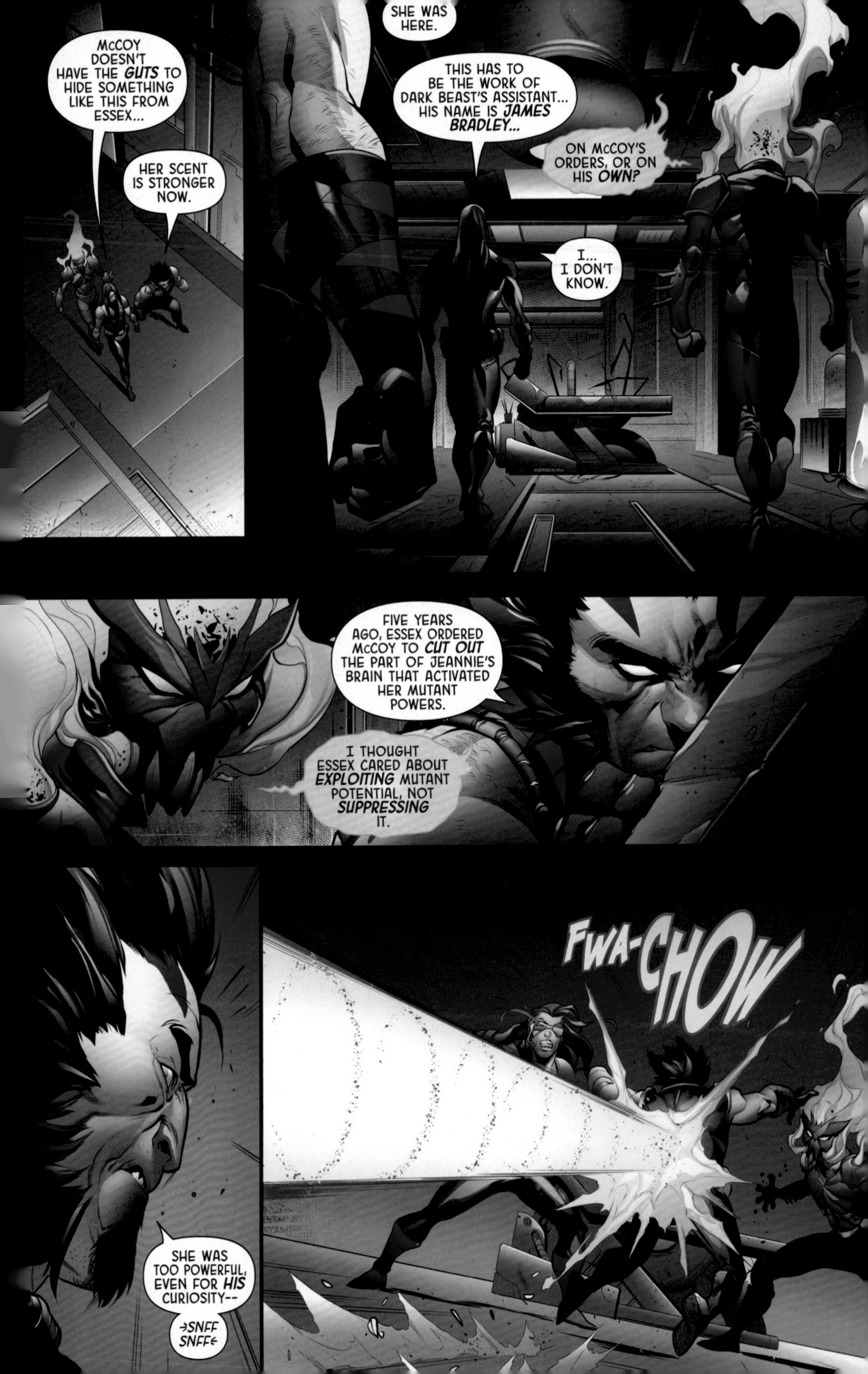
McCOY DOESN'T HAVE THE GUTS TO HIDE SOMETHING LIKE THIS FROM ESSEX...
HER SCENT IS STRONGER NOW.
SHE WAS HERE.
THIS HAS TO BE THE WORK OF DARK BEAST'S ASSISTANT... HIS NAME IS JAMES BRADLEY...
ON McCOY'S ORDERS, OR ON HIS OWN?
I... I DON'T KNOW.
FIVE YEARS AGO, ESSEX ORDERED McCOY TO CUT OUT THE PART OF JEANNIE'S BRAIN THAT ACTIVATED HER MUTANT POWERS.
I THOUGHT ESSEX CARED ABOUT EXPLOITING MUTANT POTENTIAL, NOT SUPPRESSING IT.
SHE WAS TOO POWERFUL, EVEN FOR HIS CURIOSITY--
SNFF SNFF
FWA-CHOW

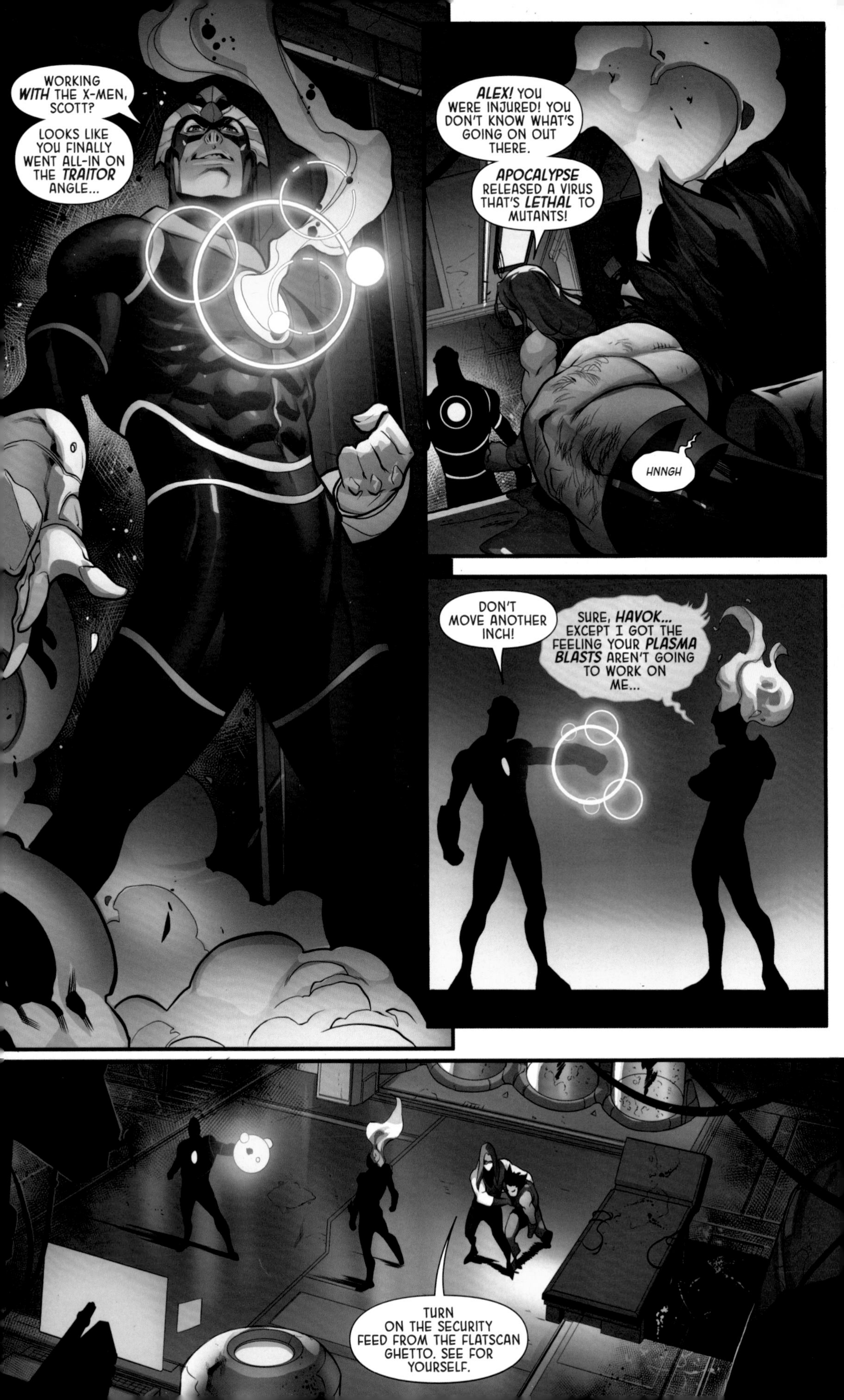
WORKING WITH THE X-MEN, SCOTT?
LOOKS LIKE YOU FINALLY WENT ALL-IN ON THE TRAITOR ANGLE...
ALEX! YOU WERE INJURED! YOU DON'T KNOW WHAT'S GOING ON OUT THERE.
APOCALYPSE RELEASED A VIRUS THAT'S LETHAL TO MUTANTS!
HNNGH
DON'T MOVE ANOTHER INCH!
SURE, HAVOK... EXCEPT I GOT THE FEELING YOUR PLASMA BLASTS AREN'T GOING TO WORK ON ME...
TURN ON THE SECURITY FEED FROM THE FLATSCAN GHETTO. SEE FOR YOURSELF.

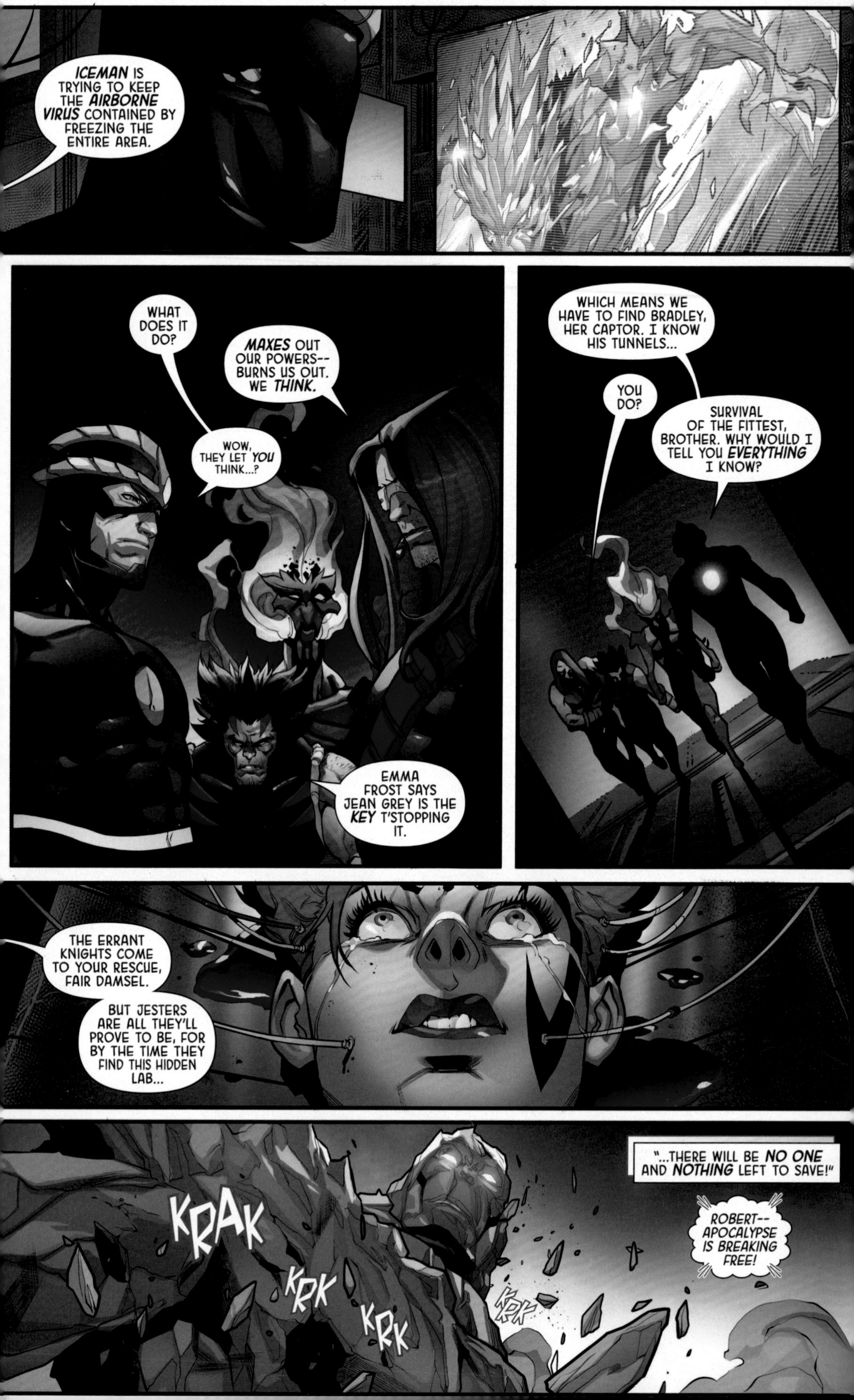
ICEMAN IS TRYING TO KEEP THE AIRBORNE VIRUS CONTAINED BY FREEZING THE ENTIRE AREA.
WHAT DOES IT DO?
MAXES OUT OUR POWERS-- BURNS US OUT. WE THINK.
WOW, THEY LET YOU THINK...?
EMMA FROST SAYS JEAN GREY IS THE KEY T'STOPPING IT.
WHICH MEANS WE HAVE TO FIND BRADLEY, HER CAPTOR. I KNOW HIS TUNNELS...
YOU DO?
SURVIVAL OF THE FITTEST, BROTHER. WHY WOULD I TELL YOU EVERYTHING I KNOW?
THE ERRANT KNIGHTS COME TO YOUR RESCUE, FAIR DAMSEL.
BUT JESTERS ARE ALL THEY'LL PROVE TO BE, FOR BY THE TIME THEY FIND THIS HIDDEN LAB...
"...THERE WILL BE NO ONE AND NOTHING LEFT TO SAVE!"
ROBERT-- APOCALYPSE IS BREAKING FREE!
KRAK
KRK
KRK
KRK

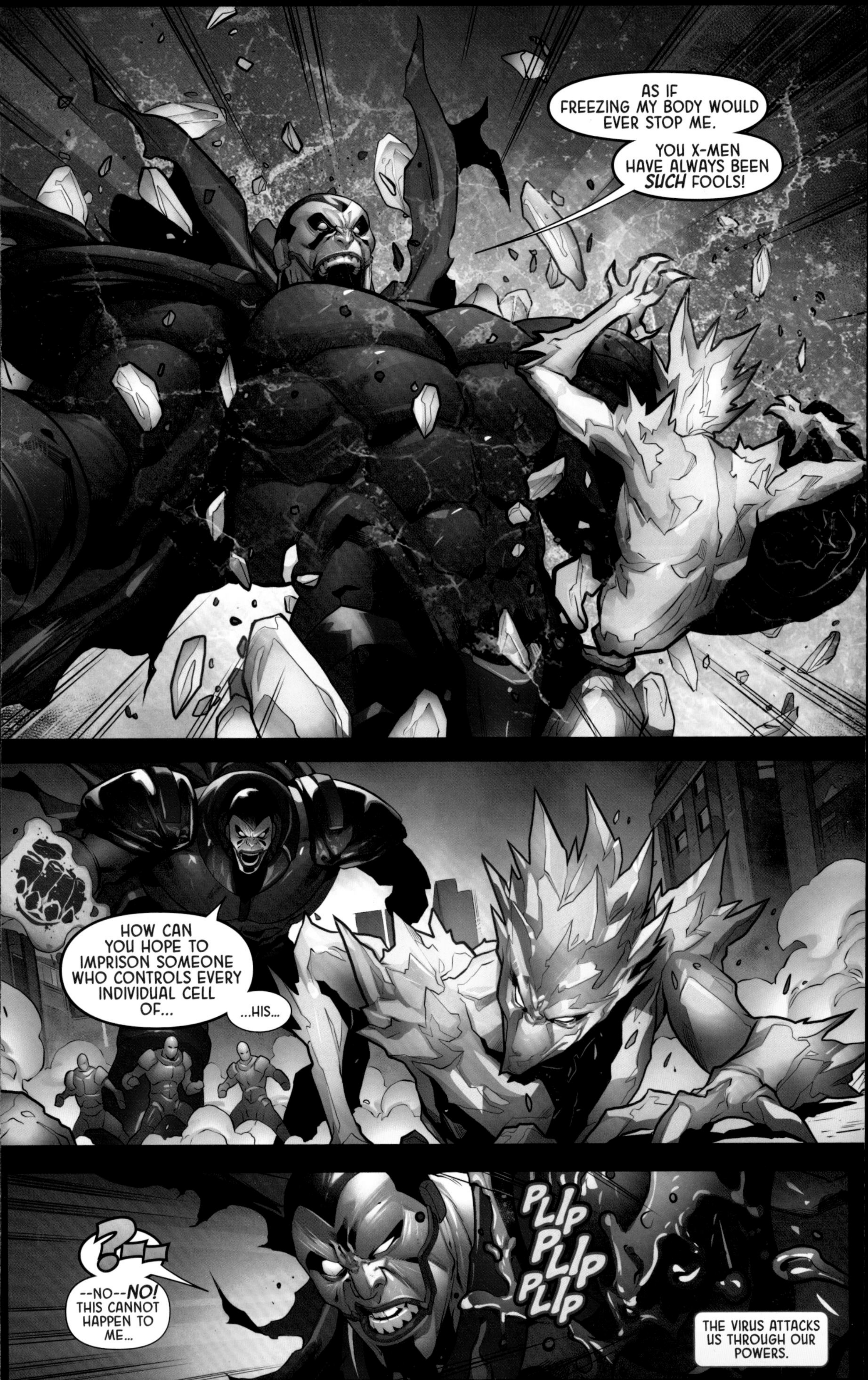
AS IF FREEZING MY BODY WOULD EVER STOP ME.
YOU X-MEN HAVE ALWAYS BEEN *SUCH* FOOLS!
HOW CAN YOU HOPE TO IMPRISON SOMEONE WHO CONTROLS EVERY INDIVIDUAL CELL OF...
...HIS...
?--
--NO--*NO!* THIS CANNOT HAPPEN TO ME...
PLIP PLIP PLIP PLIP
THE VIRUS ATTACKS US THROUGH OUR POWERS.

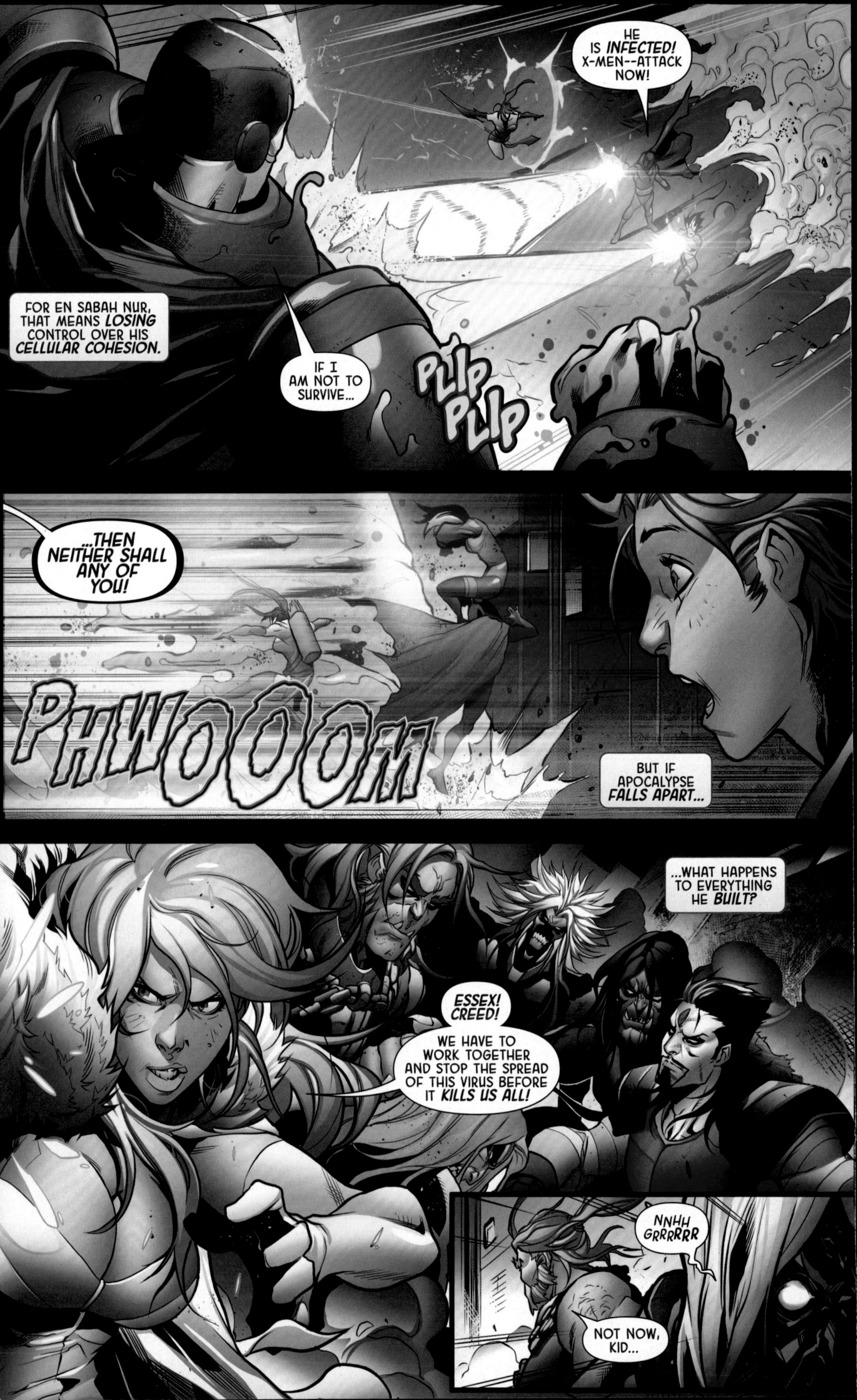
HE IS INFECTED! X-MEN--ATTACK NOW!
FOR EN SABAH NUR, THAT MEANS LOSING CONTROL OVER HIS CELLULAR COHESION.
IF I AM NOT TO SURVIVE...
PLIP PLIP
...THEN NEITHER SHALL ANY OF YOU!
PHWOOOOM
BUT IF APOCALYPSE FALLS APART...
...WHAT HAPPENS TO EVERYTHING HE BUILT?
ESSEX! CREED!
WE HAVE TO WORK TOGETHER AND STOP THE SPREAD OF THIS VIRUS BEFORE IT KILLS US ALL!
NNHH GRRRRRR
NOT NOW, KID...

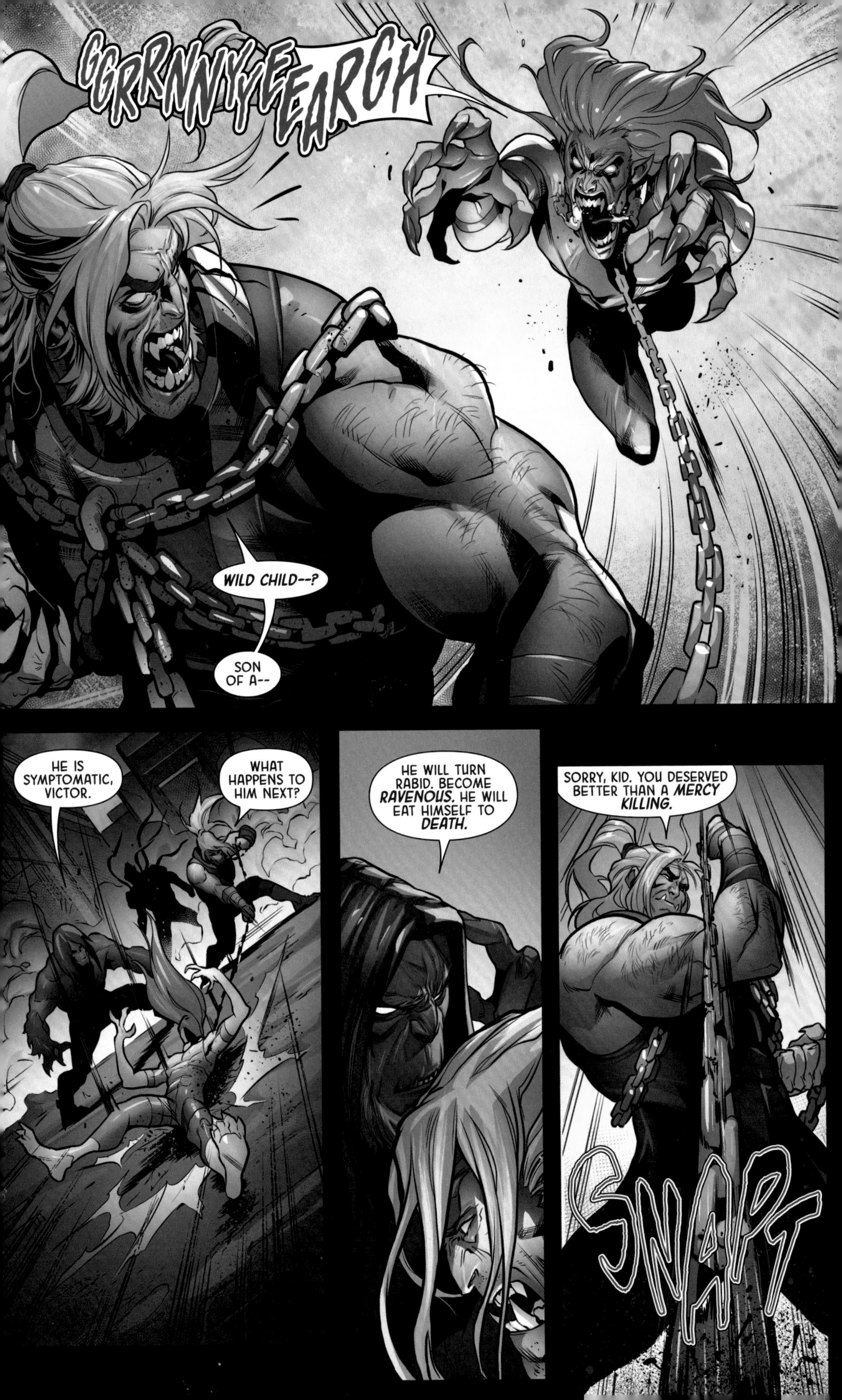
GGRRNNYYEEARGH
WILD CHILD--?
SON OF A--
HE IS SYMPTOMATIC, VICTOR.
WHAT HAPPENS TO HIM NEXT?
HE WILL TURN RABID. BECOME *RAVENOUS.* HE WILL EAT HIMSELF TO *DEATH.*
SORRY, KID. YOU DESERVED BETTER THAN A *MERCY KILLING.*
SNAP

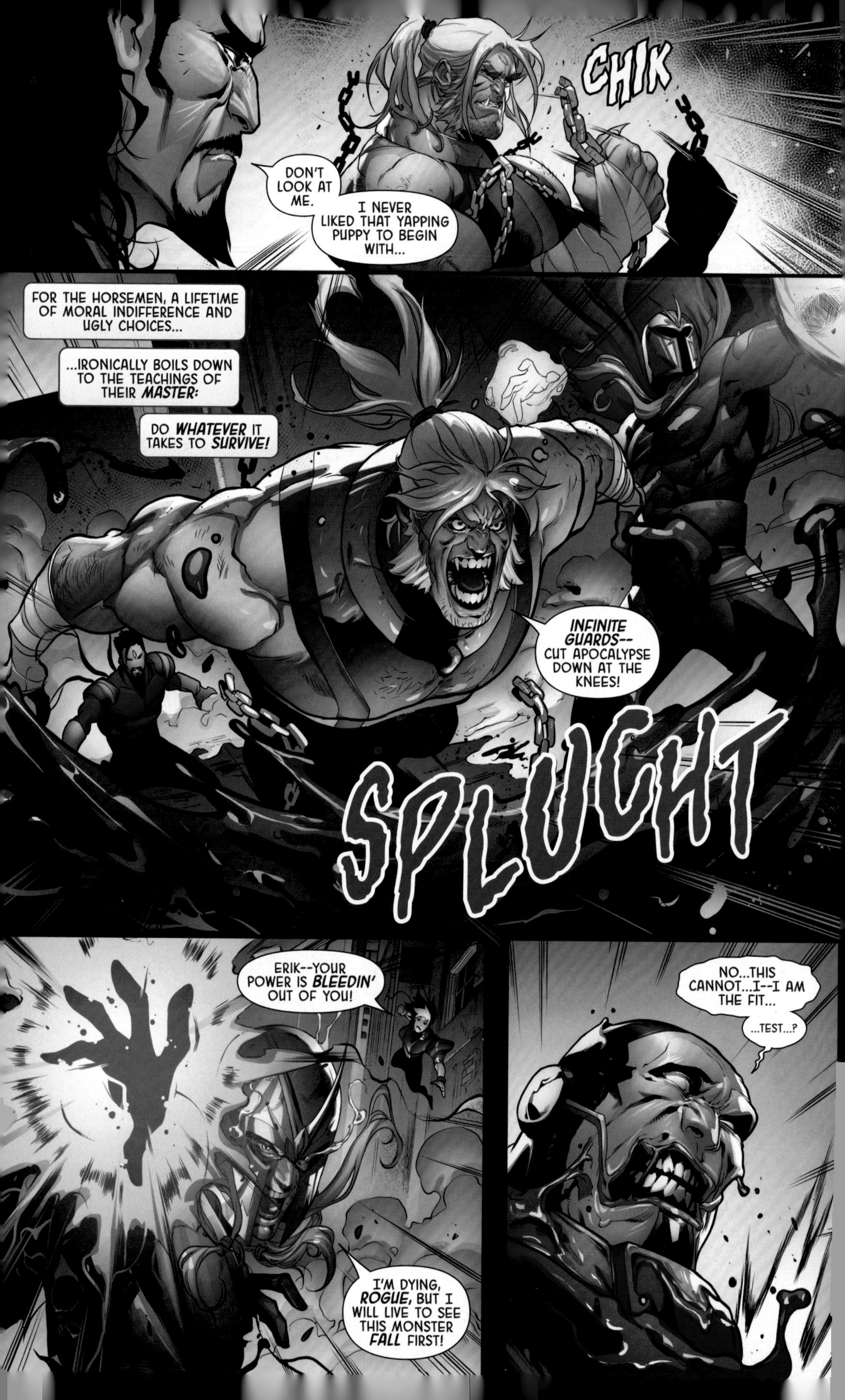
CHIK
DON'T LOOK AT ME.
I NEVER LIKED THAT YAPPING PUPPY TO BEGIN WITH...
FOR THE HORSEMEN, A LIFETIME OF MORAL INDIFFERENCE AND UGLY CHOICES...
...IRONICALLY BOILS DOWN TO THE TEACHINGS OF THEIR MASTER:
DO WHATEVER IT TAKES TO SURVIVE!
INFINITE GUARDS-- CUT APOCALYPSE DOWN AT THE KNEES!
SPLUCHT
ERIK--YOUR POWER IS BLEEDIN' OUT OF YOU!
I'M DYING, ROGUE, BUT I WILL LIVE TO SEE THIS MONSTER FALL FIRST!
NO...THIS CANNOT...I--I AM THE FIT...
...TEST...?

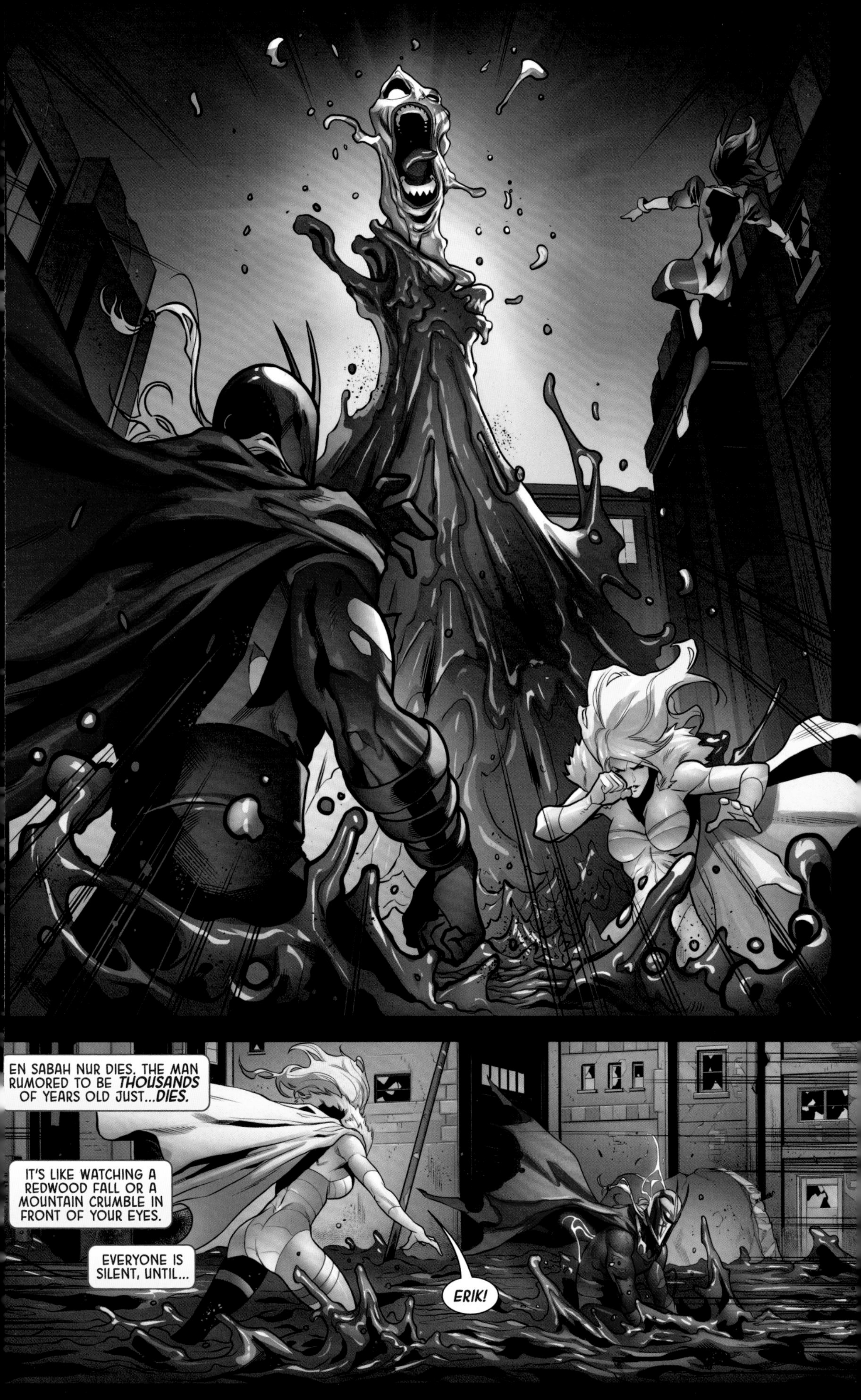
EN SABAH NUR DIES. THE MAN RUMORED TO BE *THOUSANDS* OF YEARS OLD JUST...*DIES.*
IT'S LIKE WATCHING A REDWOOD FALL OR A MOUNTAIN CRUMBLE IN FRONT OF YOUR EYES.
EVERYONE IS SILENT, UNTIL...
ERIK!

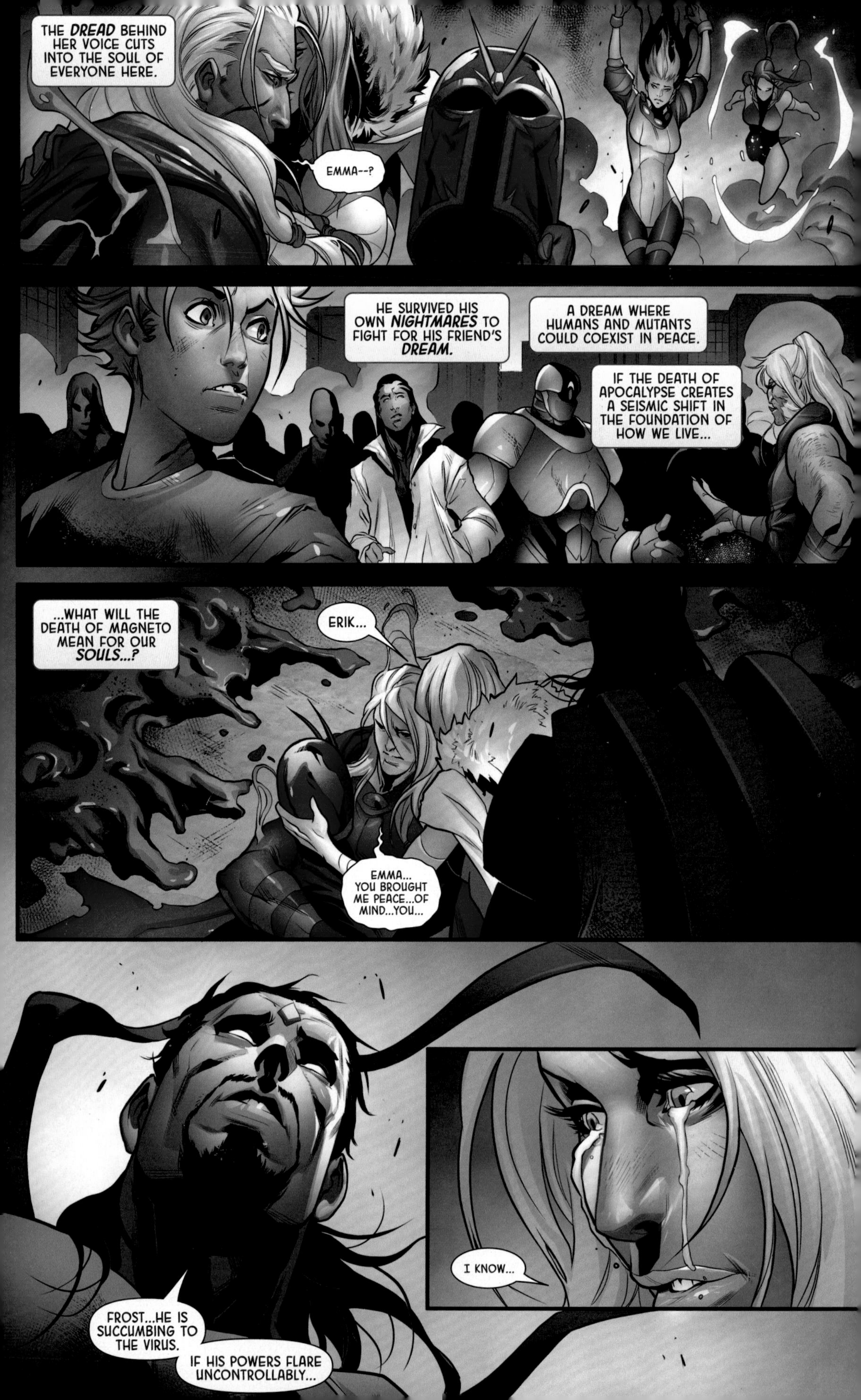
THE DREAD BEHIND HER VOICE CUTS INTO THE SOUL OF EVERYONE HERE.
EMMA--?
HE SURVIVED HIS OWN NIGHTMARES TO FIGHT FOR HIS FRIEND'S DREAM.
A DREAM WHERE HUMANS AND MUTANTS COULD COEXIST IN PEACE.
IF THE DEATH OF APOCALYPSE CREATES A SEISMIC SHIFT IN THE FOUNDATION OF HOW WE LIVE...
...WHAT WILL THE DEATH OF MAGNETO MEAN FOR OUR SOULS...?
ERIK...
EMMA... YOU BROUGHT ME PEACE...OF MIND...YOU...
I KNOW...
FROST...HE IS SUCCUMBING TO THE VIRUS.
IF HIS POWERS FLARE UNCONTROLLABLY...

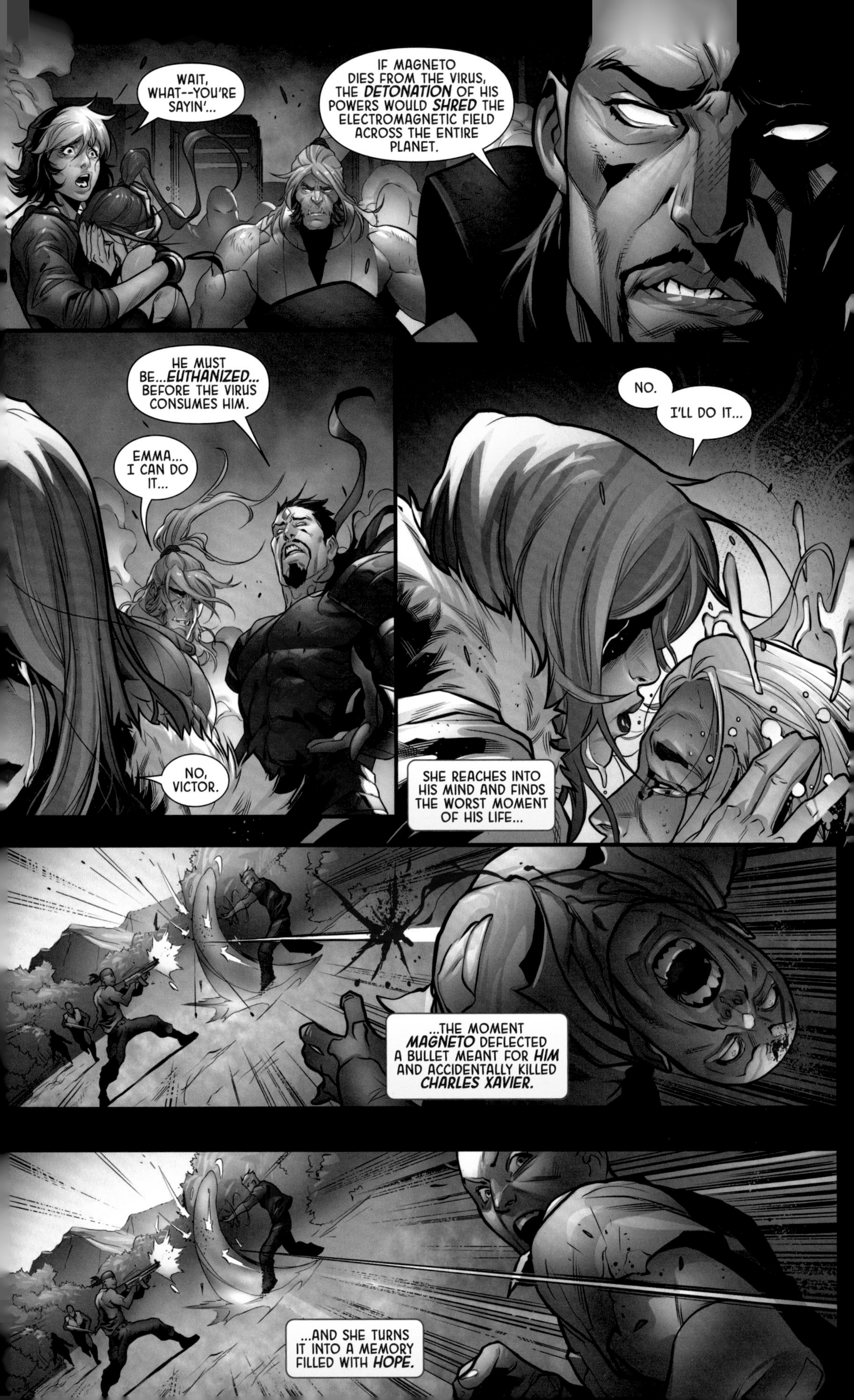
WAIT, WHAT--YOU'RE SAYIN'...
IF MAGNETO DIES FROM THE VIRUS, THE DETONATION OF HIS POWERS WOULD SHRED THE ELECTROMAGNETIC FIELD ACROSS THE ENTIRE PLANET.
HE MUST BE...EUTHANIZED... BEFORE THE VIRUS CONSUMES HIM.
EMMA... I CAN DO IT...
NO, VICTOR.
NO.
I'LL DO IT...
SHE REACHES INTO HIS MIND AND FINDS THE WORST MOMENT OF HIS LIFE...
...THE MOMENT MAGNETO DEFLECTED A BULLET MEANT FOR HIM AND ACCIDENTALLY KILLED CHARLES XAVIER.
...AND SHE TURNS IT INTO A MEMORY FILLED WITH HOPE.

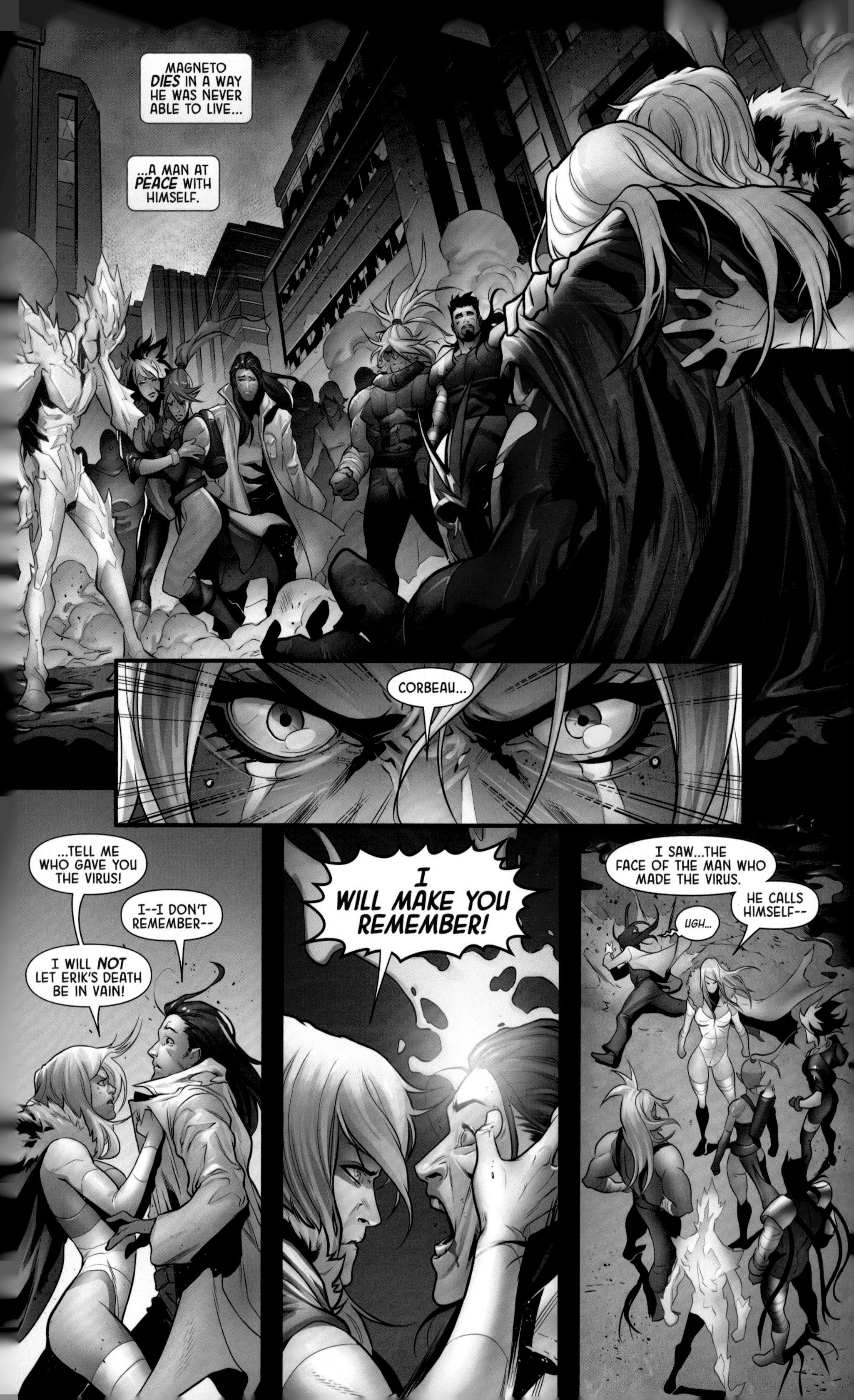
MAGNETO DIES IN A WAY HE WAS NEVER ABLE TO LIVE...
...A MAN AT PEACE WITH HIMSELF.
CORBEAU...
...TELL ME WHO GAVE YOU THE VIRUS!
I--I DON'T REMEMBER--
I WILL NOT LET ERIK'S DEATH BE IN VAIN!
I WILL MAKE YOU REMEMBER!
I SAW...THE FACE OF THE MAN WHO MADE THE VIRUS.
UGH...
HE CALLS HIMSELF--

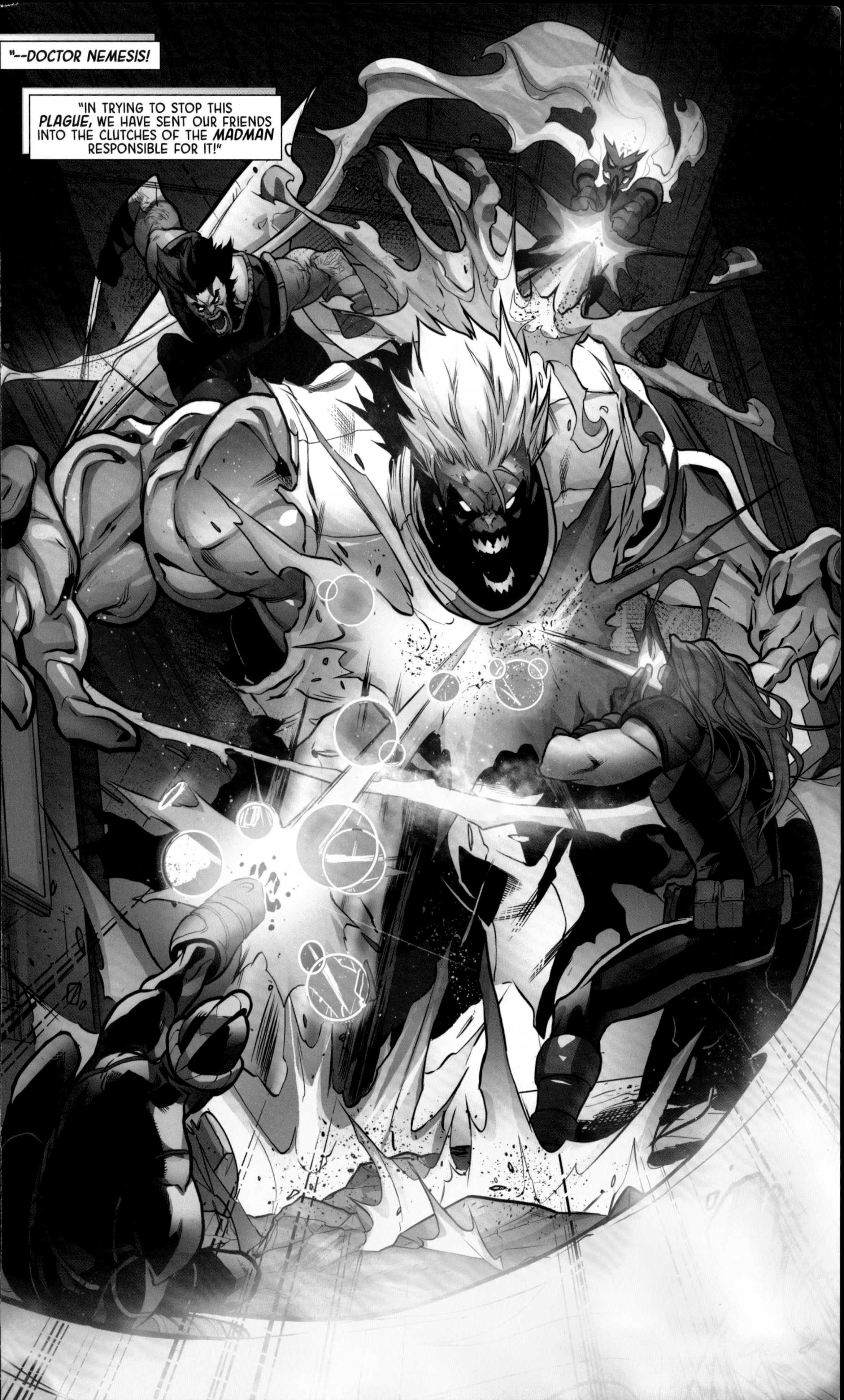
"--DOCTOR NEMESIS!
"IN TRYING TO STOP THIS PLAGUE, WE HAVE SENT OUR FRIENDS INTO THE CLUTCHES OF THE MADMAN RESPONSIBLE FOR IT!"

#1 ANT-SIZED VARIANT BY MIKE MAYHEW

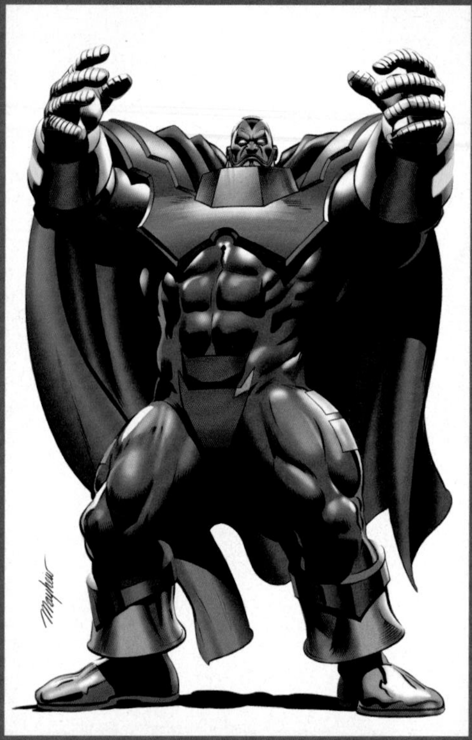

#2 VARIANT BY HUMBERTO RAMOS & EDGAR DELGADO

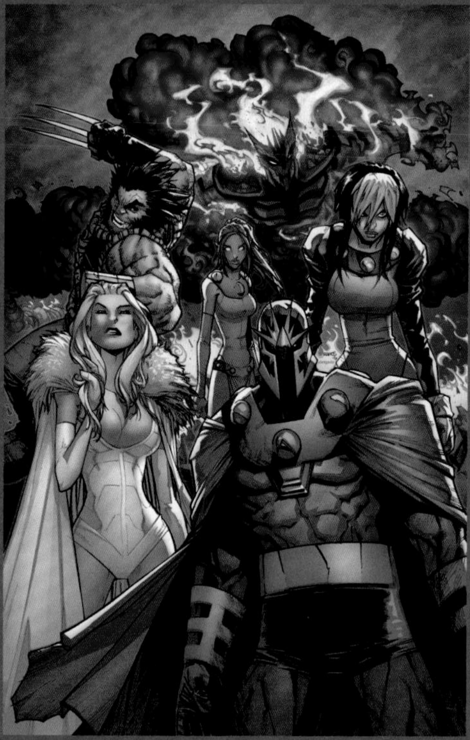

#1-5 COMBINED COVERS

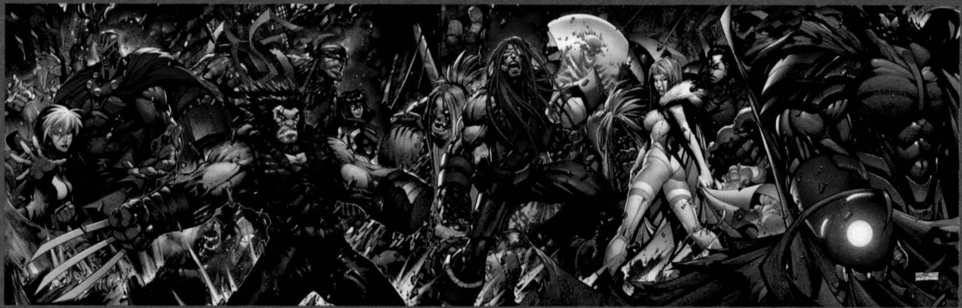

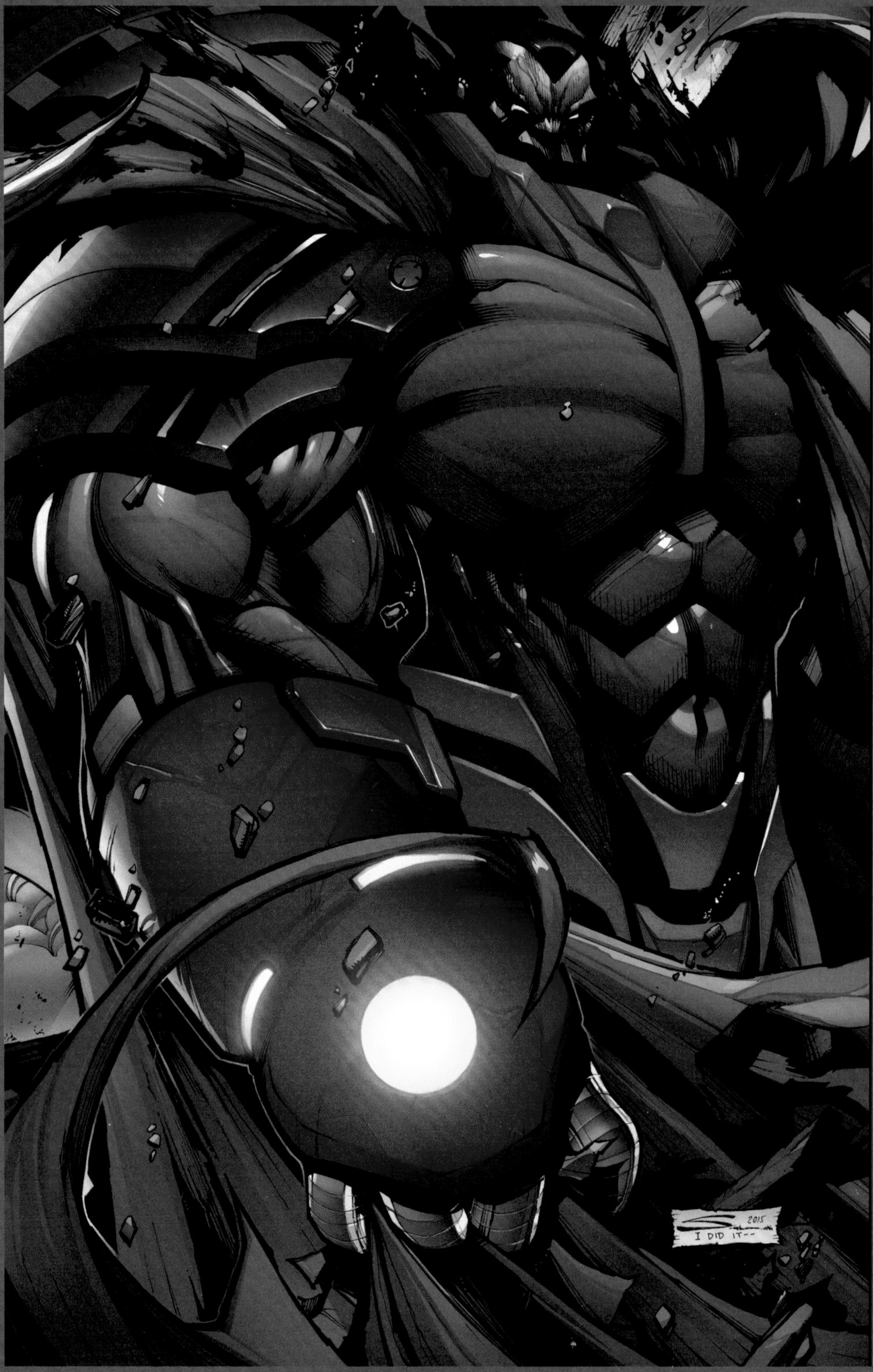
2015
I DID IT--

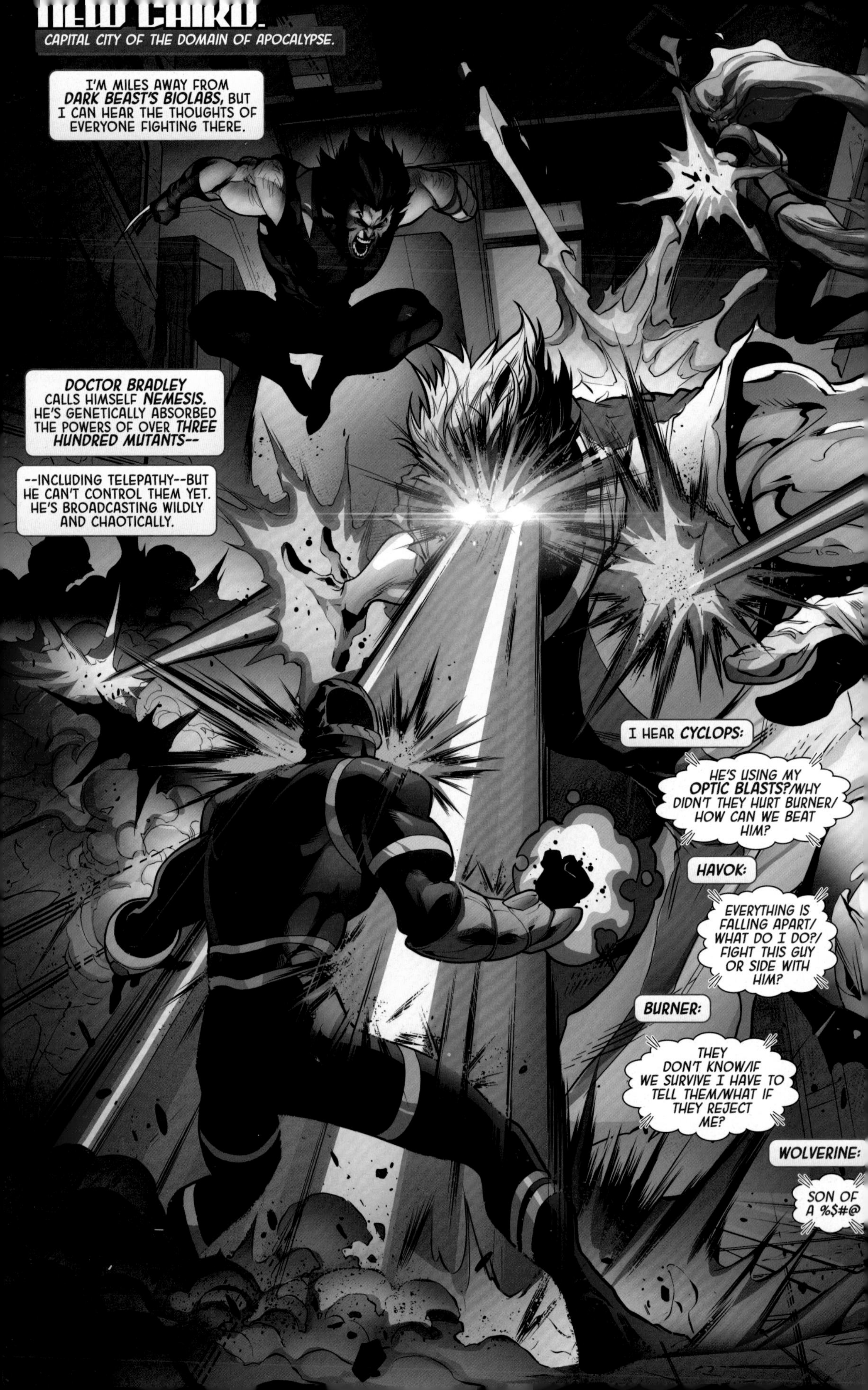
NEW CAIRO.
CAPITAL CITY OF THE DOMAIN OF APOCALYPSE.
I'M MILES AWAY FROM DARK BEAST'S BIOLABS, BUT I CAN HEAR THE THOUGHTS OF EVERYONE FIGHTING THERE.
DOCTOR BRADLEY CALLS HIMSELF NEMESIS. HE'S GENETICALLY ABSORBED THE POWERS OF OVER THREE HUNDRED MUTANTS--
--INCLUDING TELEPATHY--BUT HE CAN'T CONTROL THEM YET. HE'S BROADCASTING WILDLY AND CHAOTICALLY.
I HEAR CYCLOPS:
HE'S USING MY OPTIC BLASTS?/WHY DIDN'T THEY HURT BURNER/ HOW CAN WE BEAT HIM?
HAVOK:
EVERYTHING IS FALLING APART/ WHAT DO I DO?/ FIGHT THIS GUY OR SIDE WITH HIM?
BURNER:
THEY DON'T KNOW/IF WE SURVIVE I HAVE TO TELL THEM/WHAT IF THEY REJECT ME?
WOLVERINE:
SON OF A %$#@

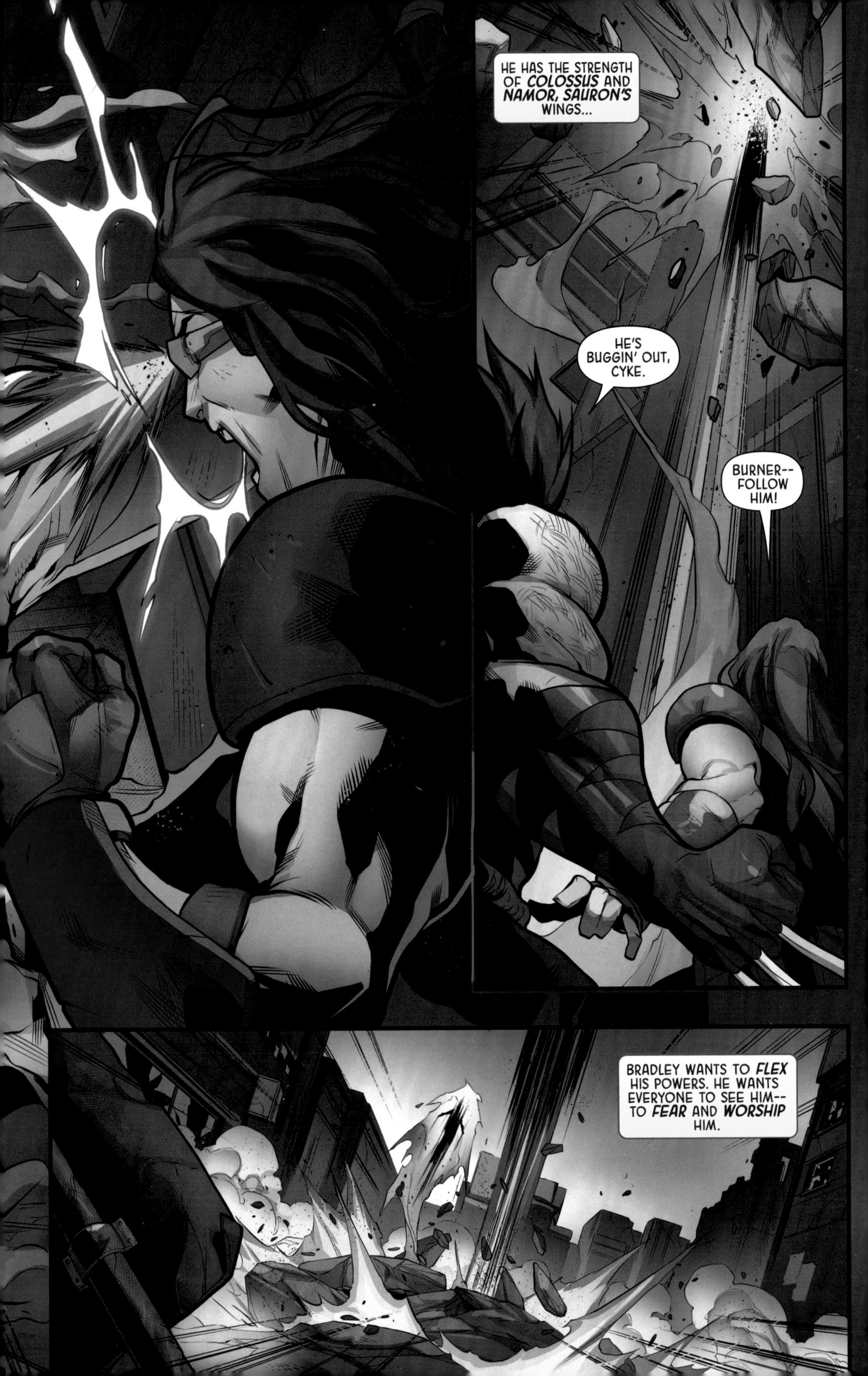
HE HAS THE STRENGTH OF COLOSSUS AND NAMOR, SAURON'S WINGS...
HE'S BUGGIN' OUT, CYKE.
BURNER-- FOLLOW HIM!
BRADLEY WANTS TO FLEX HIS POWERS. HE WANTS EVERYONE TO SEE HIM-- TO FEAR AND WORSHIP HIM.

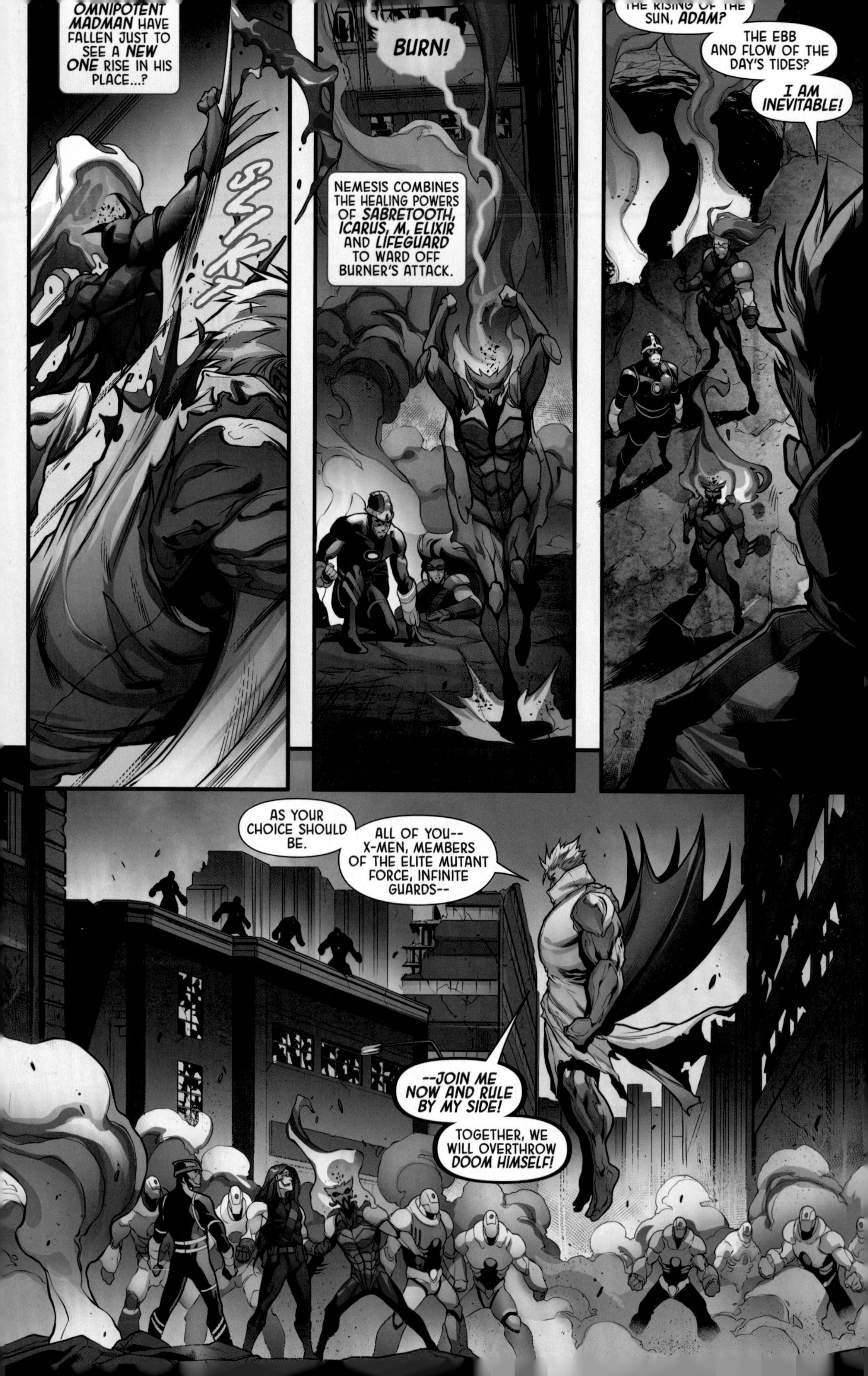
OMNIPOTENT MADMAN HAVE FALLEN JUST TO SEE A NEW ONE RISE IN HIS PLACE...?
BURN!
NEMESIS COMBINES THE HEALING POWERS OF SABRETOOTH, ICARUS, M, ELIXIR AND LIFEGUARD TO WARD OFF BURNER'S ATTACK.
THE RISING OF THE SUN, ADAM?
THE EBB AND FLOW OF THE DAY'S TIDES?
I AM INEVITABLE!
AS YOUR CHOICE SHOULD BE.
ALL OF YOU-- X-MEN, MEMBERS OF THE ELITE MUTANT FORCE, INFINITE GUARDS--
--JOIN ME NOW AND RULE BY MY SIDE!
TOGETHER, WE WILL OVERTHROW DOOM HIMSELF!

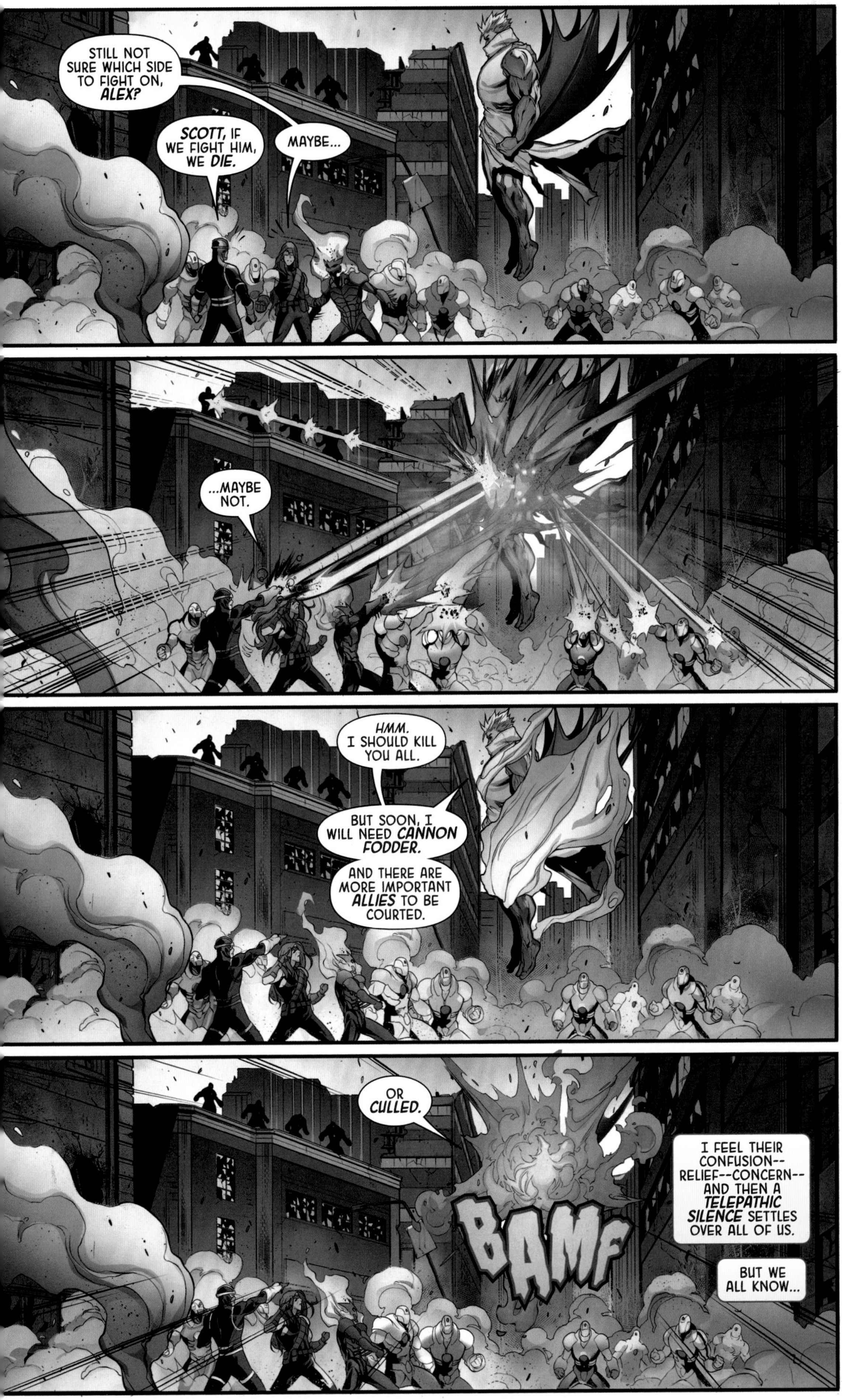
STILL NOT SURE WHICH SIDE TO FIGHT ON, ALEX?
SCOTT, IF WE FIGHT HIM, WE DIE.
MAYBE...
...MAYBE NOT.
HMM. I SHOULD KILL YOU ALL.
BUT SOON, I WILL NEED CANNON FODDER.
AND THERE ARE MORE IMPORTANT ALLIES TO BE COURTED.
OR CULLED.
BAMF
I FEEL THEIR CONFUSION--RELIEF--CONCERN--AND THEN A TELEPATHIC SILENCE SETTLES OVER ALL OF US.
BUT WE ALL KNOW...

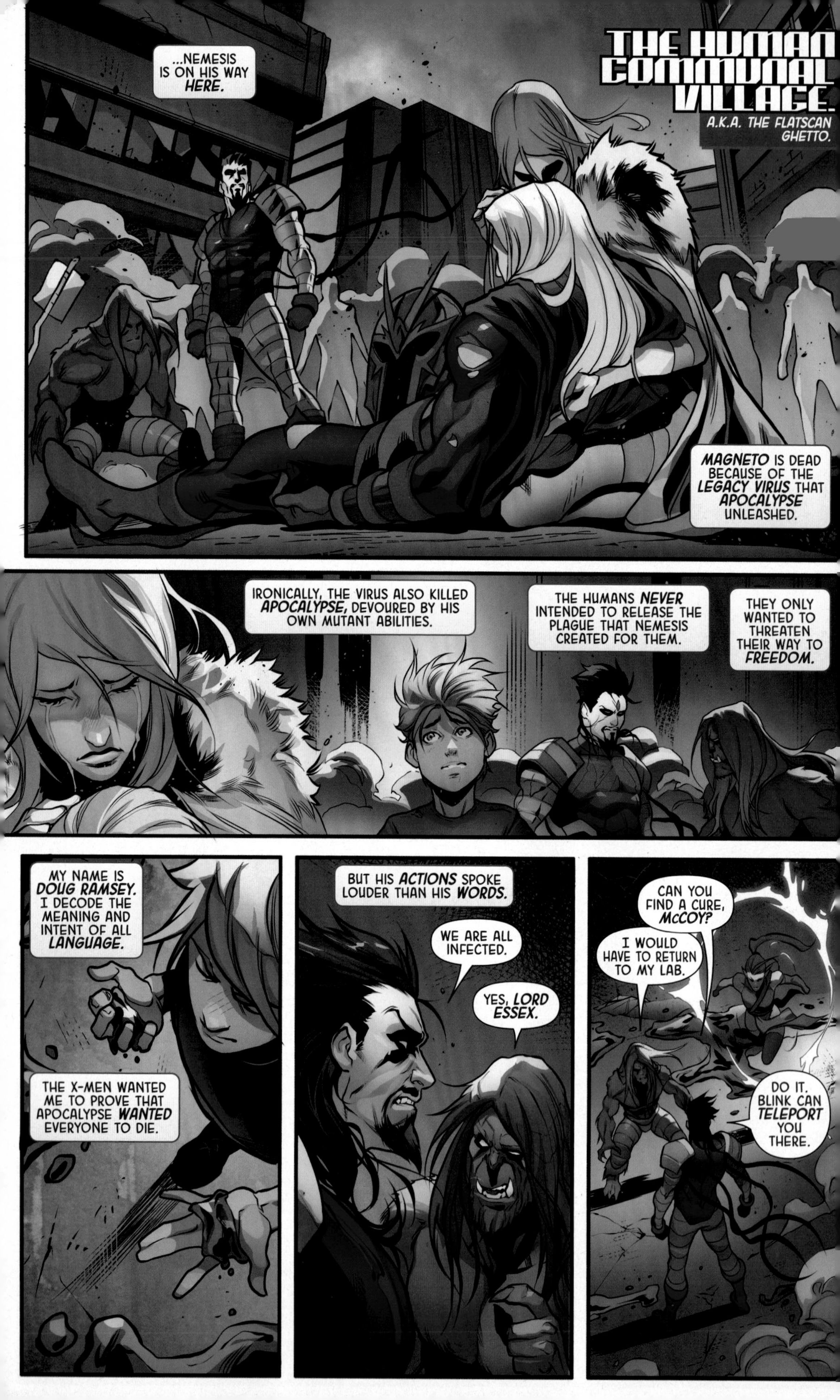
...NEMESIS IS ON HIS WAY HERE.
THE HUMAN COMMUNAL VILLAGE.
A.K.A. THE FLATSCAN GHETTO.
MAGNETO IS DEAD BECAUSE OF THE LEGACY VIRUS THAT APOCALYPSE UNLEASHED.
IRONICALLY, THE VIRUS ALSO KILLED APOCALYPSE, DEVOURED BY HIS OWN MUTANT ABILITIES.
THE HUMANS NEVER INTENDED TO RELEASE THE PLAGUE THAT NEMESIS CREATED FOR THEM.
THEY ONLY WANTED TO THREATEN THEIR WAY TO FREEDOM.
MY NAME IS DOUG RAMSEY. I DECODE THE MEANING AND INTENT OF ALL LANGUAGE.
THE X-MEN WANTED ME TO PROVE THAT APOCALYPSE WANTED EVERYONE TO DIE.
BUT HIS ACTIONS SPOKE LOUDER THAN HIS WORDS.
WE ARE ALL INFECTED.
YES, LORD ESSEX.
CAN YOU FIND A CURE, McCOY?
I WOULD HAVE TO RETURN TO MY LAB.
DO IT. BLINK CAN TELEPORT YOU THERE.

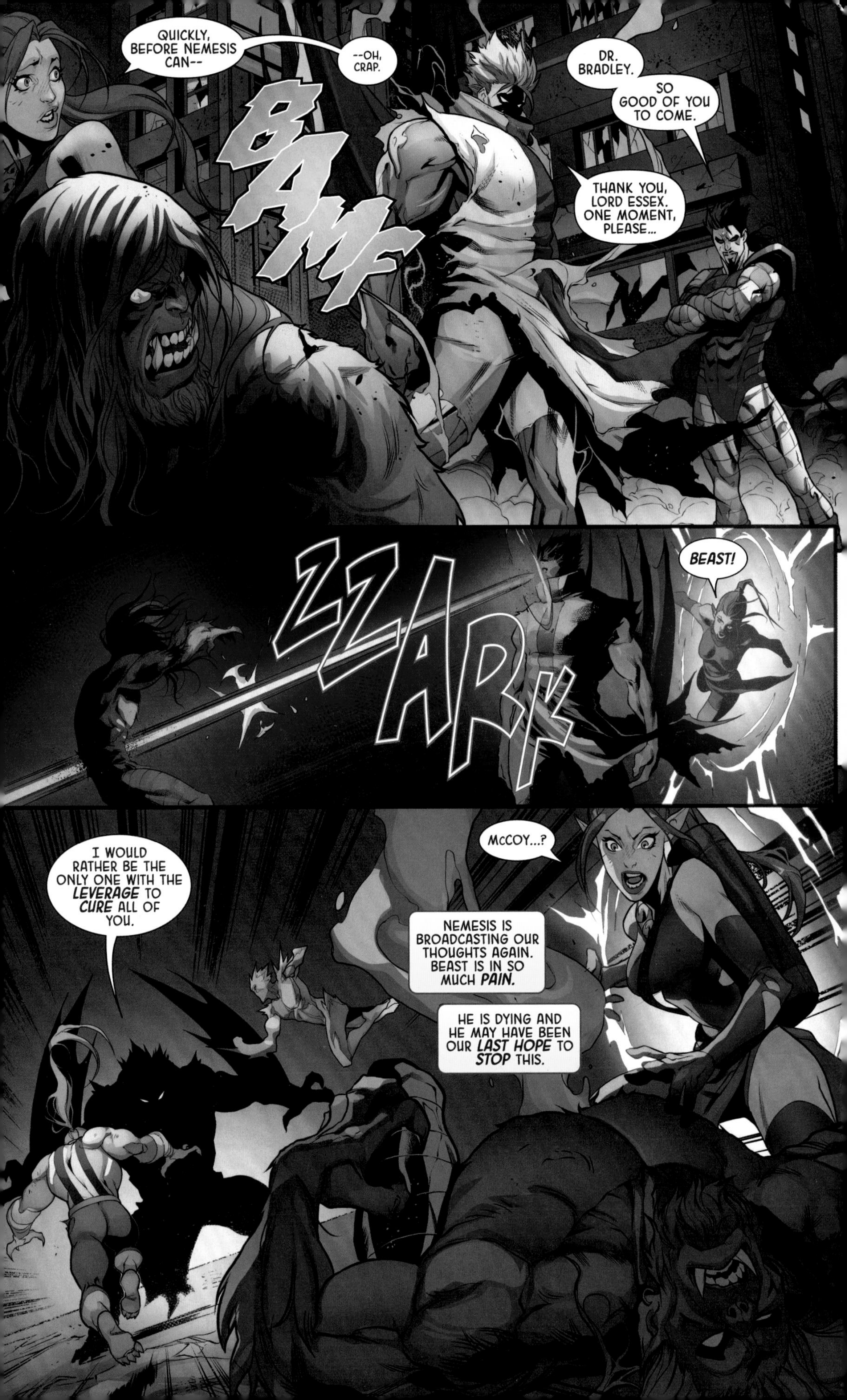
QUICKLY, BEFORE NEMESIS CAN--
--OH, CRAP.
BAMF
DR. BRADLEY.
SO GOOD OF YOU TO COME.
THANK YOU, LORD ESSEX. ONE MOMENT, PLEASE...
ZZARK
BEAST!
McCOY...?
I WOULD RATHER BE THE ONLY ONE WITH THE LEVERAGE TO CURE ALL OF YOU.
NEMESIS IS BROADCASTING OUR THOUGHTS AGAIN. BEAST IS IN SO MUCH PAIN.
HE IS DYING AND HE MAY HAVE BEEN OUR LAST HOPE TO STOP THIS.

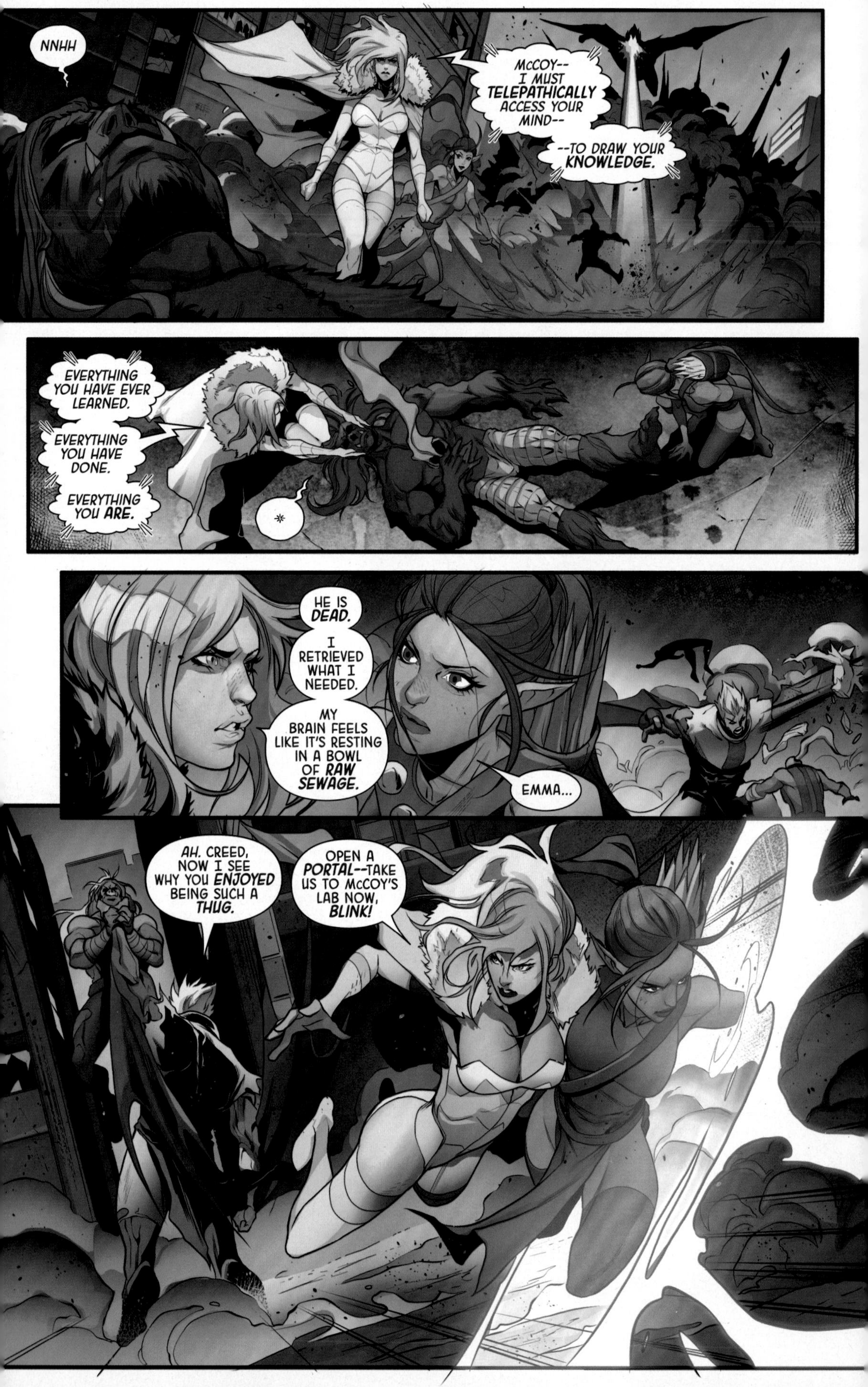
NNHH
McCOY-- I MUST TELEPATHICALLY ACCESS YOUR MIND--
--TO DRAW YOUR KNOWLEDGE.
EVERYTHING YOU HAVE EVER LEARNED.
EVERYTHING YOU HAVE DONE.
EVERYTHING YOU ARE.
*
HE IS DEAD.
I RETRIEVED WHAT I NEEDED.
MY BRAIN FEELS LIKE IT'S RESTING IN A BOWL OF RAW SEWAGE.
EMMA...
AH. CREED, NOW I SEE WHY YOU ENJOYED BEING SUCH A THUG.
OPEN A PORTAL--TAKE US TO McCOY'S LAB NOW, BLINK!

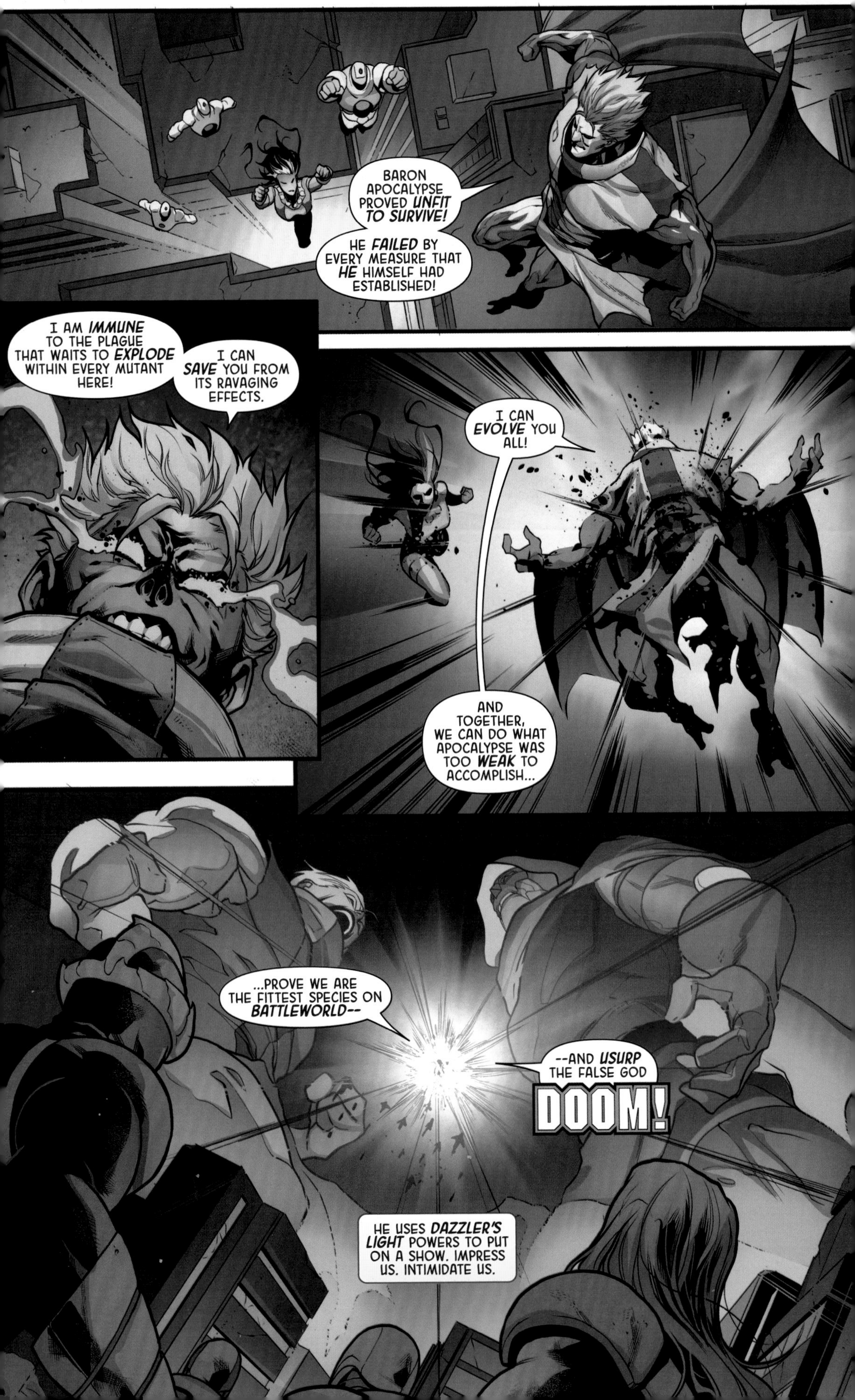
BARON APOCALYPSE PROVED UNFIT TO SURVIVE!
HE FAILED BY EVERY MEASURE THAT HE HIMSELF HAD ESTABLISHED!
I AM IMMUNE TO THE PLAGUE THAT WAITS TO EXPLODE WITHIN EVERY MUTANT HERE!
I CAN SAVE YOU FROM ITS RAVAGING EFFECTS.
I CAN EVOLVE YOU ALL!
AND TOGETHER, WE CAN DO WHAT APOCALYPSE WAS TOO WEAK TO ACCOMPLISH...
...PROVE WE ARE THE FITTEST SPECIES ON BATTLEWORLD--
--AND USURP THE FALSE GOD
DOOM!
HE USES DAZZLER'S LIGHT POWERS TO PUT ON A SHOW. IMPRESS US. INTIMIDATE US.

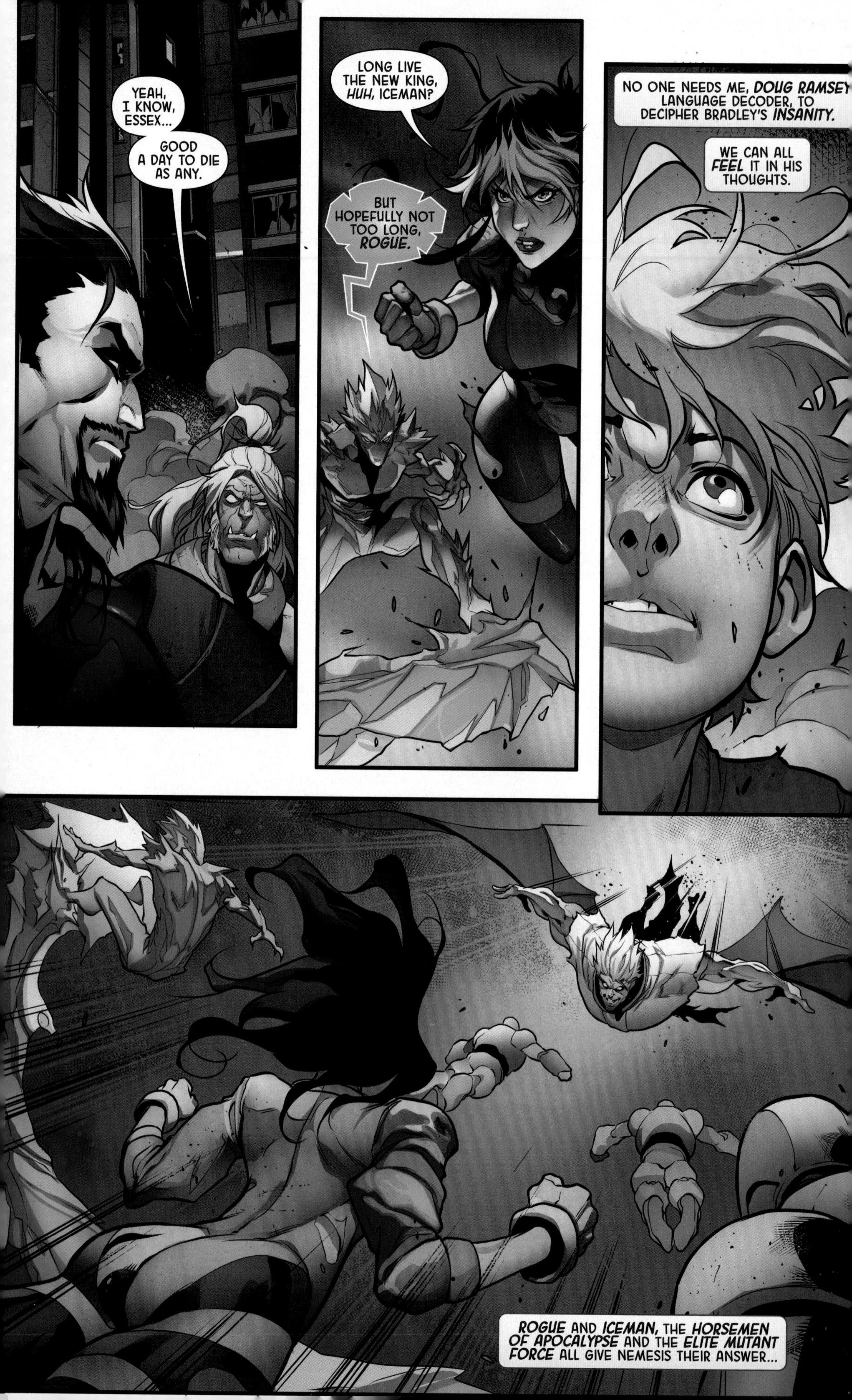
YEAH, I KNOW, ESSEX...
GOOD A DAY TO DIE AS ANY.
LONG LIVE THE NEW KING, HUH, ICEMAN?
BUT HOPEFULLY NOT TOO LONG, ROGUE.
NO ONE NEEDS ME, DOUG RAMSEY LANGUAGE DECODER, TO DECIPHER BRADLEY'S INSANITY.
WE CAN ALL FEEL IT IN HIS THOUGHTS.
ROGUE AND ICEMAN, THE HORSEMEN OF APOCALYPSE AND THE ELITE MUTANT FORCE ALL GIVE NEMESIS THEIR ANSWER...

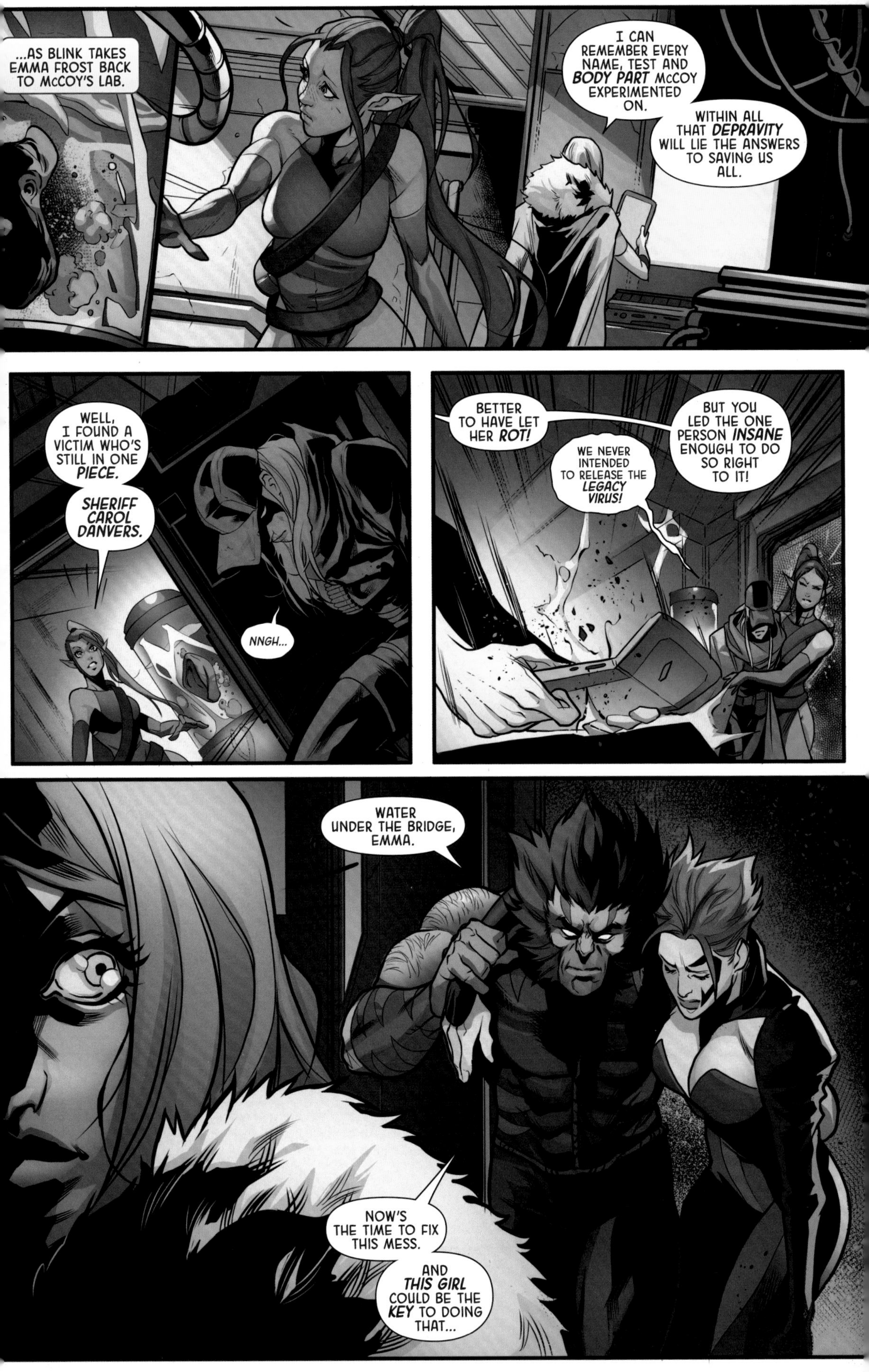
...AS BLINK TAKES EMMA FROST BACK TO McCOY'S LAB.
I CAN REMEMBER EVERY NAME, TEST AND BODY PART McCOY EXPERIMENTED ON.
WITHIN ALL THAT DEPRAVITY WILL LIE THE ANSWERS TO SAVING US ALL.
WELL, I FOUND A VICTIM WHO'S STILL IN ONE PIECE.
SHERIFF CAROL DANVERS.
NNGH...
BETTER TO HAVE LET HER ROT!
WE NEVER INTENDED TO RELEASE THE LEGACY VIRUS!
BUT YOU LED THE ONE PERSON INSANE ENOUGH TO DO SO RIGHT TO IT!
WATER UNDER THE BRIDGE, EMMA.
NOW'S THE TIME TO FIX THIS MESS.
AND THIS GIRL COULD BE THE KEY TO DOING THAT...

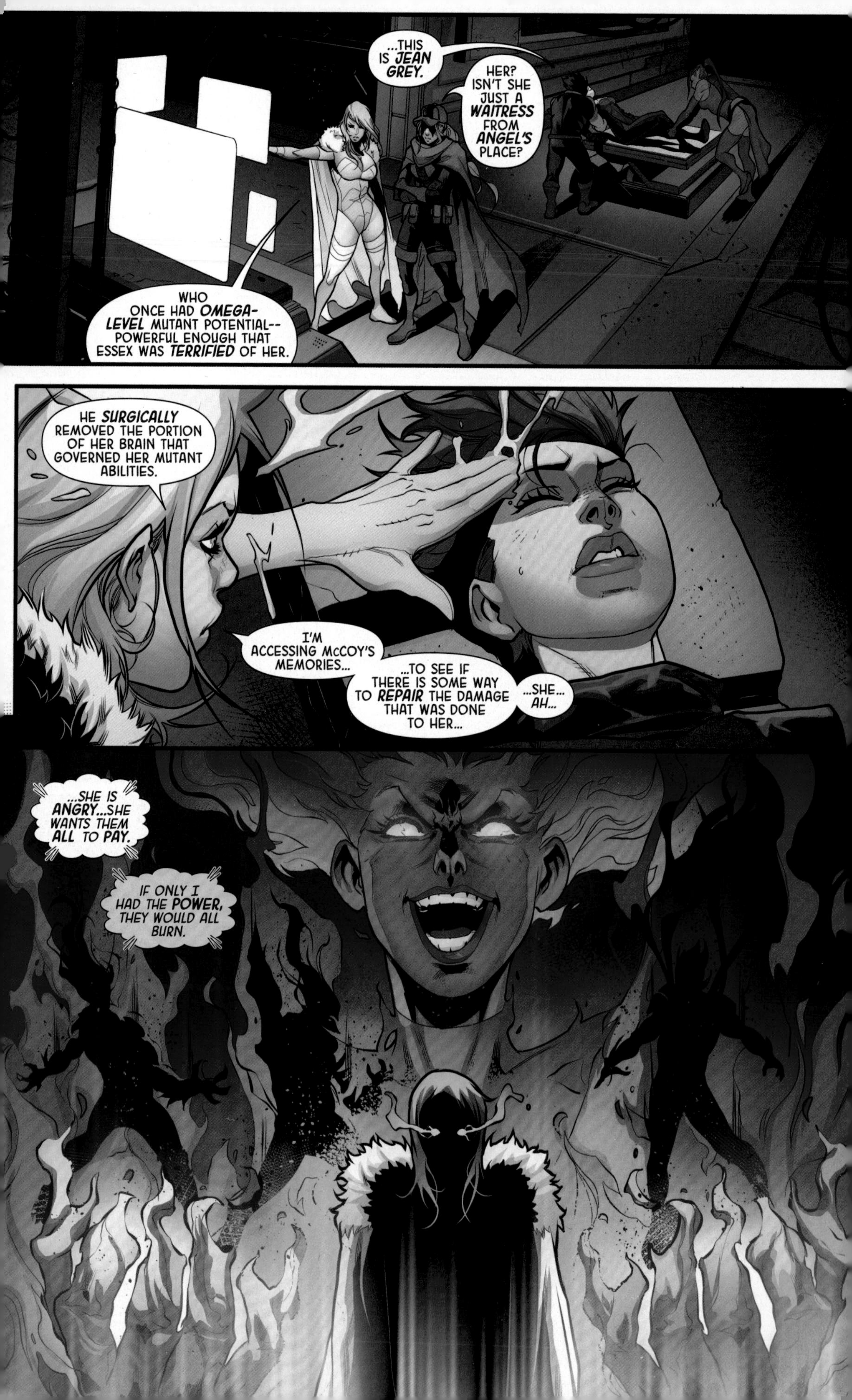
...THIS IS JEAN GREY.
HER? ISN'T SHE JUST A WAITRESS FROM ANGEL'S PLACE?
WHO ONCE HAD OMEGA-LEVEL MUTANT POTENTIAL-- POWERFUL ENOUGH THAT ESSEX WAS TERRIFIED OF HER.
HE SURGICALLY REMOVED THE PORTION OF HER BRAIN THAT GOVERNED HER MUTANT ABILITIES.
I'M ACCESSING McCOY'S MEMORIES...
...TO SEE IF THERE IS SOME WAY TO REPAIR THE DAMAGE THAT WAS DONE TO HER...
...SHE... AH...
...SHE IS ANGRY...SHE WANTS THEM ALL TO PAY.
IF ONLY I HAD THE POWER, THEY WOULD ALL BURN.

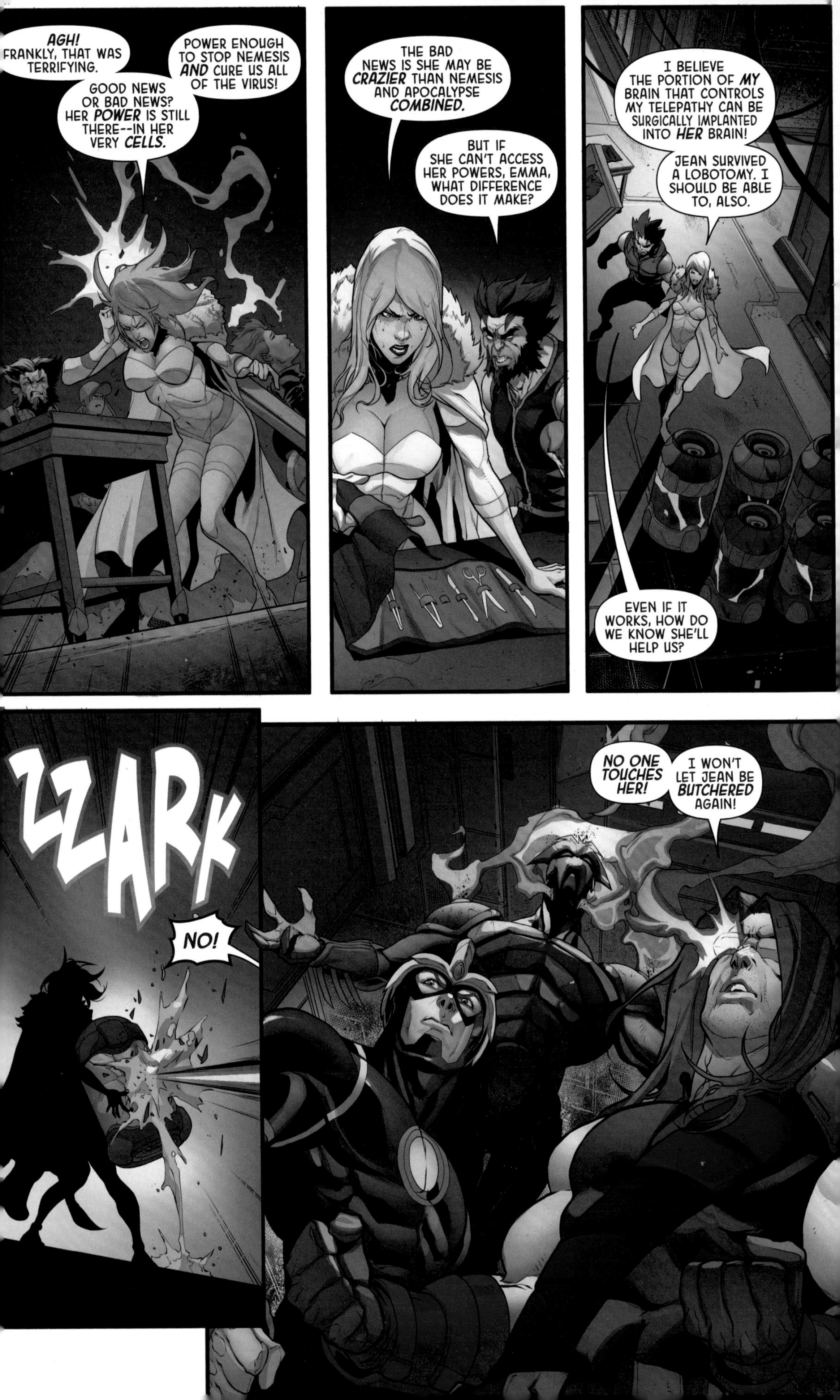
AGH! FRANKLY, THAT WAS TERRIFYING.
POWER ENOUGH TO STOP NEMESIS AND CURE US ALL OF THE VIRUS!
GOOD NEWS OR BAD NEWS? HER POWER IS STILL THERE--IN HER VERY CELLS.
THE BAD NEWS IS SHE MAY BE CRAZIER THAN NEMESIS AND APOCALYPSE COMBINED.
BUT IF SHE CAN'T ACCESS HER POWERS, EMMA, WHAT DIFFERENCE DOES IT MAKE?
I BELIEVE THE PORTION OF MY BRAIN THAT CONTROLS MY TELEPATHY CAN BE SURGICALLY IMPLANTED INTO HER BRAIN!
JEAN SURVIVED A LOBOTOMY. I SHOULD BE ABLE TO, ALSO.
EVEN IF IT WORKS, HOW DO WE KNOW SHE'LL HELP US?
ZZARK
NO!
NO ONE TOUCHES HER!
I WON'T LET JEAN BE BUTCHERED AGAIN!

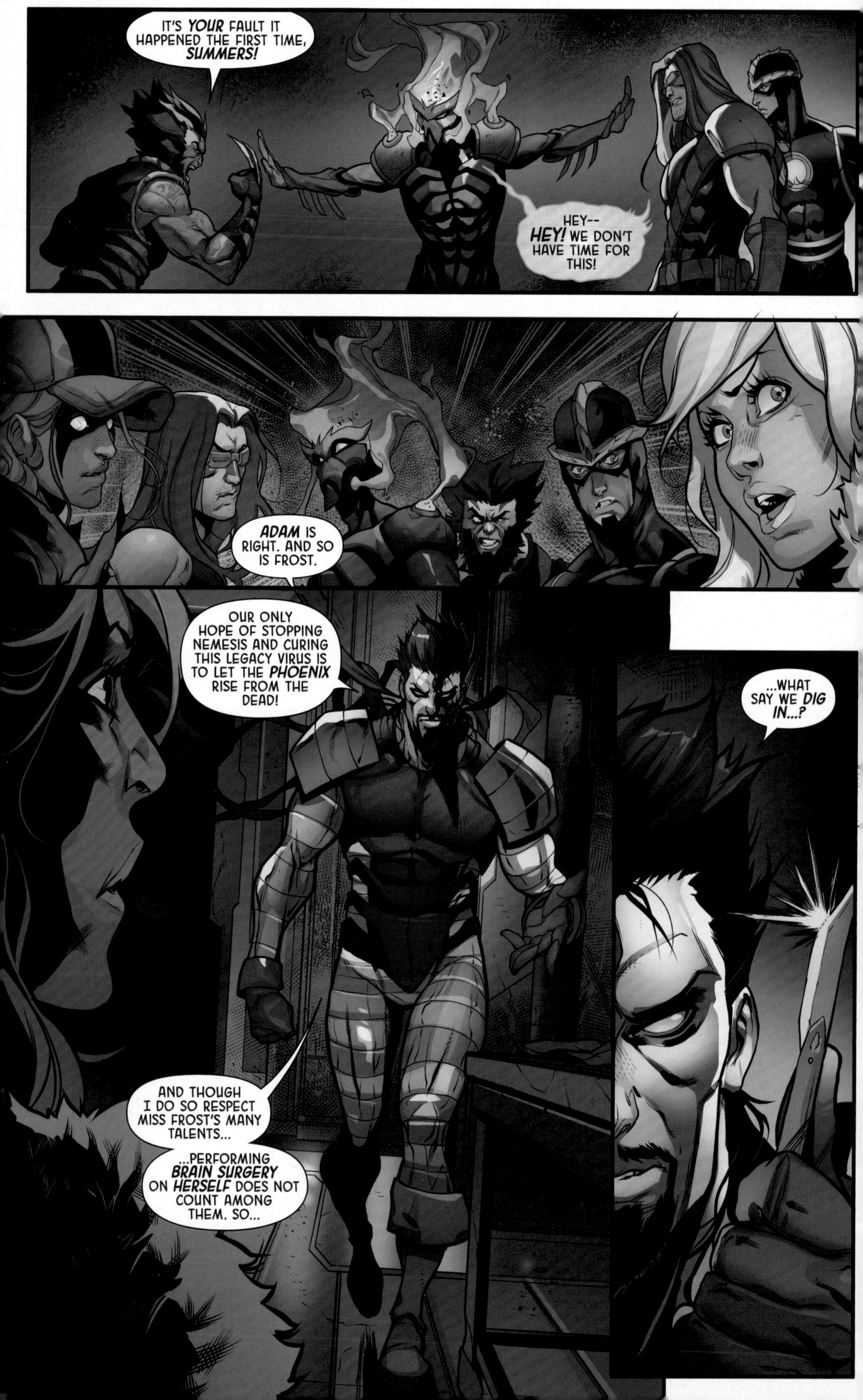
IT'S YOUR FAULT IT HAPPENED THE FIRST TIME, SUMMERS!
HEY-- HEY! WE DON'T HAVE TIME FOR THIS!
ADAM IS RIGHT. AND SO IS FROST.
OUR ONLY HOPE OF STOPPING NEMESIS AND CURING THIS LEGACY VIRUS IS TO LET THE PHOENIX RISE FROM THE DEAD!
AND THOUGH I DO SO RESPECT MISS FROST'S MANY TALENTS...
...PERFORMING BRAIN SURGERY ON HERSELF DOES NOT COUNT AMONG THEM. SO...
...WHAT SAY WE DIG IN...?

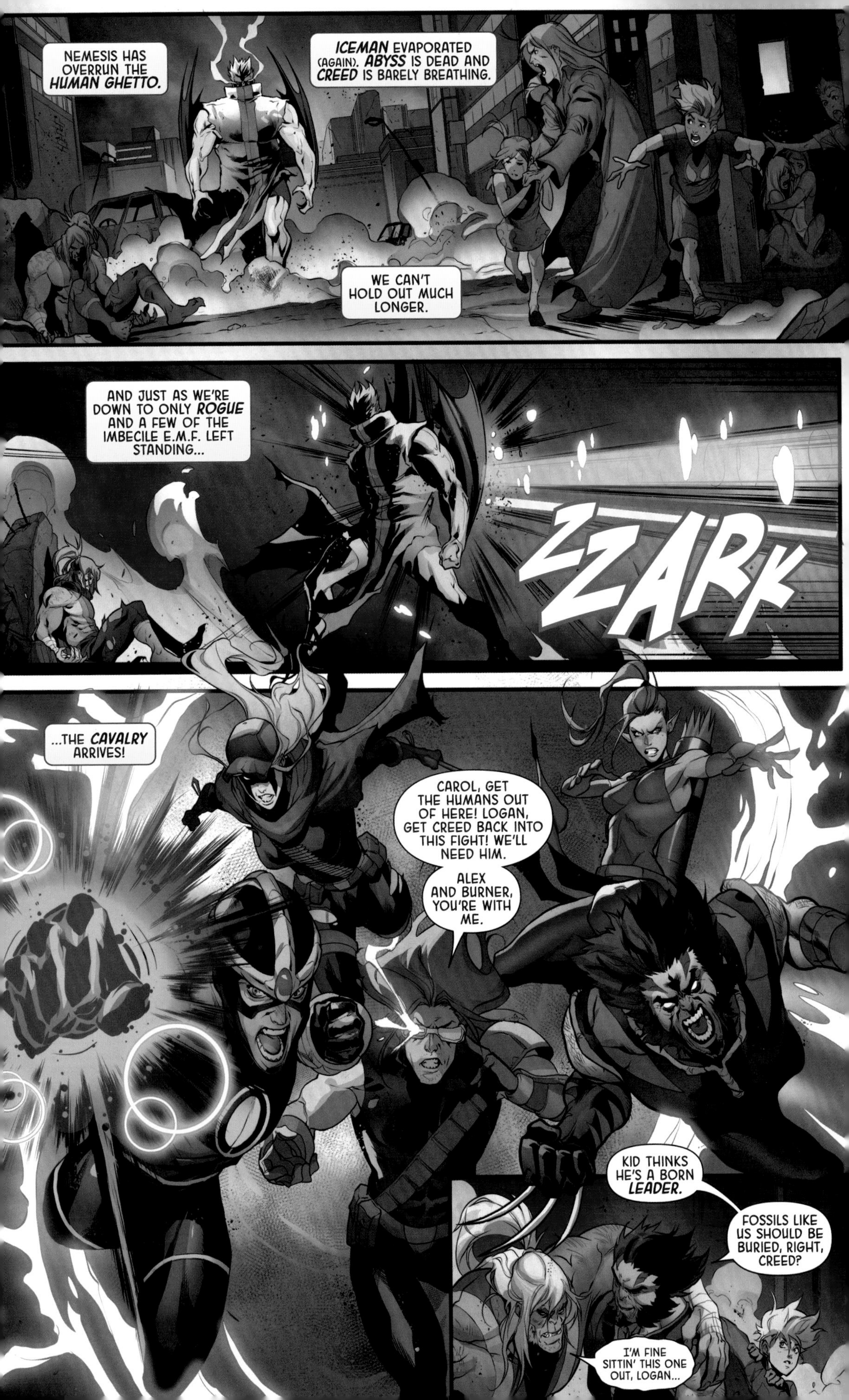
NEMESIS HAS OVERRUN THE HUMAN GHETTO.
ICEMAN EVAPORATED (AGAIN). ABYSS IS DEAD AND CREED IS BARELY BREATHING.
WE CAN'T HOLD OUT MUCH LONGER.
AND JUST AS WE'RE DOWN TO ONLY ROGUE AND A FEW OF THE IMBECILE E.M.F. LEFT STANDING...
ZZARK
...THE CAVALRY ARRIVES!
CAROL, GET THE HUMANS OUT OF HERE! LOGAN, GET CREED BACK INTO THIS FIGHT! WE'LL NEED HIM.
ALEX AND BURNER, YOU'RE WITH ME.
KID THINKS HE'S A BORN LEADER.
FOSSILS LIKE US SHOULD BE BURIED, RIGHT, CREED?
I'M FINE SITTIN' THIS ONE OUT, LOGAN...

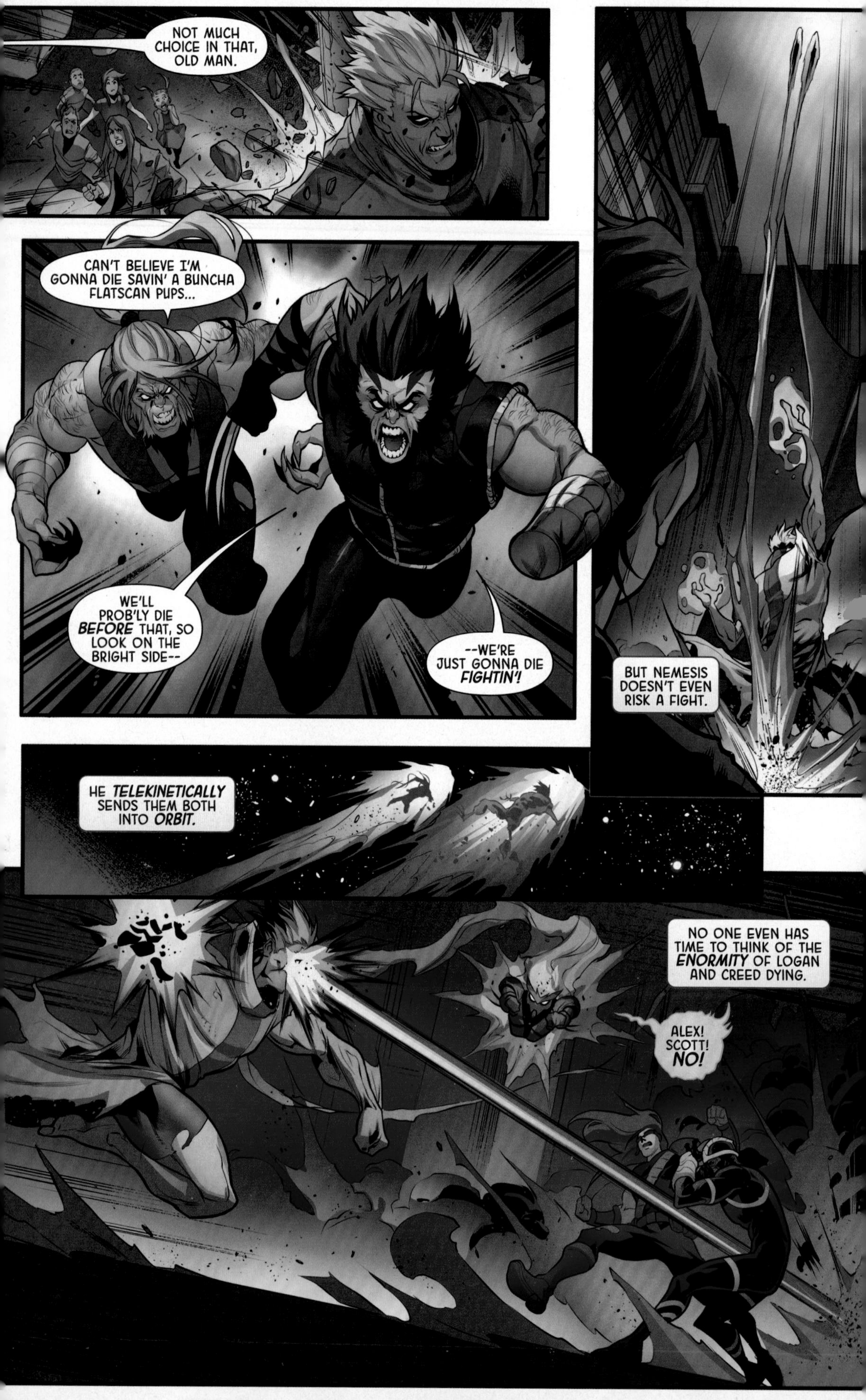
NOT MUCH CHOICE IN THAT, OLD MAN.
CAN'T BELIEVE I'M GONNA DIE SAVIN' A BUNCHA FLATSCAN PUPS...
WE'LL PROB'LY DIE BEFORE THAT, SO LOOK ON THE BRIGHT SIDE--
--WE'RE JUST GONNA DIE FIGHTIN'!
BUT NEMESIS DOESN'T EVEN RISK A FIGHT.
HE TELEKINETICALLY SENDS THEM BOTH INTO ORBIT.
NO ONE EVEN HAS TIME TO THINK OF THE ENORMITY OF LOGAN AND CREED DYING.
ALEX! SCOTT! NO!

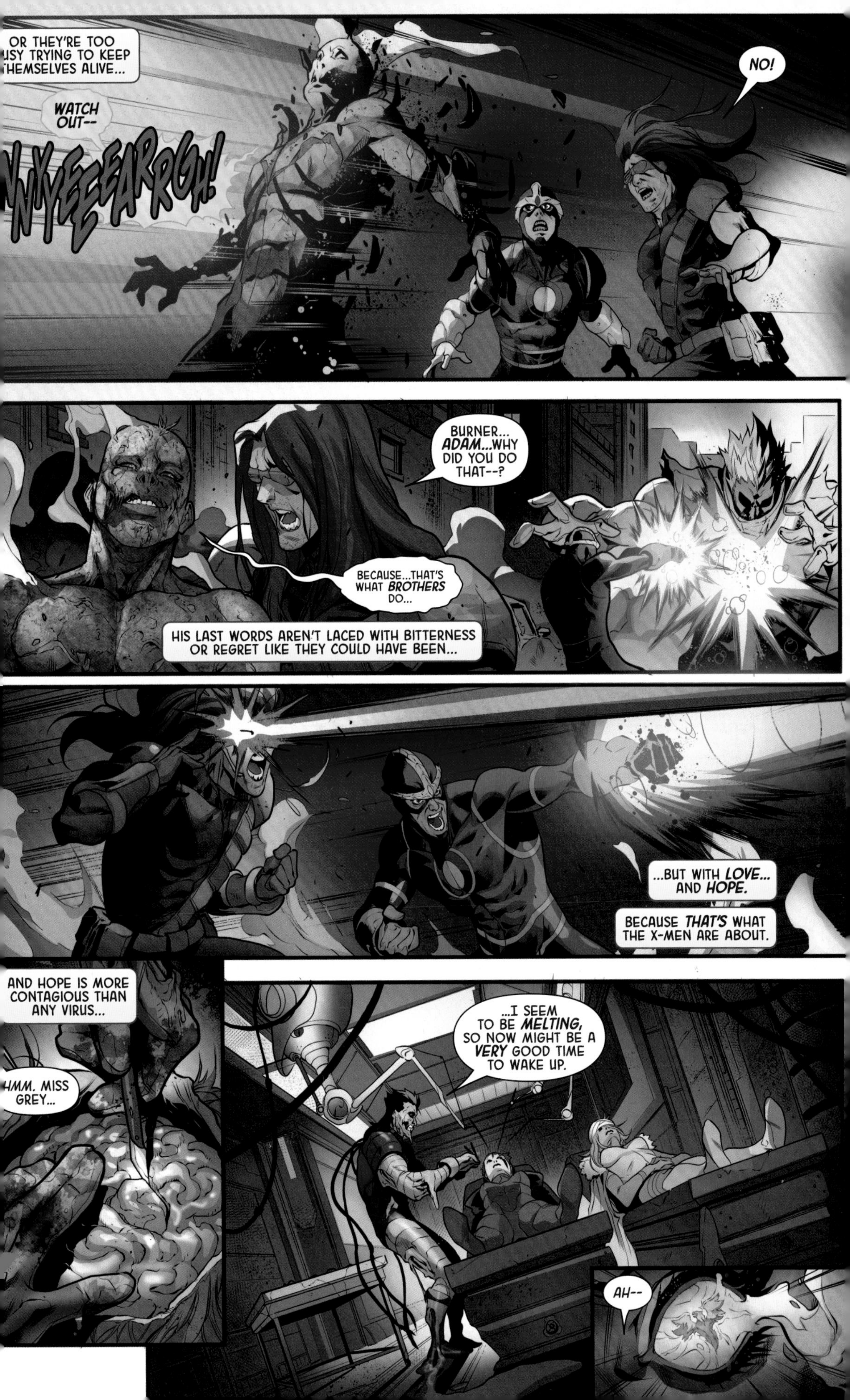
OR THEY'RE TOO
USY TRYING TO KEEP
THEMSELVES ALIVE...
WATCH
OUT--
NNYEEEARRGH!
NO!
BURNER...
ADAM...WHY
DID YOU DO
THAT--?
BECAUSE...THAT'S
WHAT BROTHERS
DO...
HIS LAST WORDS AREN'T LACED WITH BITTERNESS
OR REGRET LIKE THEY COULD HAVE BEEN...
...BUT WITH LOVE...
AND HOPE.
BECAUSE THAT'S WHAT
THE X-MEN ARE ABOUT.
AND HOPE IS MORE
CONTAGIOUS THAN
ANY VIRUS...
HMM. MISS
GREY...
...I SEEM
TO BE MELTING,
SO NOW MIGHT BE A
VERY GOOD TIME
TO WAKE UP.
AH--

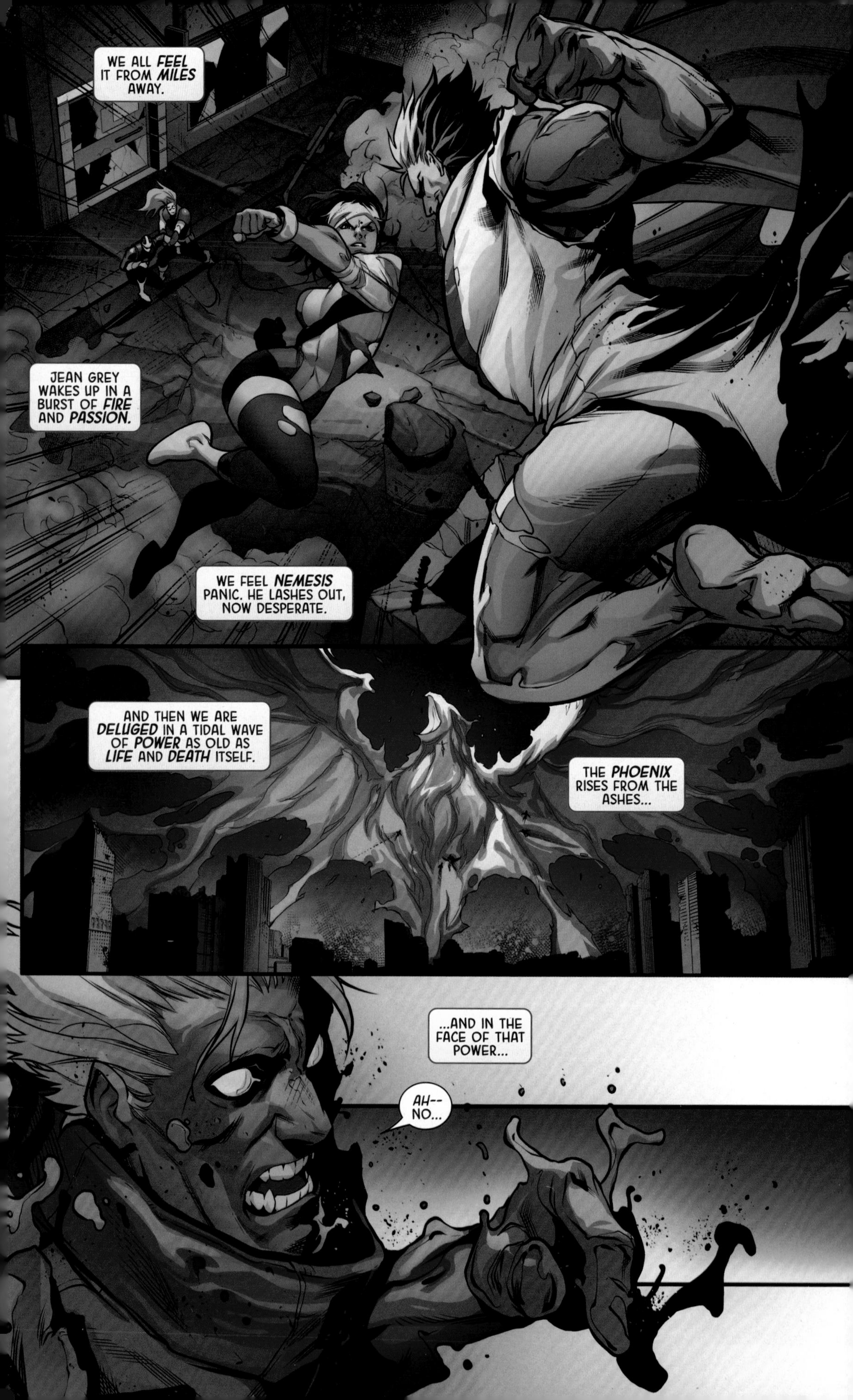
WE ALL FEEL IT FROM MILES AWAY.
JEAN GREY WAKES UP IN A BURST OF FIRE AND PASSION.
WE FEEL NEMESIS PANIC. HE LASHES OUT, NOW DESPERATE.
AND THEN WE ARE DELUGED IN A TIDAL WAVE OF POWER AS OLD AS LIFE AND DEATH ITSELF.
THE PHOENIX RISES FROM THE ASHES...
...AND IN THE FACE OF THAT POWER...
AH-- NO...

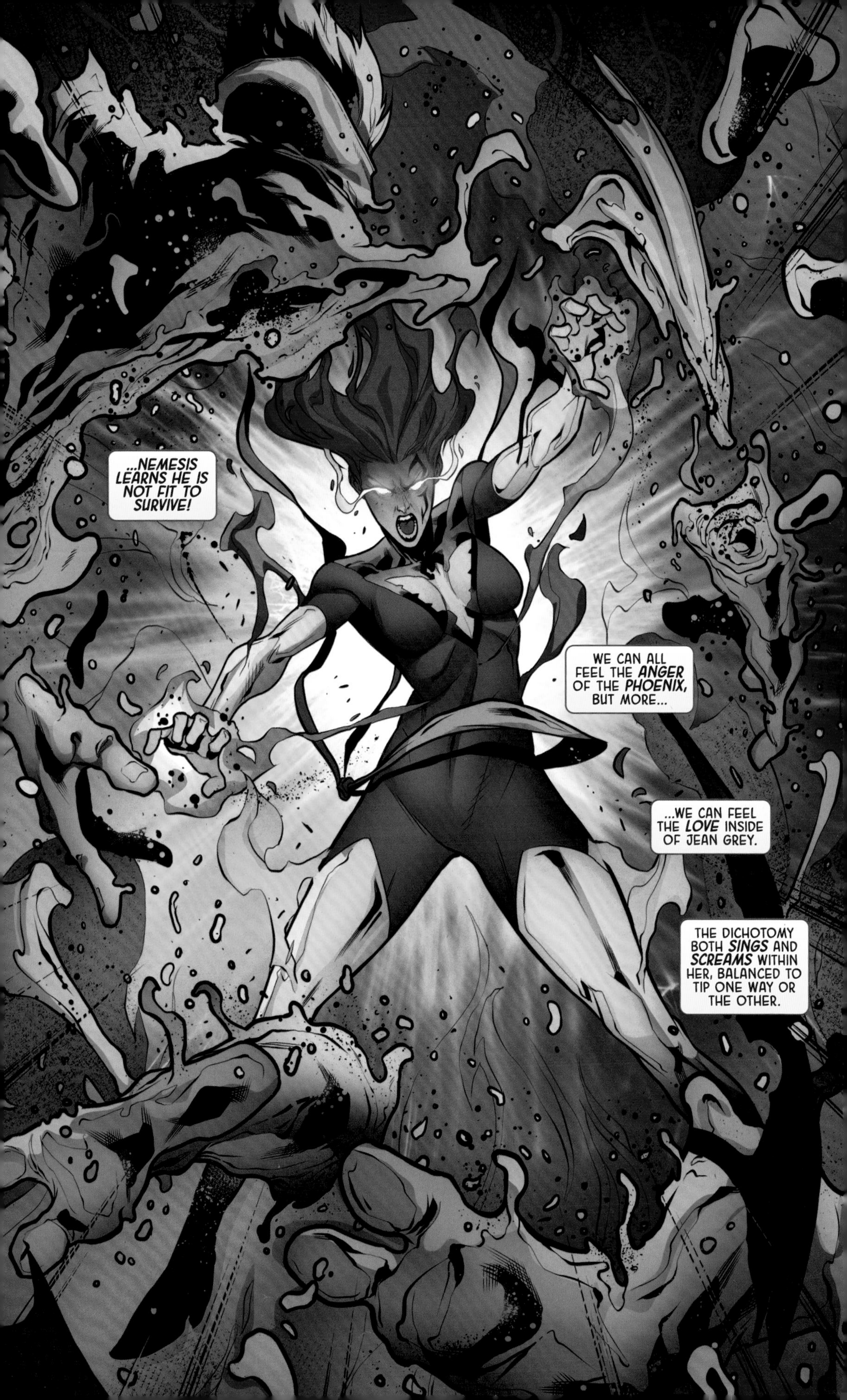
...NEMESIS LEARNS HE IS NOT FIT TO SURVIVE!
WE CAN ALL FEEL THE ANGER OF THE PHOENIX, BUT MORE...
...WE CAN FEEL THE LOVE INSIDE OF JEAN GREY.
THE DICHOTOMY BOTH SINGS AND SCREAMS WITHIN HER, BALANCED TO TIP ONE WAY OR THE OTHER.

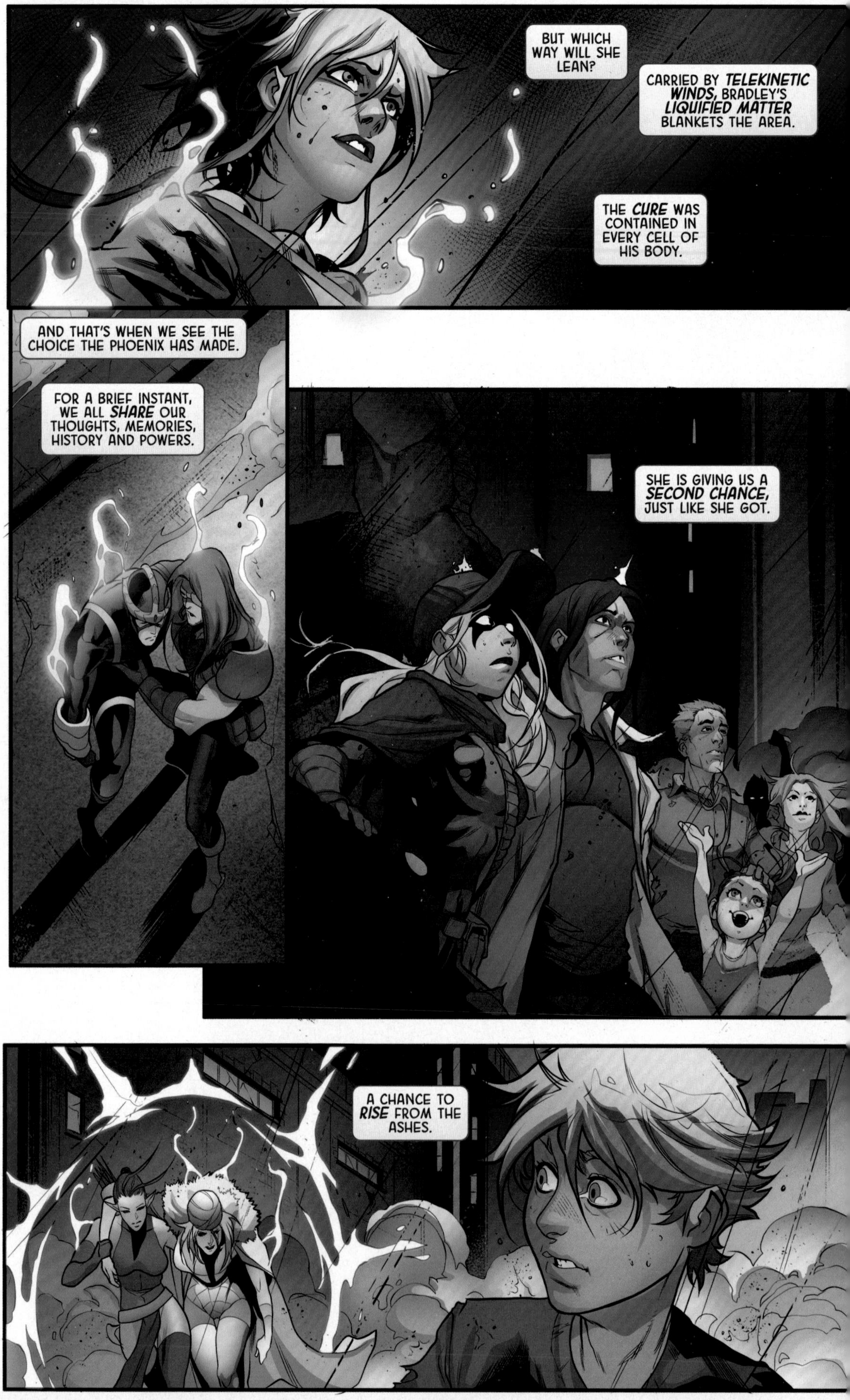
BUT WHICH WAY WILL SHE LEAN?
CARRIED BY TELEKINETIC WINDS, BRADLEY'S LIQUIFIED MATTER BLANKETS THE AREA.
THE CURE WAS CONTAINED IN EVERY CELL OF HIS BODY.
AND THAT'S WHEN WE SEE THE CHOICE THE PHOENIX HAS MADE.
FOR A BRIEF INSTANT, WE ALL SHARE OUR THOUGHTS, MEMORIES, HISTORY AND POWERS.
SHE IS GIVING US A SECOND CHANCE, JUST LIKE SHE GOT.
A CHANCE TO RISE FROM THE ASHES.

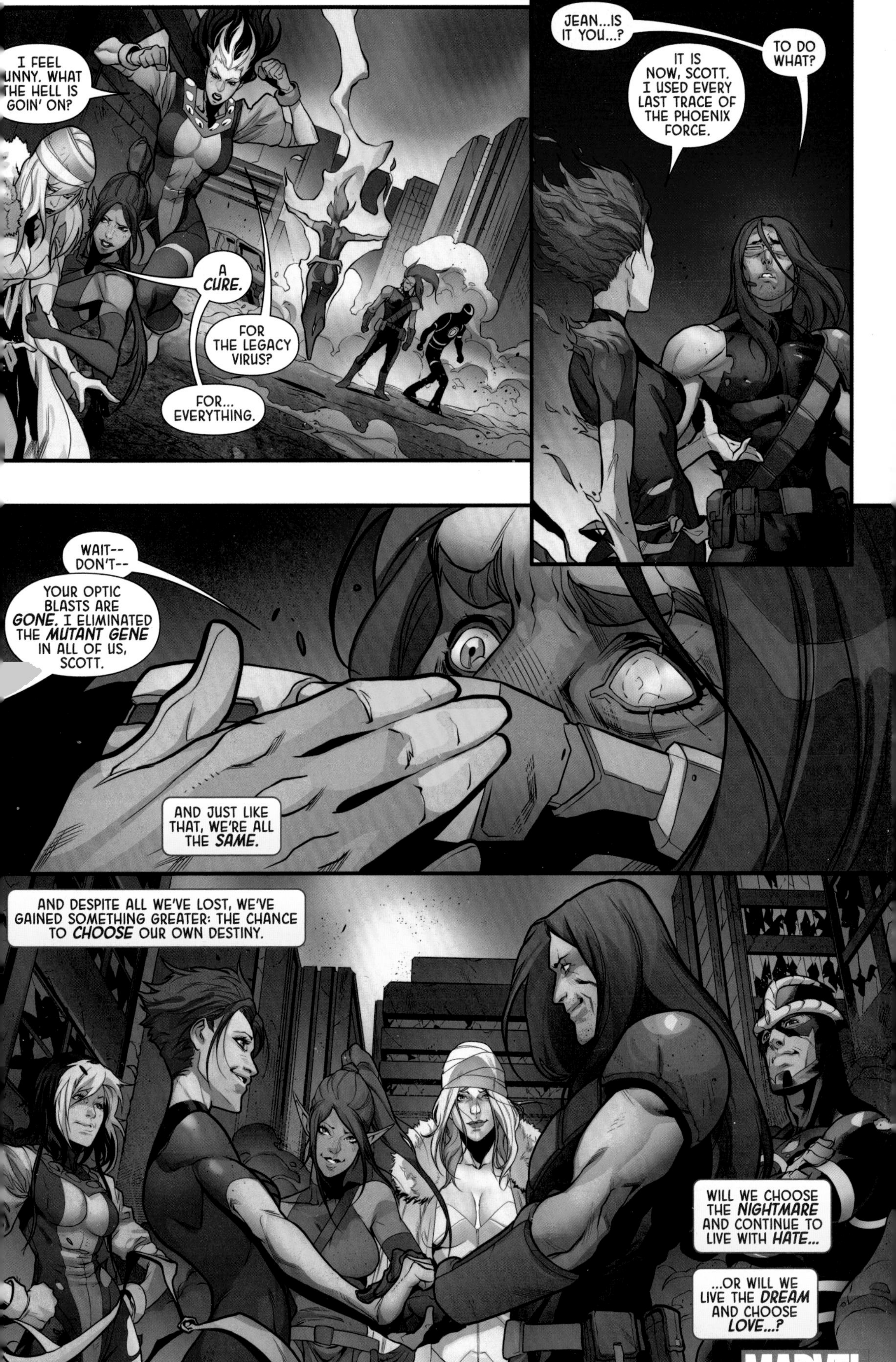

I FEEL
UNNY. WHAT
THE HELL IS
GOIN' ON?
A CURE.
FOR THE LEGACY VIRUS?
FOR... EVERYTHING.
JEAN...IS IT YOU...?
TO DO WHAT?
IT IS NOW, SCOTT. I USED EVERY LAST TRACE OF THE PHOENIX FORCE.
WAIT-- DON'T--
YOUR OPTIC BLASTS ARE GONE. I ELIMINATED THE MUTANT GENE IN ALL OF US, SCOTT.
AND JUST LIKE THAT, WE'RE ALL THE SAME.
AND DESPITE ALL WE'VE LOST, WE'VE GAINED SOMETHING GREATER: THE CHANCE TO CHOOSE OUR OWN DESTINY.
WILL WE CHOOSE THE NIGHTMARE AND CONTINUE TO LIVE WITH HATE...
...OR WILL WE LIVE THE DREAM AND CHOOSE LOVE...?
MARVEL

#3 VARIANT BY ROBBI RODRIGUEZ & MARTE GRACIA

#5 VARIANT BY ALEX GARNER

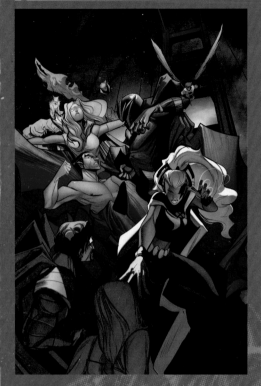

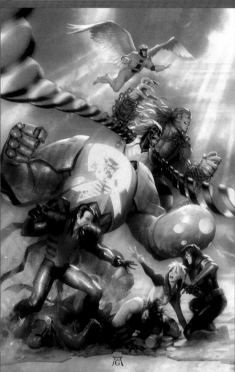

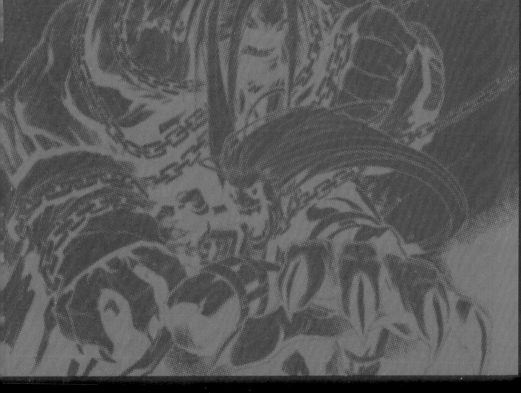